Does it bother me that after 'putting so much of myself into a piece' I have to let it go? My answer is always that I have received much joy in the making; now someone else will get joy in the using. In that way I am paid twice.

Sam Maloof, furniture maker
and craftsman

The Psychosocial Consequences of Natural and Alienated Labor

I've never liked authority. I got a taste of it in the military and hated it. Of course, that organization is bent on destruction; the organization here is designed to make money. Now I'm not sure if I know the difference, because it seems like both destroy in the end.

Jim G., production supervisor

SUNY Series in the Sociology of Work
Judith Blau, Editor

THE PSYCHOSOCIAL
CONSEQUENCES
OF NATURAL AND
ALIENATED LABOR

Michael L. Schwalbe

State University of New York Press

Published by
State University of New York Press, Albany

© 1986 State University of New York

For information, address State University of New York Press, State University Plaza,
Albany, N.Y., 12246

Library of Congress Cataloging-in-Publication Data
Schwalbe, Michael L., 1956-
The psychosocial consequences of natural and
alienated labor.
(SUNY series in the sociology of work)
Bibliography: p.
Includes index.
1. Work—Psychological aspects. 2. Alienation
(Social psychology) 3. Marx, Karl, 1818-1883.
I. Title. II. Series.
HD4904.S394 1986   305.5'62   86-5771
ISBN 0-88706-188-5
ISBN 0-88706-187-7 (pbk.)
10 9 8 7 6 5 4 3 2 1

Contents

Preface

Studying work beats doing it. Thus have I sometimes and only half-facetiously rationalized my interest in the subject. There is, however, a more serious irony in avoiding what others must endure by making a career of studying it. Why would anyone labor to explain the seemingly obvious fact that work in our society is more often drudgery than delight? What is it about this intellectual work that makes it preferable to what most people must do to survive in a capitalist society? Although my specific concerns in this book are not with differences between mental and manual work per se, some answers to these questions lie, I think, in the distinctions I have drawn here between natural and alienated labor.

One form of labor brings with it aesthetic pleasure and the possibility of enhancing human well-being and development through free, morally responsible, productive activity. The other generally denies freedom, aesthetic pleasure, and moral responsibility, thereby undermining human well-being and development. The latter is what most people experience in struggling to survive in a capitalist society. It is what I have sought to avoid in my own work and to understand and change through it.

Although I cannot separate them from my praxical concerns, my sociological concerns can be described, in distinct terms at least, as lying in how the historical social formations into which people are absorbed operate to shape their psychological development and functioning. Specifically, I am interested in how the capitalist labor process shapes the psychological development and functioning of those who are drawn into it. In trying to understand just how this occurs I have found no better set of guiding ideas than those of Karl Marx and George Herbert Mead. In this book I have tried to present these ideas accurately and clearly, with due consideration for their limitations. I have also tried, with due respect for their original formulators, to overcome these limitations, even as I hope others will do with the synthesis I have crafted here.

An explicit statement of the values underlying this work is necessary at this point. It should be apparent from the foregoing that my orientation to the capitalist labor process is a critical one. I do not pretend to approach it as a neutral analyst of history or of production systems, for no such analysis is possible. All attempts to interpret the world proceed from some set of acknowledged or unacknowledged *a priori* value commitments. I have tried, to the extent possible, to be reflexive about my own commitments in these respects.

I approach the capitalist labor process as I do because all my knowledge of it leads me to believe it is now a destructive social formation that must be abolished. While it is immensely productive in a narrow material sense, it is simultaneously destructive, on a wide scale, of what I value most in human existence: freedom of thought, regard for the mental and physical health of others, joy in creative production, and the full development of individual intellectual capacities. My values, then, are staunchly humanist; by necessary implication I am anti-capitalist. Nonetheless, I also believe capitalism must be fully and accurately understood—and its alleged destructiveness objectively documented—to accomplish its transcendence. My other commitments, as I hope will be apparent to sympathetic and critical readers alike, are therefore to principles of logic and evidence.

Not all of those who directly or indirectly contributed to this project share all of the values expressed above. Even so, I shall publicly acknowledge their contributions, which they can admit or disavow as circumstances and consciences permit.

My deepest gratitude is to my parents—for encouraging me to learn as much as I could about whatever I was interested in, for giving me the tools to do so, for instilling in me a sense of efficacy, for not going into shock when I abandoned engineering for sociology, and for unconditionally supporting my pursuit of more education than it seems anyone would rightly need. From them I also learned much about the pains and pleasures to be found in various forms of labor. This book is as much an effort to understand their experiences as my own and those of all working people.

Other debts are owed to Viktor Gecas—for being a consistently supportive and conscientious mentor, for fortifying my interests in social psychology, and for listening to my ideas about Mead and Marx when I wasn't yet sure what I was trying to say; to Joseph DeMartini and Michael Patrick Allen—for encouragement, support, and guidance throughout the course of my graduate education; to Donald Comstock—for introducing me to critical theory and giving me a sense of purpose in doing sociological work; to Lee Freese—for a valuable lesson on tenacity; to John Wardwell—for taking seriously what others would have considered a cameo role; and, reaching further back, to Woody Bishop, Robert Wolensky, and Richard Doxtator—for sparking my first serious thoughts about pursuing knowledge as a career.

Thanks are also due to Clifford Staples—for intellectual stimulation and colleagueship without which I would never have written a book such as this; to Rodney Baxter—for assistance in analyzing the survey data; to Peter Callero and Judith Blau—for helpful comments on the manuscript; to Wanda Clark, Anna Perez, and Nancy Rettig for their efforts in producing the final manuscript; and to the people who helped me obtain data for this study, especially the working people who talked to me about natural and alienated labor, if not in precisely those words.

Finally, I can but try to thank my dearest friend and spouse, Patricia Wasielewski, for her essential contributions to this book and to the motivation of its author. In addition to her expert criticism of chapter 4, only her patient tolerance of my impenetrable writing moods and incessant blathering about 'what I wrote today', made it possible to consummate this act of social science. Love, she has taught me, is what makes natural labor possible.

Introduction

> Human society, in brief, ought to be built
> around craftsmanship as the central expe-
> rience of the unalienated human being
> and the very root of free human develop-
> ment. The most fruitful way to define the
> social problem is to ask how such a soci-
> ety can be built. For the highest human
> ideal is to become a good craftsman.
>
> C. Wright Mills

To say that alienation has been a prominent concept in both Marxist and mainstream sociological studies of work is, despite appearances, incorrect. It is incorrect because there is no single concept of alienation shared by Marxist analysts of the labor process and mainstream sociologists of work. For Marxists, alienated labor is the *sine qua non* of capitalism; it is an objective fact referring to workers' lack of control over their labor. For mainstream sociologists, 'alienation' has referred to an assortment of bad feelings aroused by work. In this view alienation is not the experiential concomitant of alienated labor, but a set of negative subjective responses to work in an industrial society.

In part because of the mess mainstream sociology has made of the concept of alienation—using it to mean powerlessness, meaninglessness, normlessness, isolation, etc.—Marxist analysts of the labor process have come to avoid using it themselves, at least in any scientific way. This is unfortunate, for despite the semantic muddle surrounding the term alienation, Marx's original concept of alienated labor is still valuable for understanding the psychological consequences of the capitalist labor process. Indeed, it may be the only concept that enables us to understand these consequences in any theoretically comprehensive and coherent

1

way. One goal of this work is to reclaim the alienated labor concept in its original form, elaborate it, and put it to use.

The first step in this reclamation process is to acknowledge the limitations of the concept in its original form. With no apologies it must be said that in this form it is inadequate to account for the diverse psychological consequences of working for capitalism. In Marx's view, when workers lost control of their work they would come to loathe it. And more importantly, this loss of control would result in a mode of consciousness that perceived commodities, the products of alienated labor, as possessing an agency of their own, independent of human will. But contrary to Marx, it seems these are neither automatic nor universal consequences of the capitalist labor process. Some people loathe their paid work, some do not; some exhibit an alienated consciousness, some do not. We must ask why.

If we wish to retain the structural analysis of capitalism Marx built around his concept of alienated labor—and there are good reasons for doing so—it is necessary to somehow account for these inconsistent outcomes of working for capitalism, else the Marxist analysis cannot withstand the criticism that it merely romanticizes an ideal of artisan production and has little to do with how most people experience work in a capitalist society. To show that the concept is not merely romantic or normative, as many have labeled it, requires giving it some firmer theoretical moorings to the real world of productive activity.

This leads to the second step in reclaiming the concept: giving it an adequate social-psychological grounding. In his early writings on alienated labor Marx touched on many social-psychological matters, but explored them only superficially before moving on to other things. As a whole, the analysis he left behind (in the 1844 manuscripts) did not go much beyond philosophical anthropology. To make a more solid case for how the social organization of production can actually affect psychological development and functioning it is necessary to elaborate Marx's analysis by integrating it with a more fully developed social psychology. Further, this must be done in a manner compatible with his philosophical anthropology, which remains the essential underpinning for his theory of alienated labor.

The social psychology appropriate for this task can be found in the work of George Herbert Mead, whose own philosophical anthropology is both compatible with and complementary to Marx's. Specifically, Mead's social psychology of the self, his philosophy of the act, and his theory of aesthetic experience can provide the bases for better understanding the subjective moment of alienated labor and its significant psychological consequences. Moreover, the *natural labor perspective*, as this synthetic view will be called, can illuminate the connections between the objective reality of a labor process and its psychological effects. It thus becomes possible to distinguish the psychological effects of modernization and industrialism from those peculiarly attributable to participation in the capitalist labor process.

To describe it another way, what is constructed here is a Marxian/ Meadian theory of social structure and personality. In its present form this is not a general theory of social structure and personality, but a restricted one focusing on the sphere of production. Though it is contextually restricted, it nonetheless attempts an analysis inclusive of the capitalist labor process, productive activity within the capitalist workplace, and individual psychological functioning. Drawing on Marx and Mead it is possible to deal with such an expansive range of phenomena within a single synthetic theoretical framework. To anticipate the arguments to follow: Marx's analysis of how capitalism functions can be used to explain how it gives rise to particular forms of work experience; Mead's analysis of how humans function as social beings can be used to explain how such work experience affects people psychologically. The concern of this project is thus one which has been at the heart of sociology since Comte's time: the effects of society on the individual.

The present work is not, however, solely a theoretical treatise on Marx and Mead. Bolstering Marx with Mead's social psychology is not carried out as an end in itself, but as a means for guiding a new empirical examination of the psychological consequences of the capitalist labor process. The important theoretical groundwork for this project is laid out in chapters 1 and 2. In chapter 1 Marx's original concept of alienated labor is set forth in some detail. The emphases in this chapter are on Marx's philosophical anthropology—to establish the basis for his compatibility with Mead; and on his arguments concerning the cognitive and affective consequences of alienated labor—to establish his need for a more elaborate social psychology. In chapter 2 the basic elements of Mead's social psychology are discussed in some detail. This is to establish the fundamental compatibility and complementarity of Marx's and Mead's individual perspectives on human nature and social functioning. Then Mead's philosophy of the act is used to reinterpret alienated labor as the denial of aesthetic experience. Finally in chapter 2, Mead's ideas are used to devise a concept of natural labor, polar to alienated labor, to permit a more sophisticated analysis of forms of productive activity.

Chapter 3 on methodology bridges the theoretical work of chapters 1 and 2 and the empirical work that is the core of this project. Chapter 3 begins by linking the natural labor perspective to the real world of working for capitalism, then it prescribes a set of methods for applying the perspective to that world. In keeping with the basic premises of Meadian social psychology, it is argued that forms of productive activity can be identified as natural or alienated only by taking the perspective of the acting subject into consideration, thus dictating a phenomenological study of work experience. Further details on the specific methods used in this study can be found in appendix B.

Chapter 4 reports the results of this empirical work, focusing on the nature of those work experiences (problem solving, means-ends comprehension, self-objectification, and role taking) most important given the Meadian analysis of productive activity. This chapter also reports the results of an attempt to identify aesthetic experience inside and outside the capitalist workplace. Results of a survey undertaken to document the psychological consequences of the capitalist labor process are also summarized in chapter 4. This supplementary analysis sought to measure work-experience and psychological outcome variables and use the data to establish a two-stage link between the capitalist labor process and psychological functioning. Data collected through both fieldwork and the survey serve to qualify and largely support the natural labor perspective.

Drawing on what was learned through these investigations, chapter 5 reevaluates the adequacy and utility of the natural labor perspective for understanding the psychological consequences of the capitalist labor process. In this chapter some additions and adjustments are made to the perspective and its implications for further pursuing critical social-psychological studies of work, a broader theory of social structure and personality, and a political economy of cognitive development are discussed. Finally, a number of issues are identified as yet to be resolved through future theorizing and research.

Finally, chapter 6 considers some of the implications for action that follow from the natural labor perspective and the results of the present study.

It is my hope that the connections drawn here between the capitalist labor process, its structuring of work experiences, and the psychological consequences of these experiences, are as clear to the reader as they are to me. It is my further hope that readers, whatever their attitudes toward capitalism may be, will appreciate the analytical power of the natural labor perspective as I've constructed it. Doubtless, however, my own absorption in the perspective has made it difficult to see the gaps others inevitably will. And surely others will recognize as clearly, if not as painfully as I, the limitations of this empirical 'trial run'. But if not for loose ends there would be no new threads to follow. A pertinent bit of wisdom acquired during the course of this project came from a machine shop foreman, reputed to be a fine machinist and toolmaker, who said, "The only guy who doesn't make mistakes its the guy who isn't doing anything." This applies, as I believe Mills would agree, to all those striving to become good craftsmen.

1

Alienated Labor

*By alienating the whole of my time, as
crystallized in my work, and everything I
produced, I would be making another's
property the substance of my being, my
universal activity and actuality, my
personality.*

Hegel, *Philosophy of Right*

The ontological starting point for
Marx's system of thought is his conception of man as *homo faber:* man
the maker. Although some (for example, Israel, 1971) have argued this
represents a philosophical anthropology Marx abandoned in his later
writings, his system of thought is unintelligible without it.[1] In his later
writings Marx did not abandon this view of man, he simply presupposed
it. Purged of these philosophical underpinnings Marx can be miscon-
strued as an economic determinist, as both followers (for example, Althusser, 1969) and critics (for example, Popper, 1950) have done. In light
of his philosophical anthropology, however, Marx's predominant concern with political economy can be seen to derive not from the primacy
of economic values in this thought, but from his basic views of humans
as building animals and of labor as the central fact of human existence
(see also Avineri, 1968; Meszaros, 1970).

As a scientist and philosopher Marx rejected the metaphysical conceptions of human nature prevalent in his day. The conception of human
nature he formulated is a naturalistic one, based on historical observation. Basic to human existence throughout history, Marx observed, is labor, the transformation of nature to satisfy human needs. In Marx's view

7

> the first premise of all human existence is. . .that men must be in
> a position to live in order to be able to "make history." But life
> involves, before everything else, eating and drinking, a
> habitation, clothing, and many other things. The first historical
> act is thus the production of the means to satisfy these needs, the
> production of material life itself (*The German Ideology*, [1846],
> 1959:249).

Before all else, then, humans must confront nature and transform it to
survive. For Marx, humans are not only part of nature but shapers of it
as well.

Marx of course recognized that humans are not unique in this—
other animals also reshape nature to survive. But according to Marx, a
bird building a nest, a beaver a dam, or a bee a honeycomb all differ
from humans in one crucial respect: they act without self-consciousness.
In the *Economic and Philosophic Manuscripts* (hereafter *EPM*) Marx distinguished human and animal activity in that

> The animal is one with its life activity. It does not distinguish the
> activity from itself. It is its activity. But man makes his life
> activity itself an object of his will and consciousness. He has a
> conscious life activity. It is not a determination with which he is
> completely identified. Conscious life activity distinguishes man
> from the life activity of animals ([1844], 1963:127).

The distinguishing species-characteristic of humans is thus, in Marx's
view, the capacity to act self-consciously, to distinguish self from action.
Humans are therefore not limited to building by compulsion of instinct,
as are birds, bees, and beavers. Humans can reflect on their activity and
choose to build whatever is within their powers to build. Self-
consciousness makes it possible for humans to be "universal builders"
and to reshape nature to meet both biologically and socially determined
needs.

It is worth documenting Marx's lifelong embrace of this view. Over
20 years after he wrote the passage quoted above, a more mature Marx
wrote:

> By thus acting on the external world and changing it, [man] at
> the same time changes his own nature. He develops his
> slumbering powers and compels them to act in obedience to his
> sway. We are not dealing with those primitive instinctive forms of
> labor that remind us of the mere animal. . . . We presuppose labor
> in a form that stamps it as exclusively human. A spider conducts
> operations that resemble those of a weaver, and a bee puts to
> shame many an architect in the construction of her cells. But
> what distinguishes the worst architect from the best of bees is

this, that the architect raises his structure in imagination before he erects it in reality ([1867], 1972:232-3).

Here in the context of his economic analysis of labor power as a commodity, Marx interjected a summary statement of his earlier analysis of labor as a concrete activity.[2] In referring to humans compelling their slumbering powers to act in obedience to their sway, and to the use of imagination in human labor, Marx presupposed self-consciousness as the basis for these abilities. Clearly, only self-conscious beings can compel themselves to do anything, and only self-conscious labor can be imaginative (that is, aware of its own goals).

Perhaps the most impressive aspect of Marx's philosophical anthropology is his extension of scientific naturalism to the matter of self-consciousness. While Marx's first premise is that humans must labor to survive, he does not jump from there to self-consciousness. His second premise is, rather, that humans must labor cooperatively. It is out of the struggle to survive by cooperatively transforming nature that human sociality and self-consciousness emerge ([1846], 1959:251-2). These unique human characteristics are thus not gifts from gods, biological endowments, or Hegelian manifestations of Spirit in the World. For Marx they are species-capacities realized through cooperative labor. On this basis Marx held that human consciousness and social life were necessarily predicated on the process of transforming the material world to ensure species survival.

SELF-OBJECTIFICATION

In transforming nature to meet biological and social needs humans objectify themselves in the world; they use their mental and physical powers to turn pieces of the material world into objects with use values. Objectification occurs, for example, when humans turn mud and straw into a brick building. Marx saw this as an anthropologically necessary process through which

man really proves himself as a species-being. This production is his active species-life. By means of it nature appears as his work and his reality. For the object of labor is, therefore, the objectification of man's species-life; for he no longer reproduces himself merely intellectually, as in consciousness, but actively and in a real sense, and he sees his own reflection in a world he has constructed ([1844], 1963:128).

Again, human objectification is distinguished from instinctive transformations of nature by its self-conscious character. Self-consciousness makes it possible for humans to imagine, build, and finally perceive the things they build as separate from themselves, yet expressions of their own subjectivity.

Self-objectification occurs when humans recognize the objects they create as shaped by their own will. This means individual producers are able to see the results of their labor as expressions of their own purposive consciousness, as visible reflections of their mental and physical abilities. It is only then that nature, or rather *transformed nature*, appears to the producer as "his work and his reality." Through self-objectification humans extend their mastery over the physical world, simultaneously developing their species powers. Self-objectification thus changes not only the object (nature), but the subject (man) as well.

Marx saw the possibility for self-objectification to occur, and therefore the possibility for humans to develop their species powers, as dependent upon the social relations governing production. Under certain conditions self-objectification could be precluded; humans could create a world of objects they did not recognize as their own; the consequences of productive activity could be obscured. For these things to occur humans had only to be kept from exercising their species powers to freely choose courses of productive action, to imagine, to build creatively, and to learn by observing the results of their efforts. Capitalist relations of production, Marx argued, function in just this way to preclude self-objectification.

ALIENATED LABOR

Some commentators on Marx's concept of alienated labor claim it grew out of a romantic idealization of artisan production. While it is true Marx occasionally cited artistic production as exemplary of what "really free labor" could be ([1857], 1971:124), his concept of alienated labor was much more than an inversion of this ideal. If this were not so, Marx would not have needed the philosophical anthropology described above. He could have argued, and provoked less contention by doing so, that artisan production, with its demands for skill, commitment, and creativity, was simply the standard against which all forms of production should be measured. This, however, was not his argument, which was more powerful.

In Marx's view, labor is alienated when the social relations of production deny control over the means and ends of production to those whose labor actually transforms the material world. When this occurs people are no longer free to produce in accord with their own needs and desires, using their imagination and skills in whatever ways necessary to create objects with use values. Rather, they are forced to apply a narrow range of mental and physical powers to producing objects of value to their dominators. Such labor ceases to be an opportunity to exercise a full range of species powers through the cooperative transformation of nature. Neither can its results be seen as expressing the purposive consciousness of those who labor; self-objectification is thwarted. As Marx saw it, alienated labor thus denies the species-nature of human beings; it is more animal than human ([1844], 1963:125).

Marx's concept of alienated labor is often presented as encompassing four 'dimensions of alienation'. These are: alienation from productive process, product, self, and others. All of these can be subsumed under the points of discussion made so far. Alienated labor involves loss of control over one's productive actions and, therefore, one's products as well. This same loss of productive freedom can be described in terms of 'alienation from' process (means), products (ends), and self (species powers). Alienation from others is implicit in the ontology of alienated labor itself. That is to say, domination—without which labor cannot be alienated from anyone—is 'alienation from others.' But to be true to Marx's intent, alienation should be read as connoting a failure, rather than as in Modern English, a separation.[3] The failure is, along each of these dimensions, to engage in fully human productive activity involving free association, conscious self-direction, imagination, and self-objectification.

Marx's analyses of alienated labor and of the functioning of capitalism are of a piece: without alienated labor capitalism could not exist (although other economies could be founded on alienated labor). To make clear the connection it is necessary to briefly outline Marx's analysis of capitalism.

First, Marx observed capitalism as founded historically on the separation of laborers (predominantly agrarian) from the means of self-sufficiency. This was largely the result of the collapse of feudalism and the European enclosure movement in the eighteenth century. Both drove millions of people off the land that had previously supported them. Without the means of survival provided by feudal institutions, the displaced masses were forced by economic necessity to sell the only exchangeable commodity they possessed: their labor power (that is, their capacity to do work).

For the first time in history, then, masses of people sold their labor power at a scheduled rate, for money. This meant people sold their time and energy as commodities, in effect selling themselves as commodities. Functioning as exchange objects rather than human beings, wage-laborers became the instruments of a capitalist's will and consciousness. In this they lost their rights to choose the means and ends of their productive activity. At the same time they lost the possibility of fully exercising their species capacities through self-determined, self-objectifying labor.

In Marx's analysis, capitalism's survival depends upon workers accepting the means and ends of production dictated by capitalists. *Ends* must be accepted lest the organizing principle of production for exchange value be threatened; capitalism could not survive if workers were free to choose what they wanted to produce, for what they chose might not be profitably exchangeable. Just how objects become profitably exchangeable is, however, the heart of the matter. This has to do with why the *means* of capitalist production must also be accepted. Since, in Marx's analysis, profits derive from surplus value (the difference between the value created by labor and its under-remuneration in wages), capitalists must always struggle to maintain control of the production process in order to extract as much actual labor as possible from each unit of purchased labor power.[4] In a competitive market any individual enterprise failing to do this will weaken its position vis-à-vis other profit-making enterprises and eventually go out of business. Capitalism is thus founded on domination in productive activity and the denial of fully human labor to a class of wage-laborers (cf. Wright, 1983:92-95). In Marx's view capitalism simply cannot function in any other way.

THE COGNITIVE CONSEQUENCES OF ALIENATED LABOR

Marx was not concerned solely with the economic or philosophic implications of alienated labor. On moral grounds he was predominantly concerned with its destructive effects on human beings. In his early writings he speculated on alienated labor's psychological effects on individuals; in his later writings he described its effects on collective consciousness in capitalist societies. For Marx, both were forms of damage, in the one case to individual minds and in the other to collective rationality. In Marx's analysis both forms of damage were traceable to the denial of self-objectification enforced by alienated labor.

The cognitive effects of alienated labor on individuals constituted alienation in the clearest sense of failure. Alienated labor does not so much destroy minds, according to Marx, as it never lets them develop. Whereas self-determined, self-objectifying labor exercises and develops a wide range of species powers, alienated labor lets these powers atrophy. It keeps humans from extending their mastery over the world along both technical and intellectual dimensions. The reflexivity, imagination, and mental flexibility humans are capable of is thus never realized. In Marx's view, alienated labor produces intellectually stunted human beings suitable only for fulfilling the needs of capital. Although it is not Marx's analogy, the psychological damage wrought by alienated labor is comparable to the physiological damage wrought by Chinese footbinding; both are caused by forcibly restricting growth.

The effects of alienated labor on collective consciousness also represent failures of a sort. According to Marx, self-determined, self-objectifying labor leads humans to an understanding of the material world as reflecting their own nature. It produces a clear view of the humanly-constructed world as in fact humanly-constructed and hence subject to conscious reconstruction. But whereas self-objectifying labor enhances perception of the human agency represented in the material world, alienated labor distorts or obliterates this perception. With the loss of control over productive action comes a mode of consciousness that fails to perceive the ontological connectedness of subject and object. As Marx put it:

> The object produced by labor, its product, now stands opposed to it as an alien being, as a power independent of the producer. The product of labor is labor which has been embodied in an object and turned into a physical thing; this product is an objectification of labor. The performance of work is at the same its objectification. The performance of work appears in the sphere of political economy as a vitiation of the worker, objectification as a loss and as servitude to the object, and appropriation as alienation ([1844], 1963:122).

In his later writings Marx's concern with the effects of alienated labor on human consciousness took a slightly different turn. In *Capital*, for example, Marx attempted to demystify the value relations between commodities by showing how their value ultimately derives from labor. According to Marx this mystification arises because in commodities

> the social character of men's labor appears to them as an objective character stamped upon the product of that labor; because the relation of the producers to the sum total of their own labor is presented to them as a social relation, existing not

between themselves, but between the products of their labor ([1867], 1972:216).

Marx's point is familiar from his early writings: alienated labor makes the production process opaque, causing a failure to perceive the objects of human production as expressions of human subjectivity. But here Marx is concerned less with how people perceive their immediate relations with the objects they produce than with how they perceive relations between the objects themselves. Marx referred to the peculiar way these relations are perceived under capitalism as commodity fetishism.

Marx's analysis of commodity fetishism is essentially an analysis of the mode of consciousness created by alienated labor on a large scale. In a further passage from *Capital* the line of continuity from his early writings is clear:

> There is a definite social relation between men, that assumes, in their eyes, the fantastic form of a relation between things. In order, therefore, to find an analogy, we must have recourse to the mist-enveloped regions of the religious world. In that world the productions of the human brain appear as independent beings endowed with life, and entering into relations both with one another and the human race. So it is in the world of the Fetishism which attaches itself to the products of labor, so soon as they are produced as commodities.... This Fetishism of commodities has its origin as the foregoing analysis has already shown, in the peculiar social character of the labor that produces them ([1867], 1972:217).

Here again Marx refers to the mode of consciousness produced by alienated labor as one in which material objects appear to possess an agency of their own, independent of the human agency and social relationships that created them. In separating producer from product and denying individual responsibility for productive action, alienated labor results in a mystification of the consequences of human action; it undermines the ability to see these consequences in relation to their human origins.

THE AFFECTIVE CONSEQUENCES OF ALIENATED LABOR

Although his more enduring interest was in the cognitive consequences of alienated labor, Marx did devote some attention to its affective consequences (that is, how it makes people feel). These are not trivial consequences in Marx's view, for they concern an individual's lifelong experiences of joy or misery in labor. But they follow less clearly from the character of alienated labor than the cognitive effects discussed above, and they are less integral to the structural analysis of capitalism Marx pursued in his later works. And so Marx offered only a few passages of comment on this social-psychological dimension of alienated labor. Indeed, if there is any aspect of his early analysis of alienated labor Marx can honestly be said to have abandoned in his later works, it is this. Ironically, it is the one aspect of his analysis mainstream sociologists have embraced.

In a passage that has been taken as a summary explication of his concept of alienated labor, Marx speculated about how alienated labor makes people feel. What constitutes the alienation of labor? Marx answered himself so:

> First, that work is external to the worker, that it is not part of his nature; and that, consequently, he does not fulfill himself in his work but denies himself, has a feeling of misery rather than well-being, does not develop freely his mental and physical energies but is physically exhausted and mentally debased. The worker, therefore, feels himself at home only during his leisure time, whereas at work he feels homeless. His work is not voluntary but imposed, forced labor. It is not satisfaction of a need, by only a means for satisfying other needs. Its alien character is clearly shown by the fact that as soon as there is no physical or other compulsion it is avoided like the plague ([1844], 1963:124-5).

Marx's bold, but entirely plausible, assertions about how workers feel about alienated labor have been used as a point of departure for many studies of 'alienation' as a purely subjective phenomenon. Unfortunately, most such studies ignore Marx's analyses of human nature, productive activity, and self-objectification and, as a result, reduce alienation to having a bad attitude toward work.

Read in context, with an understanding of Marx's purposes in writing the 1844 manuscripts (largely self-clarification), the passage above is clearly an instance of Marx speculating on the psychological consequences of alienated labor as he worked out the implications of his own thought. The important element he salvages from this passage is the notion of the external, instrumental nature of alienated labor. The only new idea here is that labor of this sort must be inherently unsatisfying because it fulfills no immediate needs of the producer. Marx's point is that the self-denying character of alienated labor makes it a psychologically unrewarding activity to engage in, not that it arouses any particular set of feelings.

It is important to bear in mind, however, that unpleasant labor and alienated labor are not synonymous. Although in Marx's time the two were almost always empirically identical, theoretically they are distinct. Labor can be alienated without being dirty, difficult, or dangerous. Conversely, all such labor, despite its arduousness, it is not necessarily alienated.[5] Labor is alienated, according to Marx, when producers are forced to give up control of their productive activity, not when productive activity itself is merely unpleasant or difficult. The negative affective response to alienated labor Marx referred to—workers' loathing for work—arises from the fact of domination, which keeps workers from satisfying their own needs through their productive activity. Workers' negative feelings toward alienated labor are thus, in Marx's analysis, the necessary result of self-conscious beings being forced to act as instruments of a will they do not identify with.

ALIENATED LABOR IN LATER WRITINGS

Several points of continuity and discontinuity in Marx's treatment of alienated labor during his intellectual career have already been noted. In sum, it has been said that in his later writings Marx: (1) did not abandon the philosophical anthropology upon which his concept of alienated labor is based; (2) further developed his ideas regarding the cognitive consequences of alienated labor; but (3) deemphasized its affective consequences. In his later analyses of capitalism's structural dynamics, Marx did, however, arrive at a view of labor in industrial society that contrasts somewhat with the categorical assertions made in the *EPM*. Elements of this latter view are important to take into account in pursuing a contemporary analysis of the social-psychological effects of alienated labor.

In the *EPM* Marx analyzed human labor in universal terms, building his ontology of capitalism on this analysis. But in these early works Marx, like most young intellectuals, proceeded unencumbered by the qualifications a close examination of concrete reality might have forced him to make. Later, with his philosophical legs underneath him, so to speak, Marx undertook closer examinations of the real world. Indeed, his three volumes of *Capital* are, in a sense, empirical studies based on the theoretical work he did as a young man. While these studies did not lead him to significantly alter his theoretical framework, they did lead him to a more refined application of it. One of the important distinctions he finally arrived at is that between the 'sphere of necessity' and the 'sphere of freedom'.

The sphere of necessity encompasses those productive activities that must be undertaken to maintain the material basis of society. All large-scale construction, durable goods manufacturing, and utility services that sustain a form of collective life fall within the sphere of necessity; for example, chemicals, metals, papers, textiles and dozens of other materials must be mass produced to sustain a modern industrial society. Nor can this production be accomplished by independent artisans; it requires tremendous collective effort and massive coordination. Moreover, it must be standardized to be most efficient and its products universally useful. Because of this, Marx also recognized that in the sphere of necessity opportunities for self-determined, self-objectifying labor by *individual* producers would always be limited—even under communism.

It was Marx's conclusion that the immense productive power begotten by capital could be channelled in one of two directions: (1) into ever-increasing capital accumulation; or (2) into making the sphere of necessity as small as possible. Marx summed up these ideas in volume three of *Capital:*

> Just as the savage must wrestle with Nature to satisfy his wants, to maintain and reproduce life, so must civilized man, and he must do so in all social formations and under all possible modes of production. With his development this realm of physical necessity expands as a result of his wants; but, at the same time, the forces of production which satisfy these needs also develop. Freedom in this field can only consist in socialized man, as the associated producers, rationally regulating their interchange with Nature, bringing it under their common control, instead of being ruled by it as by the blind forces of Nature; and achieving this with the least expenditure of energy and under conditions most favorable to, and worthy of, their human nature. But it nonetheless remains a realm of necessity. Beyond it begins that development of human energy which is an end in itself, the true realm of freedom, which, however, can blossom forth only with this realm of necessity as its basis ([1894], 1972:320).

At this point Marx has recognized two important things. First, that certain exigencies of survival will always constrain the amount of self-determined, self-objectifying labor humans can engage in any historical epoch; and second, that only by mastering nature to meet these demands can the sphere of necessity be shrunk to a fraction of the size of the sphere of freedom. Thus the human struggle is always to minimize the sphere of necessity in order to maximize opportunities for exercising and developing species powers in the sphere of freedom. Of course, under capitalism increases in productivity are not converted into free time for the worker (other than in the form of unemployment), but into more surplus value for capitalists.

In his later writings, then, Marx's perspective on human labor is much more sociologically sophisticated and empirically informed than that presented in the *EPM*, as could be expected. Still, this later perspective encompasses rather than abandons the ideas developed in the *EPM*. By volume three of *Capital* Marx more fully realized the practical implications of this theoretical work when informed by a closer examination of the real world. Thus despite shifts in emphasis over the years, Marx's work possesses a remarkable theoretical integrity which makes it extremely valuable for linking the cognitive and affective consequences of alienated labor to its role as the underlying dynamic of capitalism.

ALIENATED LABOR IN CONTEMPORARY LABOR PROCESS STUDIES

While Marxist scholars have generated much theoretical writing about alienation (for example, Ollman, 1971; Meszaros, 1970; Avineri, 1968; Sève, 1978; Novack, 1970; Fromm, 1955; Marcuse, 1955), there has been virtually no development of the alienated labor concept via its application in studies of the labor process. Most such studies have simply assumed that the labor in question (under capitalism) is alienated labor and have focused on other things, such as deskilling, rates of exploitation, internal labor markets, or control strategies. None of these studies has seriously reconsidered the social psychology of alienated labor (in part because this territory has been ceded to mainstream students of 'work alienation', about whom more will be said later). Consequently, the alienated labor concept remains underdeveloped as a tool for use in social-psychological studies of the labor process (cf. Archibald, 1976; Schweitzer, 1981).

One of the most renowned Marxist analyses of the labor process is Harry Braverman's (1974) *Labor and Monopoly Capital*. This work exemplifies some of the limitations noted above. As a Marxist, Braverman accepts the principle that alienated labor is productive activity over which producers have lost control. In his view the most important historical consequence of this has been the systematic separation of mental labor (conception) from physical labor (execution). Braverman refers to this process as "deskilling," which he argues is the basis for workers' experiences of degradation under capitalism. But while his structural and historical analyses are excellent, Braverman glosses too much on the social-psychological level (see Littler and Salaman, 1982). Like Marx, Braverman refers to labor and capital in categorical terms, seldom dwelling on particulars.[6] Thus there are exceptions, complexities, and variations in the real world of work that remain undiscussed (which is not to say Braverman was unaware of them). For Braverman's general purpose of historical analysis this is not a problem; however, establishing a connection between deskilling and some set of psychological consequences— as Braverman's argument implies—requires both a closer look at the social psychology of the workplace and a theory for linking workplace experiences to psychological outcomes. In general, Braverman's analysis serves well as a backdrop to a Marxist social psychology of work, which remains to be developed.

A more recent Marxist study of the labor process that does grasp the complexities of workplace experience is Michael Burawoy's (1979) *Manufacturing Consent*. In a participant-observation study of machine operators in an engine manufacturing firm, Burawoy sought to determine why these operators worked as hard as they did. His description of the shopfloor culture, while more anthropological than social-psychological, does lend itself to some interesting social-psychological interpretations (see Gecas and Schwalbe, 1983:84). What Burawoy observes is adaptation to workers' domination by management and the coerced performance of intrinsically unrewarding labor. While Burawoy's study provides some valuable insight into how workers adapt to alienated labor by reconstituting it as a game, it doesn't explore the psychological consequences of these adaptations. Later, Burawoy's analysis proceeds outward not inward, as his purpose is to show how these adaptations reproduce capitalist relations of production, not how they produce psychological damage. Thus as far as the cognitive and affective consequences of alienated labor are concerned, Burawoy's work provides more grist for theoretical analysis than analysis itself.

In another participant-observation study, much less systematic and intensive than Burawoy's, Richard Pfeffer (1979) in *Working for Capitalism* reports on his experiences as a forklift operator in a piston ring manufacturing plant. Developing his observations from a Marxist perspective, Pfeffer offers an interesting account of workers' experience of time in and out of the factory (pp. 72-90). Although he does not explicitly link the form of this experience to Marx's concept of alienated labor, the connection is clearly implied. While Pfeffer's work makes no original discoveries, it does provide valuable documentation of some aspects of the subjective experience of alienated labor. Again, however, as with Burawoy's work, an analytic framework must be imposed upon it to understand how alienated labor produces particular cognitive and affective consequences.

These contemporary Marxist studies of the labor process are typical in their failures to draw on any body of social-psychological theory to help account for or draw out the implications of their findings (see also Zimbalist, 1979). This is attributable to a number of things, including a Marxist predisposition to ignore mainstream (social-psychological) studies of workers' responses to work, a genuine unavailability of compatible social-psychological theories to draw on, and the more obvious fact that these studies have legitimately addressed non-social-psychological matters (Thompson, 1983). In an important sense, however, these are unacceptable excuses, for no study of the labor process can escape social psychology—it can only be taken for granted. But taking too much for granted on this level has cost Marxist analysts of the labor process much credibility, especially with respect to their claims regarding the effects of work on workers. To consider this problem more closely it is useful to briefly discuss a classic mainstream study of work and alienation.

Although few who study the labor process from a Marxist perspective might agree, Robert Blauner's (1964) *Alienation and Freedom* is a valuable source for understanding the psychological effects of alienated labor. Blauner's study is not Marxist, and despite its methodological shortcomings and overstated conclusions, it still raises questions a Marxist study of the consequences of alienated labor cannot ignore. Blauner claims to begin from a position of universal skepticism, rejecting both the "automatic alienation" thesis of some Marxists and the "myth of the happy worker" espoused by capitalist apologists. While he accepts the so-called Marxian premise that there are "powerful alienating tendencies" in modern industry, he identifies the goal of empirical research as one of determining

> under what conditions these tendencies are intensified in modern industry, what situations give rise to different forms of alienation, and what consequences develop for workers and for productive systems (1964:4).

In that the objective features of work environments vary considerably, Blauner argues, there should be a "distribution of alienation" across industries.

But alienation for Blauner is not the objective condition of being denied control over one's own labor and its products; rather, it is a subjective experience, a "quality of personal experience which results from specific kinds of social arrangements." In defining alienation in this way Blauner follows Seeman (1959) in focusing not on the social relations governing production, but on the feeling-states of individuals. Thus despite his professed interests in the effects of the "socio-technical environment" on workers, Blauner does not call capitalism itself into question, nor does he look beyond particular production technologies to the capitalist imperatives that influence their use. On these grounds Blauner's analysis has been largely dismissed by Marxists. And, if judged from a Marxist perspective on these grounds alone, it deserves to be.

Nevertheless, there is at least one basic and important question raised by Blauner that cannot be dismissed, especially in an attempt to understand the psychological effects of alienated labor. That is: can the cognitive and affective consequences of alienated labor vary *within* the framework of capitalist relations of production? It seems obvious, based on the research of Blauner and many others, that these effects can and do vary within capitalist relations of production. The crucial corollary questions then become: why do these variations occur? are they explainable with reference to Marx's concept of alienated labor? or does the Marxist account of alienation deserve to be junked? Thus even though from a Marxist perspective an inquiry into the "distribution of alienation" in capitalist industry is an absurdity, it is reasonable to explore how the *effects* of alienated labor vary depending on the concrete productive activities individuals engage in. But perhaps fearing absorption in social-psychological issues, or being identified with those who study alienation as a subjective phenomenon, few Marxist analysts of the labor process have taken these questions seriously. They are questions the present study explicitly attempts to answer.

CRITICISMS OF THE ALIENATED LABOR CONCEPT

Marx's conception of alienation has been criticized—sympathetically and unsympathetically—for being normative, unscientific, rhetorical, presumptive, "shifty," and just plain confused. In assessing the merit of these charges it is important to sort the many uninformed critics from the few informed ones. The former tend to misdirect their criticisms of the contemporary, and admittedly muddled, concept of alienation at Marx.[7] Or, if they are able to distinguish Marx's notion of alienation from other versions, they still fail to understand it within the context of Marx's complete system of thought. They mistakenly believe

Marx's concept of alienation can be understood and criticized as an isolated idea, independent of his views on human nature, productive activity, and self-objectification. Still, there are valid criticisms of the
alienated labor concept, made by informed scholars, that deserve consideration. Criticisms falling into two general categories are relevant here:
those charging that alienated labor is not a useful concept for empirical
sociological research and those challenging the adequacy of its view of
the person/labor process relationship.

C. Wright Mills, a sympathetic critic, is among those who charge
that alienated labor is a concept of dubious scientific value. Mills (1956)
claims the concept of alienated labor was based on a youthful Marx's romantic idealization of artisan production—a criticism that should need
no further refutation here. Israel (1971) renders much the same criticism
of the young Marx, preferring to embrace the older Marx's "more scientific" concept of commodity fetishism. In light of a more careful reading
of Marx's early writings, both Mills's and Israel's criticisms seem a bit
abrupt, to say the least. Nonetheless, their criticisms are not groundless;
there is an element of truth in their premises. Their conclusions, however, are in error.

That Marx's concept of alienated labor has a normative basis is undeniable; that this renders it unscientific or useless for empirical research
is nonsense. If the normative basis of the concept were simply a value
proposition such as, 'human labor ought to be like x, because that's what
I'd like it to be', then this conclusion would be sound. But the standard
against which alienated labor is implicitly compared is not based on
Marx's value preferences. It is based on historical observation and analysis of what labor can be when free of domination. Thus it is true that for
Marx alienated labor represents a failure relative to a philosophically
grounded ideal. But this is true of all 'ideal-type' concepts and in no way
diminishes their scientific utility. If one's purpose, for example, is to explore how actual labor falls short of what it theoretically could be, then
there is no way to go about it but by using a comparative concept such as
alienated labor.

A related point, also made by Mills (1956), is that since Marx considered alienated labor a fact inherent in capitalism, his theory of alienation isn't really intended to be tested against reality through empirical
observation. In other words, if one accepts a Marxist perspective, alienated labor is a paradigmatically-given aspect of capitalism, not an empirical variable. In this respect Mills is entirely correct—as long as he is
referring to Marx's ontology of capitalism or to the capitalist labor process on a theoretical level. This, however, is an overly restrictive view of

Marx's thought on the matter of alienated labor (cf. Goff, 1980).

Marx's concept of alienated labor deals with more than just its role as the engine of capitalism. According to Marx, all labor involves a set of relationships between self-conscious humans, their productive activities, and the objects they create. These relations arise as humans begin to use their mental and physical powers to transform the world. There are thus two sets of relationships to be considered from Marx's point of view: human relationships with nature and human social relations. The former have to do with *productive activities*—what individuals actually do and experience in transforming nature; the latter have to do with *labor processes*—how the creation and appropriation of value is organized on a collective level. To speak of the capitalist labor process is, on the basis of this distinction, to refer to the forcible appropriation of value (in the form of congealed labor) by one class of individuals from another. To speak of productive activities under capitalism, is to refer to the mental and physical acts workers actually perform in creating objects with value.

This is an important distinction, for it shows why Mills is both right and wrong. He is right if alienated labor is taken to be synonymous with the capitalist labor process; however, if the distinction described above is made, then at least two sensible avenues for empirical application of the alienated labor concept appear. One might study, for instance, actual productive activities—what people do with their hands and minds— within capitalist relations of production. These activities are not ontological constants but empirical variables. In turn, then, one might also study the variable psychological consequences of these productive activities, as they flow from their alienated or perhaps non-alienated character. The present study uses the Marxian framework, and this crucial distinction between productive activities and labor processes, to proceed along both these avenues of inquiry.

A second line of attack on the empirical usefulness of the alienated labor concept refers to its alleged imprecision and "shiftiness" (Feuer, 1963). The most pointed statement of this criticism was made by Vilfredo Pareto, who accused Marx of using words like bats, because in them 'one could see both birds and mice'. Without understanding why this appears to be the case one can conclude there is profound confusion in Marx's treatment of alienation (see, for example, Schacht, 1970). Like the charge of scientific inpertinence discussed above, this criticism too has stuck in the minds of many mainstream sociologists. It can be dislodged only by understanding Marx's relational ontology.

Because the elements of Marx's thought exist for him as *relations* rather than ontologically distinct things-in-themselves, he often describes these elements as they entail both moments of the relation. Alienation is thus at once alienation from process, product, self, and other precisely because it exists only as a form of relation between these elements ([1844], 1963:130-1). In alternately describing alienation from each of these aspects of the relation, Marx appears to shift meanings back and forth. But within his system of internal relations (see Ollman, 1971) his usage is consistent and precise; he simply describes the same 'things' from different points of view within his system of thought. Failures to recognize this—and hence failures to understand alienated labor as a facet of a whole—underlie most criticisms of Marx as ambiguous or imprecise. Once his system of internal relations is grasped, his alleged shiftiness is no longer a problem.

If distinctions are made between labor processes, productive activities, and the psychological consequences of these activities, the alienated labor framework can indeed be useful for empirical research. Nor is this usefulness impaired by conceptual imprecision—if one operates consistently within a Marxian framework. It is the case, however, that for purposes of social-psychological research Marx's concept of alienated labor does have some serious shortcomings. These are especially pertinent to the interests of this study in the effects working for capitalism has on workers.

One of these problems is discussed by Bertell Ollman (1971), a chief expositor of Marx on the subject of alienation. Pointing to the perennial Marxist problem of working-class consciousness (that is, the lack of it), Ollman admits Marx did not have a theory of personality formation adequate to account for how specific forms of consciousness arise. In Ollman's view, generations of Marxists have ignored this theoretical deficiency because of a desire to retain faith in the revolutionary potential of the proletariat. This faith would be threatened, Ollman implies, by recognizing the psychological damage done by capitalism, damage that may undermine the capacity of the proletariat to engage in revolutionary action. Despite what followers of Marx have or haven't done, this problem has its roots in Marx's own thought, according to Ollman. Marx himself did not recognize a range of non-material human interests that can lead people to behave 'irrationally' relative to their true material interests.

Ollman's criticism rings true. Marx was not enough of a social psychologist to recognize how certain human needs (such as, for identity, self-esteem, autonomy) could actually become obstacles to 'rational' action and the formation of class consciousness. Certainly these other human needs and how they are satisfied, denied, or distorted by capitalism, must be taken into account in any Marxist social psychology. A first step in doing this, Ollman proposes, is to pursue a Marxist analysis of character structure, something not found in any adequate form in Marx's own works.

R. M. Kanter (1977:259-260) puts essentially this same criticism in another form, focusing on the Marxist view of the "person-organization relationship." In her own excellent study of the person-organization relationship, Kanter found people's orientations to the future, based on internal opportunity structures, an important factor in shaping their organizational behavior. Marxist studies of the labor process ignore these sorts of things in favor of looking at the division of labor, managerial control, and routinization. According to Kanter this results in a limited view of "the ways in which organizational structure impacts on individuals."

Kanter's general point is well taken. Marxists have ignored certain important dimensions of workplace experience and their effects on individuals. Kanter's suggestion, however, that "future orientations" or "job ladders" or whatever else, should be included in a Marxist analysis because they seem to be important for how individuals within a firm respond to their work, misses the point. From a Marxist perspective the analytical task should proceed from the outside in, to explore how the imperatives of capitalism shape workplace experiences, and how these in turn affect individuals. Reversing this approach brings with it the danger of being distracted by a plethora of social-psychological variables which may or may not be related to the functioning of capitalism in any systematic way.[8]

Overcoming these limitations requires both an elaboration and a narrowing. First, Marx must be elaborated theoretically on a social-psychological level to more clearly show how the subjective experience of alienated labor can affect psychological functioning and arouse affective responses. Moreover, this must be done in a way that maintains consistency with his structual analysis of capitalism, else the latter is lost. Second, for purposes of empirical research, this theoretical field must be narrowed to focus on a set of specifiable and examinable cognitive and affective consequences that can be shown to follow from workplace experiences and, ultimately, from the imperatives of capitalism. The next chapter is devoted to developing this theoretical field and to using it to formulate researchable questions.

A NOTE ON STUDIES OF WORK AND ALIENATION

Marxist and mainstream American sociologists sharing interests in the effects of work on workers have also shared an interest in alienation. But in the latter case this shared interest is more apparent than real. Alienation in mainstream American sociology is only nominally related to the concept of alienated labor in Marxist theory (see Fischer, 1976; Plasek, 1974; Ludz, 1976; Archibald, 1976; Schewitzer, 1981). As has been explicated in this chapter, alienated labor is an objective, publicly-observable phenomenon having to do with producers' lack of control over their labor. In mainstream American sociology, especially following publication of Melvin Seeman's influential article in 1959, 'alienation' has referred to a grab bag of unpleasant subjective feeling-states (powerlessness, normlessness, meaninglessness, and so on).[9] Thus in contrast to the Marxist perspective, alienation in mainstream sociology is largely a psychological malaise experienced by maladjusted workers.

The mainstream perspective on alienation confuses the affective consequences of alienated labor with alienation in toto. It fails to recognize the feeling-states it takes as constituting alienation as necessarily following from the imperatives of capitalist production, preferring instead to see them as endemic to work in an industrial society. Indeed, inasmuch as mainstream industrial sociology has no theory of the capitalist labor process, it cannot see beyond what is immediately apparent in the workplace. Thus the sources of these bad feelings are variously identified as technology, the division of labor, limited career opportunities, work rules, etc.[10]

Seldom are questions raised about who controls technology, who divides labor, who limits whose career opportunities, or who makes work rules. And almost never are questions raised about why technology is used as it is, and why labor is divided as it is, and so on. To answer these questions requires more than correlating workplace conditions with feelings of powerlessness. It requires analyzing the functioning of capitalism itself, a task mainstream sociologists studying "work and alienation" have unscrupulously avoided.[11]

Mainstream studies of work and alienation, most based on Seeman's social-psychological, multi-dimensional conception of alienation, have thus not been reviewed here for one simple reason: they are not theoretically relevant. (Blauner's study in the Seeman-inspired tradition was discussed because it inadvertently raised important questions about the variability of the effects of alienated labor.) To say that these studies are *theoretically* irrelevant is not, however, to deny the potential usefulness of their findings, if those findings can be meaningfully interpreted from a Marxist perspective. So too other studies of the effects of work on workers, regardless of their theoretical origins, may also contain findings of interest. As appropriate, these studies and their findings will be drawn upon and evaluated from the theoretical perspective employed here.

The purpose of this chapter has been to present the Marxist theory of alienated labor as the foundation from which this study proceeds. Drawing on both Marx's philosophical anthropology and his structural analysis of capitalism, my goal is to establish a series of connections between the imperatives of capitalist production, workplace experiences, and the psychological effects of these experiences. As acknowledged, Marx's concept of alienated labor is, in the form he left it, underdeveloped for guiding such a project to completion. Marx requires theoretical elaboration on a social-psychological level in order to formulate researchable questions about the cognitive and affective consequences of alienated labor. In the next chapter the social psychology of G.H. Mead is used to provide the necessary theoretical elaboration of Marx and to establish an operational basis for researching the psychological effects of working for capitalism.

2

Natural Labor

*The secret of how to work, which is the
secret of how to live, begins with the need
to learn.*

Carla Needleman
in *The Work of Craft*

George Herbert Mead did not so
much offer an explicit theory of human nature as he did a theory of life.
Certainly, though, Mead identified what was special about human nature, but only within a larger view of the life process. His system of
thought thus begins with the simplest organism's struggle to survive and
builds from there to account for the most complex forms of human behavior. This system of thought, much more elaborate in its treatment of
human social functioning than Marx's, provides the theoretical means to
account for the cognitive and affective consequences of human labor.

AN ADAPTING ANIMAL

Also a thoroughgoing naturalist, Mead constructed his system of
thought by analyzing the life process in terms of the behavior of organisms in relation to their environments (1934:1-41). All Mead assumed in
the first instance was that "a certain systematic physico-chemical process
arises which so selects what it reacts upon as to maintain the process, and

that this process, appearing within the physical world, emerges as life (1932:69-70)." The key idea here is selection, for what an organism is sensitive to and selects as its environment determines its life process. In Mead's words,

> Primarily living forms react to external stimulation in such fashion as to preserve the living process. The peculiar method that distinguishes their reactions from the motions of inanimate objects is that of selection. This selection is due to the sensitivity of the living form (1932:71).

Mead's point is that all living organisms select their environments by reacting to those aspects of the physical world relevant for their survival. As Mead said, they determine the objects and influences to which they will respond.[1]

Certain types of organisms are distinguishable, however, by virtue of what they are capable of reacting to in the interest of survival. As Mead went on to say,

> The conscious animal carries selection into the field of its own response. It responds to the influence or effect the outer world has upon it (1932:71).

In a nutshell this is Mead's definition of consciousness: the ability to respond to *internal* responses evoked by external stimuli. Most living organisms cannot do this and are thus bound to reacting directly to external stimuli; as such, they can never choose how to act. But neither does mere consciousness permit a choice of alternative acts, for consciousness involves only an awareness of internal states as elements of a field of stimuli. Choice in action requires that an organism be capable of selectively responding to internal stimuli, inhibiting some such responses and carrying through others. This requires self-consciousness, which involves an organism's reflexive awareness of impulses to act.

Like all living organisms, humans determine their environments based on what they must respond to in order to survive. Moreover, they are capable of perceiving and responding to their internal states. But unlike most organisms—from amoebas to the lower apes—they are not bound to a set of unmediated instinctive or conditioned responses to external or internal stimuli.[2] Rather, they are capable of differentiating between external stimuli and internal responses, and of selectively carrying through those internal responses most likely to produce desired ends. In use, this capacity is self-consciousness. In response to changing environmental circumstances such a capacity, Mead argued, has tremendous adaptive value.

According to Mead, the capacity for self-consciousness depends on the complexity of an organism's central nervous system. This is especially important in Mead's view for allowing an organism to respond in complex and discriminating ways to distant (that is, non-contact) stimuli:

> the great advance comes with the development of the encephalon. This is primarily the nerve center of the important distance senses. As these become more powerful and refined in their discriminations, the contact experiences to which they respond are delayed, and possibilities of adjustment and of choice in response are thus increased. In the innervations of the attitudes that distant objects call out the animal feels the invitation of the threat they carry with them. He experiences his own repressed responses in his response to the distant stimulation. His responses to his own tendencies to act provide the control that organizes all his responses into a coordinated act... (1932:70-71).

A highly developed central nervous system and perceptual apparatus are thus necessary for an organism to develop alternative ways of responding to the world. In Mead's view, these alternatives give rise to self consciousness, which is an adaptive response to the possibility of carrying out alternative acts of adjustment.

Equally important to Mead in this respect was the evolutionary development of the human hand, which, in making possible extremely complex manipulations of the physical world, also made possible an enormous variety of adaptive responses to it (Mead, 1934:363; 1982:119). In conjunction with this manipulatory capacity the cognitive capacity to choose alternative responses to environmental stimuli took on increased adaptive value—the adaptive value of the latter appearing only in relation to the former. In Mead's view, then, human cognitive and physiological development are interdependent evolutionary consequences of a process of adaptation; there is no split between nature and human development in Mead's system of thought.

In this framework humans are seen as distinguished by their capacities to act self-consciously and to manipulate the physical world in complex ways, both capacities being based on prerequisite physiological species characteristics. Mead did not, however, leap from physiology to self-consciousness to complex social behavior. There are several additional and critically important elements in his account of human social behavior that must be considered. But these are all based on the evolutionary, naturalist premise that humans, like all living organisms, must adapt to live. All else follows from this.

Role Taking, Self, And Community

In Mead's view self-consciousness did not arise with the mere appearance of the hand and brain as aspects of human physiology. It emerged, rather, as an adaptive response to the need for coordinated action to facilitate species survival. Along with hands and brains, the ability to coordinate action had tremendous adaptive value. It permitted early hominids to hunt, gather food, defend themselves, and otherwise transform nature with great effectiveness. Quite simply, those who could coordinate action were more likely to adapt, to survive, than those who could not. Mead's explanation of how such coordination is possible is the key to his whole account of human social behavior.

To understand this account it is useful to begin with Mead's distinction between primitive and fully social interaction (Mead, 1934: 42-134). Primitive interaction occurs when certain animals, wolves and ants for example, appear to coordinate their actions. While such animals can indeed engage in highly complex integrated behavior, what they cannot do is coordinate their actions by using significant symbols. The latter requires, according to Mead, that organisms be capable of using physical or vocal gestures to intentionally arouse particular responses in others. Although animals do arouse responses in each other, they cannot do so in this way. Their reactions to external stimuli, including each other, are instinctive or conditioned. In this type of interaction the "gesture" of one organism is a stimulus for the response of another. But the first gesture is not a symbol used with any awareness of shared meaning. It is simply a stimulus.

Animals can thus engage in what Mead called a "conversation of gestures" and so appear to coordinate action. Humans can do much more, however. They can use significant symbols to intentionally call forth particular responses in each other. This occurs only when one organism can take the attitude of the other and so anticipate the other's response to the gesture. As Mead describes this:

> Gestures become significant symbols when they implicitly arouse in an individual making them the same responses which they explicitly arouse, or are supposed to arouse, in other individuals, the individuals to whom they are addressed; and in all conversations of gestures within the social process, whether external (between different individuals) or internal (between a given individual and himself), the individual's consciousness of the content and flow of meaning involved depends on thus taking the attitude of the other toward his own gestures (1934:47).

This "taking the attitude of the other"—or role taking—is what charac-
terizes fully social interaction. It also makes possible the emergence of
the self.

For Mead, 'the self' is not simply synonymous with self-
consciousness, although they imply each other. To be a fully self-
conscious social being is to be aware of the responses one arouses in
others. This can occur only via role taking; that is, by imaginarily experiencing one's own gestures from the standpoint of the other.[3] Thus in
Mead's view the experience of self—in the sense of self-consciousness—is
necessarily predicated on experience of the other. Indeed, in this view
there can be no self without the other. As implied above, what makes all
this possible is language—a set of significant symbols used to coordinate
interaction among members of a community.[4] It is out of this interaction
that the experience of self-consciousness and 'the self' arise.

In Mead's system of thought the self is more than self-consciousness
(Mead, 1934:135-226). It consists of both a set of impulses (that is, attitudes or predispositions to act) and a body of organized, habitualized responses to the actions proceeding from these impulses. The 'impulsive'
phase of the self Mead called the "I," which embodies the responses of the
individual to the attitudes of others. The 'controlling' phase of the self
Mead called the "Me," which embodies an organized set of *others'* attitudes that the individual assumes via role taking. These two phases of the
self represent temporally alternating moments of a process taking the
form of an internal conversation of gestures. The self, in this sense, is but
the internalization of the social process (that is, acts of adjustment being
accomplished by use of significant symbols) within the individual.

Fully social interaction can therefore occur only among beings with
selves, beings thus capable of using vocal or physical gestures to simultaneously arouse functionally identical responses in themselves and others.
In this way the emergence of the self, based on the capacity to use language and thereby role-take, makes possible complex coordinated
action. Of course, the success of any particular attempt to coordinate
action depends on the role taking that actually occurs; both (or all) inter-
actants must be able to respond to their gestures from the standpoint of
the other(s). In other words, they must be able to use significant symbols
having universal meanings. Beyond individual-to-individual role taking,
then, there must also exist among any group of interacting individuals a
shared perspective.

What socially interacting individuals must share, according to
Mead, is the internalized perspective of the "generalized other"
(1934:152-164). The generalized other is an amalgam of others' attitudes
incorporated into the Me phase of the self. It is essentially the abstracted

'attitude of the community' the individual adopts in responding to his own actions. When individuals come to share a generalized other by virtue of socialization into a community, they can anticipate the responses of others to their gestures by adopting this common attitude. Because individuals can organize others' attitudes into a general community attitude, they can interact universally, insofar as those they interact with share at least a part of this general attitude (see also Stone and Farberman, 1981:2-11). The generalized other is what allows people to jointly organize their behavior in predictable, effective, and socially acceptable ways.

Social behavior in a community is thus the basis for the emergence of both the self and the generalized other that permits complex coordinated action. In this view the individual is a conscious, rational being only because he participates in the social behavior of a community. An individual does not think first and then become a member of a community; rather, he can think at all only because he is a member of a community. And he is a member of a community only because of natural evolutionary processes that realized the adaptive value of coordinated action. In the Meadian scheme of things there are thus no artificial problems of mind-body dualism or individual-versus-society ontology. Mead's analysis explains the emergence of consciousness, self, and community out of natural, unconscious processes of adaptation.

MEAD'S PHILOSOPHY OF THE ACT

Organisms must adjust to survive. This involves responding to stimuli that satisfy life-sustaining interests, as well as responding to novel conditions that may arise and impinge on the life process. Mead saw all behavior as built up out of a continual succession of acts of adjustment. Mead (1938) analyzed these acts in terms of four sequential phases: impulse, perception, manipulation, and consummation. Although contemporary social psychologists, even symbolic interactionists, have paid relatively scant attention to Mead's philosophy of the act, it is every bit as important to his system of thought as the more popular notion of the self (cf. Meltzer, et al., 1975:27-42).

The initiating phase of the act, the impulse, is present in the organism. It is a predisposition to act toward a particular stimulus in a particular way. In Mead's terminology a stimulus in an organism's environment "answers to" an impulse present in an organism. For example, an apple can be a stimulus answering to the impulse 'hunger' in an organism capable of eating apples. Under other circumstances, however, an apple might also answer to an impulse to seek a projectile for, say, self-defense. Whether an object is food or weaponry to an organism depends on the impulse the organism is attempting to satisfy with reference to the object. Such impulses can be biological or, in the case of humans, social in origin.

Perception is the first mediating phase of the act. It presupposes an impulse and, by implication, an ongoing act. Viewed in this way perception is not passive but is always linked to some purpose or interest of a perceiving organism.[5] In humans, perception is always perception of a distant (that is, as-yet-out-of-reach) object relevant for satisfying an impulse. Perception involves anticipation, prior to contact, of an object's value for satisfying an impulse. For example, perceiving an apple as a potential weapon involves anticipating its possible use in a particular act, such as throwing it. In this sense the entire act is 'collapsed' in perception of the object. Perception is referred to as a mediating phase of the act because it guides, or mediates, the progress of the act as it moves toward consummation. To put it another way, perception initially organizes behavior with respect to the potential consummatory value of an object. Thereafter manipulation becomes important.

Manipulation is the second mediating phase of the act. In manipulation, contact with the distant object is achieved and its resistance confronted. If contact brings no surprises, manipulation can bring about consummation as anticipated. But if an object's resistance is not as anticipated, it becomes necessary to reorganize behavior with respect to the object. This represents a 'problem' that must be 'solved' during the manipulatory phase of the act if consummation is to be achieved. If when contact is finally made, the apple-qua-weapon turns out to be rotten and soft, its anticipated value for satisfying an impulse to procure a weapon must be reassessed. Action toward the apple, now recognized to be worthless as a weapon, must be reorganized. Manipulation is thus also referred to as a mediating phase of the act because, depending on the resistance encountered during the contact experience it brings, it may lead to modification or discontinuation of an act. Consummation, the terminating phase of the act, is the stage of fulfillment. In consummation the impulse that initiated the act is satisfied, the act of adjustment is completed. Or, with reference to an object, it can be said that its value for satisfying an impulse is realized in consummation. So the apple, to continue the example, may literally be consumed to satisfy a hunger. One act of adjustment is thereby completed. Or, in the other case, the thrown apple may strike and deter an advancing foe, thus consummating an act of self-defense.

All acts of adjustment, however, do not necessarily involve each of these phases. The simplest *non-social act*, for example, involves only the expression of an impulse and more or less immediate consummation. By way of example Mead cited the predator killing its prey and eating it. Such an act does not involve a manipulatory phase, according to Mead, because the predator does not pause to consciously consider how to manipulate its prey so best to satisfy its hunger; for the nonself-conscious predator, the killing and the eating are one act. *Primitive social acts* also exclude the manipulatory phase. Such acts involve organisms relating to the actions and reactions of other organisms; however, the links between stimuli (one organism's actions) and responses (another organism's reactions) are direct and unmediated. No conscious consideration of alternative manipulatory strategies arises. *Social acts,* as only beings with selves are capable of, involve all phases of the act as discussed above.

The importance of the manipulatory phase of the act in Mead's system of thought is difficult to overstate. In his evolutionary view the possibility of carrying out complex manipulations of physical objects by use of the hand was instrumental to the emergence of self-consciousness.[6] Without this manipulatory capacity options for adaptive action would be limited and the ability to use significant symbols to call forth alternative responses (that is, various possible acts of adjustment) in one's self or others would be of little adaptive value. But in that possibilities for complex manipulations create possibilities for alternative acts of adjustment, the ability to use symbols to resolve conflicting tendencies to act takes on considerable adaptive value. Self-consciousness and the manipulatory phase of the act thus arose hand in hand, so to speak. Without the ability to extend the manipulatory phase of the act hominids could not have become self-conscious beings. They could not, in fact, have become human.

In Mead's system of thought the act is the fundamental unit of social behavior. All such behavior, whether as simple as eating an apple or as complex as performing brain surgery, is built up out of a continual series of impulses, perceptions, manipulations, and consummations. But not all acts proceed smoothly from impulse to consummation. As noted above, problems can arise and impede completion of the act. The ability to use language allows humans to respond to these situations in a special way: they can think.

PROBLEM SOLVING, THINKING, AND THE CREATIVE ADVANCE OF NATURE

When acts of adjustment are impeded the organism is said to confront a problematic situation. These are instances in which habit alone is an inadequate guide to action. Perhaps because of some new configuration of circumstances, changes in the environment, or changes in the organism, what always worked before no longer does. Under these circumstances nonself-conscious organisms can only discontinue an act or resort to trial and error in attempting to complete it. Beings with selves, however, are able to respond rationally, with conscious consideration of means in relation to ends.

For humans, acts are most likely to be impeded in the manipulatory phase when contact experience conflicts with the anticipated response of an object; that is, when the obdurate world and the objects in it do not respond to one's actions in a way that leads to completion of an act as anticipated. Action must then be reorganized if the initiating impulse is to be satisfied. In Mead's view, problem solving begins at this stage of reorganization. Successful problem solving consists in discovering a new course of action such that the impeded act can be completed. Unlike animals, humans need not immediately resort to trial-and-error behavior when problems arise. By means of language they can think.

Because beings with selves can carry on an internal conversation of gestures, proposing to themselves alternative courses of action when problems arise, they can carry out much trial-and-error behavior symbolically. They can use symbols to call forth in themselves alternative responses to the problematic situation (in the present), these symbols representing completed acts (in the past) and potential acts (in the future). According to Mead, using symbols in this way to overcome a problematic situation constitutes thinking; it is a process of symbolically formulating alternative lines of action that might allow an act to be consummated. The following passage from the introduction to Mead's (1938) *Philosophy of the Act* elaborates this and sums up a number of points made previously:

> In reflective thinking the organism not only responds to its own organic states but responds to its own responses. That is, the human being, because of its highly developed nervous system, is able to present to himself ideationally an entire act after the act has once been carried out and when there is a tendency to carry it out again. In other words, one can hold on to the past by

employing symbols, such as those used in language, which are representative of acts. Such a consciousness of an act makes possible a distinction between past and present; and, when past action is broken up and reorganized in an attempt to respond successfully to an anticipated, oncoming event, the future likewise becomes prominent in thinking. Thus a psychological specious present may be extended into both a past and a future, and, although reflective thinking is dependent upon both inorganic and organic processes, it transcends both and is the highest type of sociality involving communication or role taking, meaning, knowing, and inference. In fact, reflective thinking is the highest development of the general method of adaptation necessary to adjustment and the survival of emergent forms (193:ixv).[7]

According to Mead, then, thinking is an attempt to solve a problem by the "symbolic indication of possible futures" to one's self (see also Blumer, 1969:61-77). In this process the past can be reconstructed as symbols are cognitively manipulated in trying to guide an act toward consummation in the future. Beings with selves, capable of using language, are thus not bound to acting solely on either a trial-and-error basis or on the basis of conditioned responses. They can use symbols to construct novel acts out of past experience and can thereby transcend both habit and instinct when neither proves to be an adequate guide to completing an act. Of course, the alternative ways of consummating an act humans can propose to themselves (what Mead called hypotheses) are not guaranteed solutions to problems but only possible ones. Ultimately, problems are 'solved' only when an impeded act is consummated.

Most human action is not this complicated, however. Much of it is no more complicated than animal behavior. Habit does, indeed *must*, suffice for guiding most acts to completion. If it did not, humans would be caught up in endless problem solving such that basic acts of adjustment, eating for example, would be delayed to the point of threatening survival. In Mead's view habit is just as important as problem solving. Indeed, it is the express function of problem solving not only to bring acts to completion, but to form habits. These habits, represented by memories of successful acts, can then serve to guide action in the future. In short, this is how humans learn and 'accumulate knowledge'. In this way problem solving contributes to more than just the formation of habit; it contributes to the creative advance of nature.

When humans freely pursue satisfaction of diverse biological and social impulses they continually confront the resistance of objects in the world. In this process novel situations inevitably arise, problems must be solved, behavior must be reorganized. When reflective thinking produces a line of action effective in overcoming a problem, this represents, in Mead's terminology, "reorganization of a perspective." This means the relationship between an organism and its environment is altered. Alterations that serve the life process constitute creative advances of nature.

For humans a creative advance of nature brings into being new perceptual objects and new possibilities for action. The reorganized perspective, which is a reorganized relationship between subject and object, brings with it possibilities for experience that did not exist previously. These experiences are the novel, emergent aspects of human life. While creative advances of nature can occur without reflective thought—as in the case of an adaptive mutation—beings with selves can pursue such advances intentionally. They can consciously try to reorganize perspectives and bring themselves into more adequate relationships with their environments. To do so humans need only actively confront the world and struggle to solve the problems that inhibit satisfaction of their numerous and diverse impulses.

AESTHETIC EXPERIENCE

In Mead's philosophy of the act consummation is the stage of fulfillment. Mead saw this stage of the act as bringing with it natural pleasure in attaining the reward value in the stimulus to the act. Based on his philosophy of the act, Mead's view of aesthetic experience is straightforward: it is the penetration of the consummatory phase of the act into the manipulatory phase (1938:445-457). That is, aesthetic experience is a prescient experience of the pleasure of consummation during the manipulatory phase of the act. As Mead described it:

> What is peculiar to [aesthetic experience] is its power to catch the enjoyment that belongs to the consummation, the outcome, of an undertaking and to give to the implements, the objects that are instrumental in the undertaking, and to the acts that compose it something of the joy and satisfaction that suffuse its successful accomplishment (1938:454).

Like consciousness, aesthetic experience is explained in Mead's system of thought as a natural phenomenon. It is simply the appreciation of the end value of an act as the act is being carried out. It is not a mystical or spiritual arousal. But while this account of what constitutes aesthetic experience is simple enough, it does have some more complex entailments.

Aesthetic experience requires, first of all, that the relationship between manipulation and consummation be understood and appreciated. Merely fondling an object during the manipulatory phase of the act won't necessarily evoke aesthetic experience. If aesthetic experience is to arise, an understanding of how manipulation might bring about consummation is essential. In other words, aesthetic experience involves calling forth the pleasureful response of consummation during the manipulatory phase of the act—but the prerequisite for this is a grasp of how manipulation can lead to consummation. By way of example Mead cited the artisan who stops his act of production to appreciate his tools and the results they allow him to achieve. In so doing the artisan enters what Mead called an "aesthetic mood."

By implication aesthetic experience requires a self and role taking. Only by imagining the future can an individual experience the joy of consummation in manipulation. And only beings with selves can imagine the future. But to restate an important point: the mere capacity to imagine the future, or the endpoint of an act, is not sufficient to engender aesthetic experience. When manipulatory activity is not understood as related to satisfaction of an impulse (that is, when such activity is meaningless), no aesthetic experience can arise.[8] Aesthetic experience depends on understanding and appreciating the relationship between the means and ends of an activity.

Since, according to Mead, aesthetic experience arises in the manipulatory phase of the act, there is also a correlation between problem solving and aesthetic experience. When action is guided by habit alone, the pause to appreciate one's tools is less likely to occur. While it is by no means impossible for aesthetic experience to arise in habitualized action, it is simply less likely to occur because the reflective thinking that establishes the imaginary links between manipulation and consummation is not called for. The appearance of a problem, however, is cause for stopping to reflect on one's tools (or actions in general) and the effects one is trying to produce. In general, the reflective thinking that constitutes problem solving calls into imagination numerous links between manipulation and consummation. As such, aesthetic experience is more likely to arise in what is commonly thought of as challenging activity than in highly routinized activity.

Finally, Mead seems to imply there is a necessary moral dimension to aesthetic experience. More than just understanding the relationship between the means and ends, Mead suggests one must be satisfied with the means and ends themselves. In this regard Mead commented:

> But those that can import the aesthetic experience into activity must be fortunately engaged and engaged in rewarding undertakings. And this means more than the mere adaptation of means to end, the mere successful co-operative fashioning of the goods which are enjoyed in common. The enjoyment of its ultimate use must be suggested by the intermediate steps in its production and flow naturally into the skill which constructs it. It is this which gives joy to creation and belongs to the work of the artist, the research scientist, and skilled artisan who can follow his article through to its completion (1938:457).

Although David Miller, a foremost Meadian scholar, contends this is essential to aesthetic experience as Mead defined it, Mead's own position does not seem so clear (but see Miller, 1973:218-227).

Logically, within Mead's system of thought, complete moral satisfaction with means and ends is not necessary for aesthetic experience. All that is necessary is that an act—wherein there is consciousness of a relationship between manipulation and consummation—satisfy an impulse of an actor. By implication, if an impulse is being satisfied, the ends in question are already accepted. While it seems reasonable to suppose that strong moral commitment to particular means and ends might intensify aesthetic experience (by enhancing the joy of consummation), based on Mead's own framework it cannot be held as essential to it. What is obviously true, however, is that aesthetic experience is unlikely to arise any time people are forced to act contrary to their wills, thus satisfying no impulses of their own; or when necessity demands the use of manipulatory strategies conflicting with normal moral standards.

THE MEAD AND MARX CONNECTION

Based on the foregoing, several important points of convergence between Meadian and Marxian thought should be apparent. Perhaps the foremost point of convergence is at the level of philosophical anthropology. As naturalists, both Marx and Mead saw humans as animals specially distinguished by capacities for self-consciousness, reflective thinking, symbol use, and imagination. While Marx began with self-conscious humans transforming nature to survive, Mead, even more basically, began with primitive, unconscious adaptation. Starting at this point allowed Mead to construct not just a philosophical anthropology but a whole cosmology. Within this broader view Mead, in a manner highly complementary to Marx, was able to offer an account of things Marx took for granted. Thus, for example, while both men saw self-consciousness as emergent out of the cooperative activity necessary for survival, Mead's view explains how self-consciousness arose and how it functions in human social life. In this respect Mead nicely illuminates the basement of Marx's philosophical anthropology.

The emphasis both men placed on manipulatory activity is also interesting and important. Marx began his analysis with manipulatory activity: the transformation of the material world. While Marx recognized that self-consciousness was linked to the process of cooperatively transforming nature, his analysis proceeded in an historical rather than social-psychological direction. He therefore never developed a complete theory of consciousness or personality formation. Mead, on the other hand, probed more deeply and was able to explain the ontogenetic and functional relationships of manipulatory activity to human thought. Along these dimensions Mead's analysis is perfectly compatible with Marx's. It is just more elaborate.

Two further points of convergence and one point of alleged divergence between Meadian and Marxian thought deserve discussion. First, Mead and Marx shared not only a similar philosophical anthropology, but a similar sociological perspective on human nature. Both saw humans as having a general, non-historically contingent nature, and a socially constructed nature contingent on historical circumstances. Such characteristics as self-consciousness, the need to build, the capacities to imagine, use symbols, and think, are part of a general human nature found in any historical period. But the actual contents of consciousness and imagination, the symbols used, and modes of thought prevailing in any historical period can and do vary. Both Mead and Marx recognized these aspects of human nature as historically variable depending on the actual experiences of individuals in the world. Failing to distinguish philosophical anthropology from sociology in this way has led to distorted portrayals of the Marxian view of human nature as infinitely malleable. In fact, the Marxian view is much like the Meadian view, which sees people (selves) as malleable in content but not in basic form or function. This distinction is emphasized here to clear the ground for later merging Meadian and Marxian views on how actual experiences in the world affect consciousness and psychological functioning.

A further point of convergence concerns the notion of self-objectification. While Mead did not develop the idea of self-objectification in quite the way Marx did, his concerns with the matter of creativity reveal a similar orientation. In Mead's view, despite the thoroughly social nature of the individual, the individual remains the locus of creativity, which consists in a unique response to some stimulus or problematic situation. Such a response might take the form of a work of art, a mathematical equation, or a novel scientific hypothesis. If an individual can take the role of the other and recognize his response as an expression of the "I" phase of the self, the Meadian equivalent of self-objectification has occurred. It consists in the Me seeing the I reflected in the world (Mead, 1934:196-197; 214-22). Although the terminology is different from Marx's, the experience in question is essentially the same.

Finally, there is a point of alleged divergence between Meadian and Marxian thought that merits comment. Some have noted the incompatible views of truth characterizing Pragmatism (Mead) and Materialism (Marx). Ropers (1973:48) makes this point succinctly: "For Marxism truth is discovered in practice, for Pragmatism it is created in practice." Even if one were comparing the commonly understood Pragmatist and Materialist (not *Marxist*) notions of truth, this distinction would be debatable. If one is comparing Mead and Marx no debate is warranted at all.

To make a case for this as a point of divergence between Mead and Marx one must construe Mead as an idealist who sees truth as subjective or 'lodged in the mind' (see for example, Lichtman, 1970). Such a construal is entirely inaccurate; Mead is no such idealist philosopher. What humans take to be true is, for Mead, a product of shared perspectives and forms of life. While it is correct to say, albeit in dangerously abbreviated terms, Pragmatism sees truth as "created in practice," Mead himself said it a bit differently:

Knowledge is a process in conduct that so organizes the field of action that delayed and inhibited responses may take place. The test of the success of the process of knowledge, that is, the test of truth is found in the discovery or construction of objects as will mediate our conflicting and checked activities and allow conduct to proceed (1932:68).

Thus in a Pragmatist tradition, Mead says the *test of truth* lies in action; those understandings of the world that "allow conduct to proceed" (that is, those that work) will be *taken as true* by those sharing a common perspective (see also Mead, 1932:161-175). But truth is not solely dependent on collective imagination. For Mead the world is really 'out there' existing independently of human consciousness. Moreover, it consists of an obdurate material reality that resists human action. Effective understandings of the world—those that can compete for the label 'true'—must therefore reflect its material character. In Mead's view such understandings must ultimately be grounded in contact experience with the world.

This understanding of how truth is "created in practice" is hardly at odds with Marx's. In his second thesis on Feuerbach Marx wrote:

> The question whether objective truth can be attributed to human thinking is not a question of theory but is a practical question. Man must prove the truth, that is, the reality and power, the this-sidedness of his thinking in practice. The dispute over the reality of or non-reality of thinking which is isolated from practice is a purely scholastic question ([1845], 1972:108).

Thus despite an attempt to drive a wedge between Pragmatism and Materialism on the issue of truth, this is a non-problem for making the Mead/Marx connection (see also Goff,1980:91). Both men saw truth—and the process whereby truth is created—as rooted in action and communal life.

Numerous theorists have recognized the complementarity of Meadian and Marxian thought (Batuik and Sacks, 1981; Goff, 1980; Blake, 1976; Ropers, 1973; Janousek, 1972;Anderson, 1971; Lichtman, 1970; Baumann, 1969; Berger and Luckmann, 1967; Gerth and Mills, 1953). But few have gone beyond either noting the compatibility of Mead and Marx with respect to their conceptions of human nature, or asserting the desirability of infusing structural Marxism with a concern for subjective reality via symbolic interactionism.The strategy here is different. By focusing on Mead and Marx themselves and ignoring their followers for the moment, I have tried to demonstrate their fundamental compatibility and complementarity. But this has not been done in the interest of turning Marx into a symbolic interactionist or Mead into an historical materialist. Rather, the interest is in organizing a new perspective, based on the original insights of these two powerful thinkers, that can account for the structure of a labor process and the ways in which this structure affects individuals. The next step in this reorganization is to begin tying together some of the major ideas presented thus far.

Alienation As The Denial Of Aesthetic Experience

In alienated labor producers do not control the means and ends of their productive activities, they do not use all their mental and physical powers to bring into being objects with use values, nor do they experience self-objectification. As argued in the previous chapter, all this follows from the fact of domination in production. This domination reduces potentially free-choosing humans to acting as the instruments of another's will. Marx argued the experience attendant to performing such labor was joyless and produced a mode of consciousness through which subject and object were perceived as unconnected. To offer a more detailed explanation than Marx as to why alienated labor should produce such effects, it is useful to reanalyze alienated labor in terms of Mead's philosophy of the act.

Alienated labor, first of all, satisfies no immediate impulse of a producer. This is by definition the case when one is acting as the instrument of another's will. It is obviously true, however, that even alienated labor must satisfy some impulse, else no one would engage in it at all. This impulse is, in a general sense, to maintain the life process. Individuals enter into dominant-subordinate relations of production to satisfy impulses to acquire objects such as food, clothing, and housing which are necessary for survival. But such impulses cannot be satisfied *in* waged labor (as they could be in the labor of growing one's own food, making one's own clothes, etc.). Rather, they can be satisfied only outside the labor process via wages. A person entering a wage relationship to build widgets, for example, does not seek to satisfy an impulse to build widgets; no such impulse is typically present. The impulse is to procure, say, an automobile, which can be purchased with wages.

Because alienated labor does not satisfy any immediate impulse of a producer, its results are not expressions of the "I." The individual does not perceive what he does as an expression of his unique self. What he does express, rather, is his need to obtain the means of survival. In a Meadian sense this is the meaning of alienated labor; its meaning does not lie in expressing the I in any unique way, but in merely maintaining the life process. Strictly speaking, then, alienated labor itself is not devoid of meaning, its meaning is simply equivalent to that of any other animal function necessary to survival. This is the Meadian corollary to Marx's point that alienated labor involves no self-objectification and, as such, does not constitute a uniquely human activity.

It should be acknowledged at this point, however, that even alienated labor involves impulses, perceptions, manipulations, and consummations—as it must. The important questions are: which impulses are being acted on? how are they being acted on? and what kinds of acts are being consummated? Answering these questions—something that cannot be done immediately—requires making a distinction between the many acts involved in actual productive activity and the 'meta-act' involved in participating in a labor process. Actually building a widget, for example, is likely to involve many sub-acts: procuring raw materials, shaping these materials, assembling them, and so on. If one does all this to build one's own widget, these acts constitute a meta-act consummated in using the finished widget. If one does all this for wages—to procure an automobile—the meta-act is consummated in using the auto procured with wages. (The relationships between acts, meta-acts, productive activities, and labor processes are schematically illustrated and discussed in appendix A.)

At this point it may be useful to apply the Meadian analysis to a hypothetical labor process and set of productive activities. For purposes of illustration, then, imagine a wage labor process in which productive activities: (1) are not under the control of the producers involved; (2) require no imagination or creativity; and (3) are fragmented and routinized. The approximation of these hypothetical circumstances to what Marx observed to be the case under capitalism should be apparent. From a Meadian perspective what such conditions of production do is preclude, or severely inhibit, aesthetic experience.

With reference to this hypothetical example aesthetic experience would be inhibited in three ways. First, the lack of producer control over the means and ends of production (in a wage labor relationship) implies productive activities are not oriented to satisfying producers' own impulses; in this case those whose acts transform nature achieve no consummation of their initiating impulses in those acts. The meta-act involved here would be consummated only when productive activity ceased, wages were paid, and various objects thereby acquired. It is possible, however, for a type of consummatory pleasure to arise in such activity. This could occur if a wage laborer imagined the relationship between the time spent working and, say, the size of a paycheck ["Another hour of overtime and my check will hit $500"]. It could also occur if the relationship between time spent working and procurement of a desired object were imagined ["Each hour of overtime brings me closer to having a new car"]. But in neither case is this aesthetic experience arising naturally in productive activity oriented to satisfying an immediate need. It is more like an attempt to find some satisfaction in an inherently unsatisfying activity via mental gymnastics.

Second, in the absence of a requirement for imagination or creativity, aesthetic experience is minimized because an individual need not call forth an image of an object-to-be-created. To say no imagination or creativity is required is to say ends are predetermined; there is thus no need for images to be called forth to guide the act to completion. Forethought becomes superfluous. This being the case, aesthetic experience is unlikely to arise since it depends on symbolically exploring the relationship between an imaginary object-to-be-created and the means of its creation.[9]

Again, however, this is not to say aesthetic experience cannot arise in mundane or routine transformative acts. In principle it can.[10] But since it depends on individuals reflecting on the relation between means and ends—either to solve a problem or to produce a creative effect—it is less likely to arise in unimaginative work where means, reduced to mere behavior, overshadow predetermined ends.

While lack of control and predetermination of ends can inhibit aesthetic experience, it seems fragmentation and routinization might preclude it entirely. A highly fragmented (that is, highly sub-divided) production process does this by undermining a producer's understanding of the production process as a whole. In such a situation workers need not understand the whole process; all they need to know to participate competently is how to perform a single task. The relations of their task to other tasks, to the process as a whole, and to the final product are functionally irrelevant. These conditions are hardly conducive to developing an understanding of or appreciation for the unitary relationship between means and ends. Without this, the pleasure of consummation cannot be imported into the manipulatory phase of the act. Fragmentation can thus preclude aesthetic experience by preventing understanding and appreciation of the means-end relationship.

Fragmentation would also preclude aesthetic experience in another way. Sub-divided production tasks do not result in finished objects; workers merely perform limited operations. Rather than producing a complete widget, a worker merely contributes in some minor way to its overall production. Workers thus produce no objects with use values, but make partial contributions to the ultimate exchange value of a final commodity, which is the sum of a series of incomplete productive acts. Most importantly, under such conditions workers cannot take the role of the user of an object they produce, for they are producing, in their immediate activity, no finished objects with consummatory value. The consummatory phase of the act cannot be imported into the manipulatory unless this role taking is possible. Productive activity such as this, wherein the production of objects with definite use values is replaced by the performance of operations, precludes the aesthetic experience derivable from imaginary consummation through role taking.

Routinization, by itself, constrains opportunities for aesthetic experience to arise because it obviates the need for problem solving. As such, it eliminates occasions where one must reflect on one's tools, methods, and goals, and in this dwell on relationships between means and ends. Routinization thus eliminates the need for reflective thinking and so eliminates from production the cognitive activity giving rise to aesthetic experience. Taken together, fragmentation and routinization can attenuate the manipulatory phase of the act to the point where little or no thinking is necessary at all. Productive tasks of this sort not only preclude aesthetic experience, they nearly preclude the need for human intelligence. In the extreme this is the implication of the hypothetical production situation analyzed here.

This example also illustrates several things with regard to a Meadian analysis of alienated labor. It shows, first of all, that both the structure of a labor process and the form of productive activities it encompasses can affect the constitution of producers' acts. It also shows the importance of distinguishing between a labor process and a set of productive activities. A labor process impinges on individual producers only indirectly, via the work experiences it broadly enables or constrains. What affects individuals directly are the activities they engage in, for only in these do psychologically consequential experiences arise. Only by focusing on the latter can the psychological consequences of a labor process be sensibly analyzed. Taking aesthetic experience as the focal point for considering problem solving, role taking, means-ends comprehension, and self-objectification in productive activity is one way to approach this analysis.

By interpreting alienation as the denial of aesthetic experience it is possible to assimilate Marx's understanding of the subjective dimension of alienated labor to the Meadian view. But to analyze the psychological effects of productive activities in the real world of work something more is necessary. Merely analyzing productive activity as 'alienated or not' leaves an analysis open-ended, unable to account for the consequences of whatever it is that constitutes non-alienated productive activity. An adequate analysis must be anchored at both ends, so to speak. It must describe the dimensions of subjective experience involved in both alienated and non-alienated productive activity. The next step in developing a theoretical framework adequate to guide such an analysis is, therefore, to elaborate a concept of non-alienated or natural labor.

A CONCEPT OF NATURAL LABOR

Alienated labor has been analyzed in Meadian terms as a denial of aesthetic experience. It seems appropriate therefore to begin developing a concept of natural labor by considering the necessary characteristics of activity that engenders and sustains aesthetic experience. As noted above, these characteristics must include understanding and appreciation of the means-ends relationship, action oriented to satisfying one's own impulses, and role-taking and problem-solving demands. The next step is to consider each of these characteristics in specific relation to productive activity.

In general Meadian terms, to understand and appreciate the means-end relationship is to be able to anticipate the responses of objects in the environment to one's actions on those objects. Aesthetic experience becomes possible, in principle, as soon as an individual can imagine a desired outcome and can select a line of action likely to produce it. This requires a minimal level of technical mastery over the environment and objects in it. An artist, for example, exercises this mastery when he desires to create a particular effect and can select and manipulate the tools and materials necessary to do so. But without either the appropriate skills or tractable materials, no aesthetic experience is possible for the artist or any producer. Two preconditions for aesthetic experience in productive activity are thus technical mastery and the availability of objects over which mastery can be exercised. Skills and objects must correspond to each other. In this sense these preconditions are 'relational' and situationally specific; they arise only out of the relation between a specific producer and a specific material environment.

By way of example consider first the cabinetmaker's apprentice, who can derive little pleasure from manipulating tools and materials in a production process he does not yet fully understand. The apprentice may well be able to envision a desired end (a finished cabinet), but the connection between action and that end is not yet grasped. In gaining mastery over his tools and materials the apprentice learns what effects he can create, why certain actions must be performed and how they will bear on the finished product. Until this mastery is achieved his actions will be awkward and frustrating, providing little aesthetic experience. Once it is achieved, however, the apprentice can then move from impulse to consummation in imagination and so experience aesthetic pleasure in both the imaginary and material expressions of his own will and consciousness. Now consider the journeyman cabinetmaker deprived of his tools or materials. Save for imagination, his skills can provide him no aesthetic experience without objects upon which to exercise them. Obviously this does not apply only to cabinetmakers and their apprentices. The same principles apply to any kind of productive activity.

Aesthetic experience also requires an individual be producing to satisfy impulses of his own. Aesthetic experience can therefore never arise in forced labor. But this is seldom a clearcut matter, for freedom or coercion is in the nature of the act as the actor perceives it. For example, an individual whose "I" is completely identified with the will of a group or another individual may experience no sense of coercion in working to satisfy impulses emanating from another "I." If so, there is no obstacle to aesthetic experience nor to self-objectification. Aesthetic experience thus presupposes acceptance of, or identification with, the impulses one seeks to satisfy via productive action. By implication, productive activity cannot be identified as alienated or natural without taking the perspective of the subject into account.

Aesthetic experience further depends on the possibility for role taking to occur. As discussed earlier, role taking is essential to importing the pleasure of consummation into the manipulatory phase of the act. This sort of role taking in productive activity depends on a producer's ability to conceive, in imagination, a finished product. Moreover, the product so conceived must have use value within some act imaginable by the producer. An object having no such value for a producer, even if this is only imaginary, makes it impossible to role-take with respect to the object. In other words, the object answers to no impulse of the producer; there is no attitude or role the producer can take toward the object wherein it possesses consummatory value. The object is such a case is meaningless.

Two examples may help clarify this. Imagine first the work of a knifemaker. In conceiving a new design he must orient himself to the obect-to-be-created as its potential user. Because he can do this, the imaginary knife-to-be-created is a meaningful object. While actually producing it the craftsman must continually orient himself to the object being formed from the perspective of its user. This makes it possible to continually move back and forth in imagination between manipulation and consummation. Aesthetic experience thus pervades this type of artisan production. Imagine now the drill press operator boring holes in steel plates. Although he may be able to imagine the object he is trying to create (a plate with a hole in it), it is doubtful whether he can take the role of its user. If a perforated steel plate has no use value within any act the operator can imagine, he cannot take the role of its user. Nor, therefore, can he import any consummatory pleasure into the manipulatory phase of the act. The finished product in this case is meaningless and can provide no basis for aesthetic experience.

A final point of clarification should be made regarding actual consummation by the producer versus imaginary consummation via role taking. Many systems of production, particularly those oriented to exchange, do not involve producers directly consuming or using their own products. A knifemaker may form many blades he will not use; a baker may bake many loaves he will not eat. In either case the consummatory values of the objects produced are not realized by their producers. Only via role taking can those consummatory values be appreciated. This represents no obstacle to aesthetic experience—if an object being created has potential use value within an act imaginable by its creator, role taking is possible and so too aesthetic experience. When production is oriented to exchange, a second act is 'mapped over' the imaginary use of the object—this is the act that is consummated when a final exchange occurs (see also appendix A). In other words, objects produced for exchange have value within multiple acts (see Mead, 1938:452-3). Production for exchange thus does not preclude aesthetic experience if the objects produced have potential consummatory value for their producers.

Finally, aesthetic experience can arise only when productive activity demands reflection on the means-ends relationship. This means productive activity cannot be so habitualized that thinking is no longer necessary. The manipulatory phase of the act must require calling forth an image of the final product to guide completion of the act, else there is no imagined consummation to import into the manipulatory phase of the act. These two phases are collapsed when no thinking is required. As noted above, what gives rise to aesthetic experience is the demand for thinking about one's tools, methods, and intended products. What gives rise to thinking is the need to solve problems. When productive activity requires no problem solving it can no longer be a source of aesthetic experience. To restate this in positive terms: for productive activity to sustain aesthetic experience it must demand occasional problem solving.

It should be noted that the problem solving which gives rise to aesthetic experience is not necessarily found in 'complex' productive activity. Since an activity, no matter how complex, can eventually be mastered and habitualized, complexity alone is no guarantee an activity will be a source of aesthetic pleasure. The problem solving that sustains aesthetic experience depends on novelty and variety in productive activity. When individuals are free to pursue diverse impulses in their productive activity, thereby providing themselves novelty and variety, problems will arise naturally. But when productive activity is organized to preclude novelty and variety, when it is routinized, aesthetic experience will be precluded by elimination of the need for occasional problem solving.

In sum, then, productive activity that fosters understanding of the means-ends relationship, that allows expression of the "I," that demands role taking and problem solving, will evoke and sustain aesthetic experience. But such activity also has another important consequence: the creative advance of nature. It is the creative advance of nature along with aesthetic experiences that constitute natural labor.

The creative advance of nature involves reorganization of a perspec-

tive, reorganization of the relationship between an organism and its environment. In conscious human activity this may involve a change in the
individual such that his capacities for manipulating the environment are
enhanced, thereby increasing the power to satisfy impulses. Or it may involve a changed environment such that it answers more satisfactorily to
impulses in the individual. In the context of productive activity a creative
advance of nature may consist in the development of a new skill, idea,
tool, or product. This is much like Marx's idea of human species-powers
being developed through labor. But it is more than that. Here not only
are *individual* powers developed, but nature itself; the adequacy of the
organism-environment relationship for sustaining life and satisfying impulses is objectively improved.

What then is natural labor? It is labor that expresses and satisfies an
individual's own impulses, that demands use of human capacities for
imagining, role taking, and problem solving, and that results in a creative advance of nature—a more satisfying and better life-sustaining relationship between humans and their environments. Aesthetic experience
is the subjective moment of natural labor; the creative advance of nature
is its objective moment.

THE COGNITIVE AND AFFECTIVE CONSEQUENCES OF NATURAL AND ALIENATED LABOR

Two distinct forms of productive activity have been discussed
above. Each stands in opposition to the other: alienated labor denies
what natural labor engenders and sustains. Each form thus involves a
substantially different set of experiences for individuals as they go about
transforming the world. Those engaged in natural labor, free from domination, can role-take, solve problems, reflect on the ends of their activities, and see expressions of themselves in their products. Those engaged
in alienated labor might experience none of these things; or they might
experience them in dramatically different ways. In any event it would
seem reasonable to suppose these experiences might have consequences
for an individual's worldview, cognitive development, psychological
functioning, and feelings about work. Some probable consequences of
performing natural and alienated labor are explored below.

Natural labor involves aesthetic experience and the creative advance
of nature. For purposes of considering its cognitive and affective consequences, aesthetic experience—the experience of the individual

producer—is what must concern us. The consequences of this experience can be explored by considering what it comprises (role taking, problem solving, means-ends comprehension, and self-objectification) and asking: if these things occur, what cognitive and affective consequences can be expected to follow? And conversely, what happens when they do not occur?

First of all, then, what might the consequences be of role taking in productive activity? One possible consequence is an increase in interpersonal sensitivity. Simply by virtue of learning, having to imagine how others will react to the results of one's work may bring this about (cf. Breer and Locke, 1965:270). It seems reasonable to suppose, in other words, that demands for role taking in work might sharpen an individual's role-taking skills; that is, make him a more adept role-taker. Or this demand might lead to an increased propensity or inclination to role-take; that is, increase his readiness to look at things, especially the consequences of his actions, from other points of view. In turn this might enhance an ability to role-take via the productions of others, to be able to see through objects to the human agency underlying their construction. The cognitive activity of role taking in productive activity might thus be expected to make individuals more sensitive to the perspectives of others, especially with regard to the consequences of their actions. And it might also predispose them toward seeing the human constructedness of other objects in the world, not just objects of their own creation.

If an individual does not have to role-take in production some opposite effects might be expected. If an individual need not be concerned with how anyone else will use or react to the results of his work, then sensitivity to the perspectives of others might be dulled. The individual's ability and propensity to role-take with regard to the consequences of his productive actions might thus be diminished, as might his ability and propensity to role-take via the productions of others. The human agency underlying such productions would therefore be less well perceived. In this analysis, then, a failure to role-take in productive activity is seen as contributing to the development of a reified mode of consciousness, one less likely to perceive expressions of human agency in the shape of the world.[11]

The above is closely related to an individual's own experience of self-expression in productive activity. In natural labor this self-expression is apparent in the results of one's productive activities. Through natural labor one learns that the world is shaped by human agents—oneself and others. An individual who can recognize the expression of his own interests in the world might be more likely to recognize the expression of other interests in the world. In this way self-expression, or in Marx's terms, self-objectification, is thus also a potentially important experience for determining an individual's mode of consciousness. In natural labor these experiences contribute to a way of seeing the world that makes its human origins visible. In alienated labor the lack of such experiences leaves this vision undeveloped or clouded. Thus whereas natural labor teaches an individual to see the human constructedness of the world, alienated labor denies this and leads to the formation of a reified consciousness.

Other cognitive consequences might also be expected to arise out of the experience of natural labor. These would be associated with problem solving in productive activity. Since problem solving involves different types of thinking depending on the type of problem one is trying to solve, its cognitive effects—in the form of thinking skills—could not be expected to be uniform or easy to predict. But since all problem solving involves reflection on one's activity with respect to the goal(s) of that activity, it is possible to suggest some general consequences of this.

In solving problems an individual must propose alternative hypotheses (ways of proceeding) to himself. This cognitive activity involves adopting multiple perspectives; that is, taking different attitudes toward the problematic situation in the search for a way to proceed. It seems plausible, assuming only that people can indeed develop cognitive skills, that the demand for this type of cognitive activity might result in a greater ability to look at things from different points of view. In other words, the demand for problem solving in productive activity might reasonably be expected to enhance an individual's problem-solving abilities.[12] Another consequence of the demand for adopting multiple perspectives might be a form of 'intellectual flexibility', which, from a Meadian perspective, would be virtually synonymous with the ability to adopt multiple points of view (in this case, however, the *ability* to adopt multiple points of view needs to be distinguished from the *propensity* to do so).

In contrast, productive activity requiring no problem solving would not require an individual to adopt multiple points of view. As a result, an individual's ability to adopt multiple perspectives might remain undeveloped; he might thus exhibit less intellectual flexibility.[13]

Comprehension of the means-ends relationship is also part of natural labor. But it seems unlikely that in itself this would have any consequences over and above role taking and problem solving, both of which imply a grasp of the means-ends relationship. As part of the same set of concomitantly arising cognitive experiences, reflecting on the means-ends relationship might thus also enhance an individual's general awareness of the consequences of his actions. Such reflection might also enhance awareness of the consequences of others' actions. Role taking, problem solving, and reflecting on means-ends relationships are thus simply different aspects of the same process of coming to understand the world as a reflection of human interests and social relationships. By virtue of the different cognitive experiences each form of labor gives rise to, individuals engaging in natural labor might be expected to possess a greater understanding of these things than individuals engaged in alienated labor. Indeed, theoretically this must be the case, since it is only through natural labor one can come to know the world at all.[14]

The foregoing discussion refers to the cognitive consequences of natural and alienated labor. The affective consequences of natural and alienated labor can be treated more briefly. If productive activity is oriented to satisfying one's own impulses, then such activity should arouse a positive affective response—people should like it. Indeed, this is implicit in the whole notion of aesthetic experience, which is pleasure-in-anticipation, but real pleasure nonetheless. The absence of aesthetic experience in productive activity is the absence of pleasure in productive activity. It is the absence of intrinsic reward. In natural labor, complete with aesthetic experience, should be found pleasure, intrinsic reward, and satisfaction; in alienated labor, devoid of aesthetic experience, should be found no intrinsic pleasure or satisfaction (but not necessarily misery). The affective responses to such forms of activity should follow accordingly: natural labor ought to make people feel good about it, and alienated labor, since it does not satisfy a producer's own impulses in labor itself, ought to arouse dislike.

By virtue, then, of the self-objectification, role taking, problem solving, and means-ends comprehension natural labor comprises, it should theoretically result in: (1) greater ability to perceive the human constructedness of the world; (2) a propensity to role-take and be sensitive to others' reactions to one's own actions; (3) an ability to adopt multiple perspectives or to be intellectually flexible; and (4) a tendency to enjoy the work itself. The first three of these can be considered cognitive consequences in that they concern ways of seeing the world and cognitively responding to it. The latter can be considered an affective consequence in that it refers to feelings toward work itself. In opposition to the expected consequences of natural labor stand those of alienated labor: reified consciousness, a diminished propensity to role-take (egocentrism), a diminished ability to adopt multiple perspectives, and a dislike for work itself. These are perhaps best seen as failures relative to the potentialities represented by the consequences of natural labor. In short, to come full circle to Marx again, these failures constitute alienation.

The arguments linking natural and alienated labor with these psychological consequences are based, first of all, on a Meadian view of how productive activity is experienced by beings with selves, and second, on the assumption that the different experiences associated with natural and alienated productive activity will have different effects on the psychological development and functioning of individuals. Given the Meadian perspective developed here, and the reasonable assumption that experiences in the world affect people psychologically, these connections are theoretically sound. What remains to be done at a theoretical level is to link these experiences to the capitalist labor process. And then, if this theoretical framework is to guide empirical inquiry, some methodological translation is necessary to connect the framework to the real world of work. Both tasks will be taken up in the following chapter.

This chapter has presented the basic elements of G.H. Mead's social psychology. Like Marx, Mead developed not just a handful of loosely related analytical concepts but a coherent system of thought. As such, it was necessary to begin with Mead's understandings of adaptation, the self, and community to demonstrate the fundamental compatibility and complementarity of the Meadian and Marxian perspectives. Mead's further understandings of the act, aesthetic experience, and the creative advance of nature were then applied to an analysis of alienated labor. While this provided a social-psychological elaboration of Marx along one dimension, it was still incomplete. It was argued that a similar elaboration was necessary to understand non-alienated or natural labor. Drawing on Mead's social psychology, both forms of labor were described and distinguished in terms of their sustaining conditions, the individual experiences they involve, and their differential cognitive and affective consequences. The theoretical analysis in this chapter was thus directed inward, toward the individual. In the next chapter it will be redirected outward, toward the labor process, and then translated into terms suitable for guiding empirical research.

3

Methodology

You'll say, "Well, if you get paid for your work, is that prostitution? No indeed. But how are you gonna prove it's not?
Nick Lindsay, carpenter
quoted in *Working*

The basic theoretical tools for analyzing the psychosocial consequences of natural and alienated labor were developed in chapters 1 and 2. Now it is necessary to devise a strategy for using them. But before proceeding, two preemptory theoretical issues remain to be addressed. These are issues pertinent to how an analysis of natural and alienated labor can be carried out in accord with the theoretical perspective being advanced here. The first concerns the relationship between the structural imperatives of the capitalist labor process and opportunities for aesthetic experience. The second concerns the nature of work experience itself and how it must be approached to understand its psychological effects.

THE CAPITALIST LABOR PROCESS AND OPPORTUNITIES FOR AESTHETIC EXPERIENCE

The previously made distinction between labor processes and productive activities bears repeating here. A labor process, it was said, encompasses both a mode of production and the social relations that govern it. It is a system for the collective creation and appropriation of value as embodied in transformed nature. Productive activities are what individuals engage in—the things they do with their hands and minds in the workplace. The latter are what may or may not provide aesthetic experience. A labor process enables or constrains this experience but does not determine it. Understanding how this occurs is essential to understanding the more complex connection between social structure and personality.

To make the initial connection between social structure and *experience*, we must return briefly to the Marxist analysis of the capitalist labor process.

From the Marxist perspective the capitalist labor process involves the extraction of surplus value by capitalists from workers. This occurs when workers invest more value (labor) in the objects they create than their capitalist employers pay them for. The difference is realized as profit when capitalists eventually sell the objects workers create (see Burawoy, 1979:13-30). Maximizing profit, the motivating interest of capitalism, depends in large part on keeping wages low while extracting from workers as much useful labor as possible. Workers' interests thus conflict with those of their employers in at least two respects. First, workers' interests in higher wages conflict with capitalists' interests in higher profits. And second, capitalists' interests in extracting as much labor from workers as possible conflict with workers' interests in performing no more alienated labor than necessary. These inherent conflicts make it imperative for capitalists to maintain control of both the labor process and of people, else profit could not be realized and capitalism could not survive.[1]

The ways in which capitalists seek to extract surplus value efficiently while maintaining control of the labor process are fundamentally important for the organization of work. For example, subdividing labor is a control strategy of immense consequence for both capitalists and workers. By breaking a production process down into simple, component parts, capitalists accomplish a number of things: (1) downward pressure is exerted on wages since easily trained operatives can be used to replace expensive skilled workers; (2) productivity is enhanced because each operative can develop maximum competence at a narrow specialty; and (3) control of the fragmented production process is secured because, in the absence of skilled workers, employers can assume the role of coordinating it (Stone, 1974; Marglin, 1974; Gartman, 1978).

Task routinization is another expression of the control imperative. Although work can be routinized without being highly subdivided, routinization and fragmentation tend to covary, with the former used to enhance the capitalist advances of the latter. Like fragmentation, routinization can depress wages because it allows an employer to minimize dependency on the discretion of skilled workers; it also serves to keep control of production in the hands of those who establish routines for others to follow. Neither fragmentation nor routinization are accidents of industrial development. They are concrete manifestations of system imperatives for extracting surplus value efficiently and, concomitantly, maintaining control of the labor process (Braverman, 1974; Noble, 1979; Edwards, 1979; Gorz, 1976).

As discussed earlier, both fragmentation and routinization can have consequences for people's opportunities to derive aesthetic experience from their work. A detailed sub-division of labor can diminish problem-solving demands, undermine means-ends comprehension, deny self-objectification, and make role taking impossible. Routinization can have similar effects, especially with regard to diminishing problem-solving demands. The important point here is that the imperatives of capitalism directly affect the organization of work, which in turn constrains opportunities for people to derive aesthetic experience in the workplace. The capitalist labor process thus does not make labor alienated in only some abstract, theoretical sense, but in a very concrete, immediate sense by virtue of what it compels individuals to do, and what it keeps them from doing.

These imperatives do not, however, make alienated all productive activities occurring in the capitalist workplace. While they do exert pressures to organize work in ways that minimize needs for many workers to solve problems, role-take, think creatively, or comprehend the entire production process, they do not rule out these experiences for everyone. Some workers may experience considerable demands for problem solving, means-end comprehension, creativity, and role taking. Others may experience few such demands. Those who do have opportunities for problem solving, developing means-ends comprehension, and creating objects with use values (which necessitates role taking), may derive a great deal of aesthetic pleasure from their work. As per the arguments advanced in the previous chapter, the cognitive and affective consequences of these work experiences should vary accordingly. In other words, as Blauner argued, the capitalist labor process per se should not be expected to have uniform consequences for all who participate in it.

One crucial implication of this guides the empirical analysis to follow; that is, the cognitive and affective consequences of work follow from what people actually do and experience in the workplace. Although they are perhaps the best structural variables for predicting what people will get a chance to do and experience in the workplace, neither class position nor occupation directly determines the psychological effects of work.[2] Rather, class and occupation structure opportunities for engaging in certain kinds of productive activities, which, in turn, may have predictable psychological effects. Social structure, a metaphor for stable patterns of practical and symbolic behavior, is therefore seen as doing just that: structuring opportunities for groups of people to engage in work that either stimulates or retards their psychological development.

To understand how this occurs, at least on the social-psychological level of concern here, it is essential to examine what people actually do and experience in the workplace. The remainder of this chapter is an attempt to come to grips with how such an examination can be undertaken in keeping with the Marxian/Meadian, natural labor perspective.

THE PHENOMENOLOGY OF WORK

Many studies of the psychological consequences of work identify so-called objective conditions of work (for example, organization size, reward systems, technology-in-use) and search for their alleged subjective consequences. While significant correlations can be found between such things as "levels of automation" and "feelings of normlessness" (see Susman, 1972; Form, 1973), this hardly amounts to a theoretically sound way to demonstrate how workplace experiences affect psychological functioning. Such approaches lack a theory of how particular workplace experiences can produce particular psychological outcomes. Without it they misspecify a direct relationship between occupational conditions and psychological outcomes. These approaches also typically lack an appreciation for the phenomenology of work—the reality of work as people experience it. This reality consists of the meanings people give to their work and occupational conditions, not the meanings researchers give to them. The theoretical framework on which the present study is based demands consideration of these meanings.

Two things are of primary importance for individual psychological development from the Meadian perspective: practical activities (that is, struggles to manipulate the material world) and symbolic activities (that is, struggles to organize experience and coordinate action by using signs). From this perspective any attempt to understand the psychological effects of work must consider both the practical activities people engage in and the meanings they rely on to guide their individual and collective action. Practical activities are interpretable, however, only via the meanings social actors give to them (see Schwartz and Jacobs, 1979:107-130, for a discussion of this in a methodological context). In other words, all human social behavior is infused with meaning such that behavior per se cannot be understood at all apart from its meaning (except perhaps in some biological sense). This means that focusing on technology, routinization, the division of labor, control strategies, etc., as they ostensibly affect psychological functioning, makes sense only if we consider how they enable and constrain certain practical and symbolic activities.

The activities of special interest here are those involving problem solving, role taking, self-objectification, and means-end comprehension. Although these activities are no less objectively real than a machine, they are not publicly-observable in the same way a typewriter or drill press is. Overt behavior is observable, of course, but an internal conversation of gestures is not. To tap this experience one must share the perspective of the individual confronting and attempting to solve a problem. Obviously this cannot be accomplished experientially; but it can be accomplished functionally by coming to understand the covert symbolic activities of an other. Fortunately, this is precisely what beings with selves, who share a language and a culture, do all the time when symbolically interacting. The same mutual understanding this requires (that is, sharing a perspective) is necessary to identify instances of problem solving, role taking, self-objectification, and means-ends comprehension, as such things arise only within the perspectives of selved organisms.

However theoretically abstract this argument may seem, it has some quite concrete methodological implications. The importance of phenomenological understanding in analyzing the psychological effects of work can be illustrated in two contrasting ways by considering the research of Kohn and Schooler (1973, 1978, 1983) and that of Michael Burawoy (1979).

During the past decade Melvin Kohn and Carmi Schooler have been perhaps the most prominent sociological researchers of the relationship between work and personality. Their analyses have uncovered a number of interesting relationships between occupational experience and psychological functioning. One of the most interesting of these is a positive association between the substantive complexity of work and "ideational flexibility."[3] On the basis of their research Kohn and Schooler have concluded that the opportunity to use initiative, thought, and independent judgment in one's work is more important than ownership, status, income, or interpersonal relations in terms of effects on psychological functioning (1973:116). According to Kohn and Schooler, the connection between occupational experience and psychological functioning arises because the job confronts the individual with "demands he must try to meet."

If problem solving can be assumed to be implicit in using initiative, thought, and independent judgment in one's work, then Kohn and Schooler's explanation of their findings is entirely consistent with the perspective advanced here. But their work exhibits serious theoretical and methodological weaknesses (despite its statistical sophistication). First, they do not operate within any theoretical framework that would allow them to identify particular aspects of work as psychologically consequential in any specifiable ways.[4] Thus it is not clear how "substantive complexity" (rated by the researchers) translates into demands on individuals and, in turn, into psychological effects. Second, this theoretical gap reflects a more problematic methodological one: Kohn and Schooler, relying almost entirely on survey data, typically deal in third- and fourth-order reconstructions of work experience; they do not seem to take the perspective of the subject very seriously. If they did, they might find their focus on complexity to be misleading. If the intellectual demands of work are of foremost importance, surely these demands must be assessed from the perspective of the worker. From the worker's perspective complexity per se may be less important than demands for problem solving.[5] As discussed earlier, even seemingly complex work can be mastered such that its demands for problem solving become negligible.

The problem is that Kohn and Schooler have largely ignored the phenomenology of work. In their research, what people actually do and experience in the workplace remain obscured behind computer-generated measurement models and path-diagrams of structural and psychological outcome variables. One is hard pressed to find people in these analyses. Michael Burawoy's research stands in contrast in this respect. Although, as noted in chapter 1, Burawoy (1979) does not attempt to identify psychological outcomes of work, he does provide some valuable insight into what people actually do and experience in the workplace. By penetrating the phenomenology of work Burawoy's research illuminates some less obvious but no less important ways in which work experience can affect people psychologically.

In his study of machine operators in a large engine manufacturing firm, Burawoy sought to determine why workers who performed exploitive and uninteresting piecework worked as hard as they did. One explanation for this, at the level of the shopfloor culture, could be found in the way workers responded to the deprivations of their work by reconstituting it as a game of "making out." In this game workers competed with themselves and each other in trying to maximize their payoff—with minimal effort—under the piece-rate pay system. Winning at this game vis-à-vis one's fellow workers was a source of self-esteem and status on the shopfloor. Workers thus literally reconstructed the meaning of their activities in order to derive some satisfaction from them. This practice of turning simple, otherwise boring work into complex, challenging games appears quite common (see also Roy, 1959; Balzer, 1976; Terkel, 1972:xviii).

From the theoretical perspective advanced here, this can be seen as a reconstitution of the act within the productive process in order to satisfy impulses other than those oriented to production or procurement of wages. These game-playing activities are important as more than coping strategies, however. They are also potentially consequential for psychological development and functioning. If it is possible for such alternative acts to be carried out in the workplace, then it is also possible for problem solving, role taking, self-objectification, and means-end comprehension to be a part of them. Thus even in the face of severe objective constraints individuals may find ways to derive aesthetic experience from their workplace activities. Because these are not part of work as officially defined does not mean they have no cognitive or affective consequences. Indeed, such consequences might be even more significant than those of 'real' work.

Burawoy's research, like that of others who have penetrated the phenomenological reality of the workplace, demonstrates how misleading it can be to make assumptions about how work is experienced based on objective conditions alone (researchers of work stress and job satisfaction have known this for a long time; see House, 1974; Seashore and Taber, 1975). Burawoy's research also makes another important point with respect to understanding the psychological effects of work: we cannot safely take for granted what work is; in a very real sense it must be discovered. The machine operators in Burawoy's study did not merely perform simple machine work during the day, they also performed a complex, challenging game. This unofficial work of making out was no less real than the official work of making engine parts. And although it remains to be documented, it seems this unofficial work or game playing may have significant psychological consequences. It is important to remember, then, that meanings are not simply 'attached to' work, they determine what it is. It is thus only within the phenomenological field of the worker that what he or she actually does and experiences can be understood.

From the natural labor perspective there are thus two levels on which the psychological effects of work must be understood. First, on a structural level, the capitalist labor process compels the organization of work in ways that enable and constrain certain kinds of work experiences. The organization of work makes it possible or impossible for some individuals to engage in natural productive activities and thereby derive aesthetic experiences from their work. At this level the consequences of the capitalist labor process must be discerned from a sociological perspective on an entire production system. What is visible from this perspective is how the system absorbs and transforms masses of people to satisfy its needs for particular kinds of labor. Second, on a social-psychological level, actual experiences in the workplace are what shape the psychological development and functioning of individuals. But at this level analysis can proceed only by penetrating the phenomenology of work and thereby seeking to understand how individuals constitute their acts in response to the possibilities created by a particular production system.

The empirical study prescribed below takes up only a limited set of analytical tasks suggested by the theoretical perspective developed here. This study is intended to provide a basis for initially assessing the usefulness of the perspective and for refining it at key points. More specifically, attempts will be made to: (1) identify natural and alienated productive activities in the capitalist workplace; (2) to describe the conditions under which they occur; and (3) to provisionally document their cognitive and affective consequences in accord with theoretical expectations.

STUDYING PRODUCTIVE ACTIVITIES AND THEIR CONSEQUENCES

The first goal of this research is to identify natural and alienated productive activities in the capitalist workplace. This calls for examining if and how people solve problems, role-take, objectify themselves, and comprehend means-end relationships in their work. The second goal of this research is to identify the conditions under which these experiences arise. The conditions of interest are those that can be shown to enable or constrain problem solving, role taking, and so on. Although some of these conditions have been identified theoretically, they should be documented empirically as well. Meeting these goals requires gaining access to the capitalist workplace(s), interviewing workers about their work experiences, and observing their work and the conditions under which it occurs.

Prior to considering the problem of access, some consideration must be given to the matter of sampling. Is it important which capitalist workplaces and which workers are studied? In principle, no; any capitalist workplace wherein *some* natural productive activity might occur would be suitable. Similarly, any group of workers, some of whom might engage in natural productive activity, would be suitable. Logically, however, neither a suitable workplace nor group of workers could be selected prior to determining what this study seeks to determine; hence, some sampling decisions must be made based on prior knowledge. Since the first phase of this study is intended simply to identify and describe a set of social-psychological phenomena in a natural setting, probability sampling is not an issue. Based on theoretical and practical considerations, however, some selectivity is in order.

Since many of the examples used in previous chapters dealt with manufacturing activity, it seems appropriate to continue to focus primarily on manufacturing settings: workplaces where people make things (while the theoretical framework developed here is no less applicable to service work, that application would require some translation, and it is perhaps best not to complicate things too soon). But at the same time it makes sense to examine substantially different kinds of work within these settings. This should enhance the likelihood of observing both natural and alienated productive activities and, by virtue of the comparisons it would allow, serve to highlight relationships between forms of labor and the conditions under which they occur. For present purposes this can be accomplished by focusing on distinct job groups (and, ideally, by minimizing variation within them while maximizing variation across them). Sufficient numbers of individuals in each group should be included to gain a reasonably comprehensive view of the work characterizing a particular job within a particular workplace. And again, since the purpose here is to develop a basic understanding of the *qualities* of certain work experiences, not to make inferences about their distributions in a larger population, probability sampling is not an issue.

Gaining access to the capitalist workplace could be accomplished in a number of ways. One could, for example, collect data as a participant-observer, concealing one's research interests from both employer and fellow employees.[6] This would facilitate penetrating the phenomenological reality of the workplace and gaining an intimate understanding of the experiences of some of those in it. But it would carry the disadvantages of restricted access to employee groups of interest, heavy time demands relative to the range of data thereby obtainable, and the obvious problem of getting hired in the first place. An alternative is simply to request ac-

cess via managerial authority. This would offer the advantages of access
to all employee groups of interest, optimal time demands relative to the
data thereby obtainable, and access to other potentially useful information. The disadvantages of this front-door strategy lie in getting the door
open initially, and in establishing rapport with workers while appearing
to represent management interests. However, given the desirability of ac-
cessing a variety of workers and the need to obtain data that cannot be
obtained unobtrusively, the front door seems the preferable, if not ideal,
entry point.

Once access is obtained, gaining an understanding of how people experience their work requires no less than face-to-face interaction, prefer-
ably at the work site. In the capitalist workplace, where time is value,
restrictions are likely to be imposed on this interaction (that is, in the interest of minimizing the time lost to the research project). Brief, focused
interviews may thus be most appropriate for primary data collection.
While this may not permit in-depth probing of workers' work experiences, the need to observe as well as interview demands this tradeoff
(otherwise the entire study could be conducted outside the workplace).
Observation itself offers some compensation for limited on-site interviewing time; and, once access is obtained, subjects can be recruited for
more in-depth off-site interviews. In combination, on-site interviews and
observations, plus off-site interviews, should provide an adequate basis
for identifying the productive experiences of interest, as well as the conditions that shape them.

Talking to people, formally or informally interviewing them, to find
out if they derive aesthetic experience from their work is not an easy
task; few people could describe their work experience in such terms. Obviously, then, some translation will be necessary to determine whether
people's verbal reports of their work experience reflect natural productive activity. Focusing on the component experiences of natural productive activity may make for easier translation. For example, determining
whether people must solve problems in their work might be accomplished by directly asking them if and when they do; direct questioning
about role-taking demands might be fruitless, however. Asking about demands for "considering how someone else will use or react to the results
of your work" should, on the other hand, yield interpretable and relevant responses. Similarly, asking people about self-objectification might
be unproductive, but asking about "seeing how your work contributes to
a final product of some kind" should not. This is simply to put role taking, self-objectification, and means-ends comprehension into the language of everyday life. People's verbal reports of their experiences are
thus the raw data for this phase of the study.

While verbal reports are useful for learning about how or whether people solve problems, role-take, and so forth, they are less useful for learning about the conditions under which they do so. This is because the conditions of interest are not always part of the everyday consciousness of the worker. For example, to understand the division of labor in any given instance requires looking at a production process as a whole—precisely what an individual performing limited operations within that process might be unable to do. In other words, while an individual can validly report on his experience within a social context, he cannot necessarily report on the context itself, which comprises more than an individual's immediate experience of it.

To understand the workplace sociologically requires more than an insider's report of how it looks or feels from the inside. To understand how its structural features shape experience within it requires both an insider's view and an outside sociological view. To put it another way, both interpretive and explanatory analyses are required. People's work experiences must be interpreted using the Meadian concepts presented in chapter 2. Moreover, these experiences must also be explained using the Marxian concepts presented in chapter 1. Failing to do the latter would produce a scientifically truncated, acontextual and ahistorical analysis of work experience.

In sum, then, the first phase of this study requires: (1) gaining access to capitalist workplaces in the manufacturing sector; (2) gaining access therein to a variety of workers performing different types of work under different conditions; (3) soliciting verbal reports of relevant work experiences; (4) observing the conditions under which these work experiences arise; and (5) interpreting these reports and observations from the theoretical perspective developed here. In this initial phase of analysis the component experiences of natural labor will be 'dependent variables', the precise character of which, must be discovered. In the second phase of analysis they will become 'independent variables' as an attempt is made to document their effects on psychological functioning as per theoretical expectations.

The second goal of this research is to provisionally document relationships between problem solving, role taking, means-ends comprehension and their theoretically expected cognitive and affective consequences. As discussed earlier, the cognitive consequences of interest include a reified mode of consciousness, propensity to role-take, and intellectual flexibility. The affective consequence of interest is work enjoyment. Somehow, then, some documentation of the existence or non-existence of these predicted relationships must be obtained. Although this could be accomplished by various means, an analytic survey of workers included in the initial study phase is perhaps the most efficient means for doing so.[7]

Although the use of survey data may seem inconsistent with the methodological premises established above, this is really not so. There is no contradiction involved in combining interpretive analysis with quantitative analysis, if the latter grows out of the former. In this case questionnaire responses can be seen as narrowly delimited verbal reports, which are first aggregated and then disaggregated in searching for patterned regularities in responses to items concerning work experiences and various psychological dispositions. With no pretense that such patterns are self-evident and not the products of particular interpretive frameworks, and without illegitimately elevating their ontological status beyond that of covarying verbal reports, they can be used to provide evidence for the social-structure-and-personality relationships expected to obtain in the real world. Given the inherent limitations of survey data, however, no more than this status as supplemental documentation is granted them here.

RESEARCHABLE QUESTIONS

The broad goals of this study have been set forth as identifying forms of labor in the capitalist workplace, describing the conditions under which they occur, and documenting their psychological consequences. More specific questions can be posed, however. And indeed they must, for only by attempting to answer specific questions can the utility of the theoretical perspective developed here be assessed and its analytic power enhanced.

With regard to problem solving in the workplace, the Meadian perspective suggests a number of interesting questions: how do people experience problem solving demands in their workplace? what kinds of problems must they solve? who must solve what kinds of problems? what kinds of thinking do these problems require to solve them? Although there is an immense body of experimental research on problem solving (in the field of cognitive psychology), very little research has been done on problem solving in natural settings (see Mayer, 1983). And even in social psychology there is scant theoretical or empirical work that could be said to constitute a social psychology of problem solving (see Straus, 1968, for one of the few studies in this area). The questions posed above have thus scarcely been considered from a sociological perspective, Meadian or otherwise.

Parallel questions can be raised with regard to role taking in work. Role taking via objects of production was identified as important, theoretically, for shaping a producer's mode of consciousness. But certainly other kinds of role taking occur in the workplace, even as people do nothing more than talk to each other. Thus it is appropriate to ask: in what ways do people experience role taking in their work? do they role take at all via the objects they produce? whose roles (perspectives) do they take, those of co-workers, subordinates, bosses, customers? who must take whose perspective in the course of his or her work? why? From the theoretical perspective advanced here these are key questions; answering them is essential to understanding how work shapes social consciousness via role-taking experiences.

A number of previously unasked questions about self-objectification can also be raised. While it is almost axiomatic in the work motivation literature that people want to see the results of their work, this experience has not been adequately analyzed in social-psychological terms (cf. Rosenberg, 1979:34-38, on ego-extensions). From the perspective developed here it is important to ask in this regard: how do people perceive the contribution of their efforts to a final product of some kind? what do they perceive as a final product? who perceives what as a final product? The things people perceive as the final products of their work must affect the role taking they can potentially do via those products. How they are able or unable to perceive the contribution of their work to a final product must also affect possibilities for aesthetic experience and thus possibilities for work enjoyment. But just how workplace conditions shape these experiences remains to be discovered. In the same vein it is reasonable to further ask: do people especially enjoy certain tasks because of the aesthetic experience they provide? or do other social-psychological processes appear to be more powerful influences on task liking? Answers to such questions could have significant implications for basic social-psychological understandings of human motivation.

While partial answers to some of these questions could perhaps be drawn out of research undertaken from other analytic perspectives, answers to questions posed specifically in terms of aesthetic experience must be pursued across unbroken ground. Mead's theory of aesthetic experience simply has not been used in any empirical studies of work, or anything else for that matter. In the interest, then, of better understanding aesthetic experience itself, still other questions can be asked, such as: how do work and off-work activities differ with respect to the opportunities they provide for aesthetic experience? do people derive aesthetic experience at all from their off-work activities? do their work experiences affect their abilities to derive aesthetic experience from their off-work activities? Obviously, definitive answers to all of these questions will not be forthcoming from a single research project. Tentative answers to these guiding questions can surely be generated, however, based on the methods prescribed above.

A FINAL NOTE ON RESEARCH INTERESTS

The data generated by this study (see appendix B for further details) are not intended to provide conclusive grounds for accepting or rejecting the natural labor perspective. After all, the data could always be held to be flawed in some way, the sample could be argued to be too limited for adequately testing the theory, or the theory itself could be stretched to accommodate any unruly findings. Since theories are always underdetermined by facts, it is rarely impossible to somehow rescue a theory from inconsistent data.[8] In making this point I am not trying to insulate my arguments from the liability of potentially unsupportive findings. Rather, it is to underscore the importance of being forthright about the interests underlying empirical research, especially an attempt to 'test a theory'. This requires a brief excursis on epistemology.

It should be noted first that, properly speaking, one does not test a theory; rather, one tests hypotheses derived from a theory. While particular hypotheses may be consistent or inconsistent with observations of the real world, the theories from which they derive may be only more or less useful. The usefulness of a theory depends on how thoroughly it makes sense of how-the-world-seems-to-work and how consistently it leads to effective action. Given this Pragmatist orientation, what then is the purpose of bringing data to bear on the natural labor perspective? Perhaps the best way to describe the interests of this research is by using a mapmaking metaphor.

Like maps, theories are representations of a territory, attempts to describe states-of-affairs or operative processes in the world. And like theories, maps may be more or less useful depending on how effectively they allow one to deal with some territory, some geographic reality. Further, maps and theories are constructed in analogous ways: by reproducing internal schemas (formalizing common sense), by logically extrapolating from the known to the suspected (deduction), and by exploring the territory to be mapped and discovering its configurations (induction). None of these methods is necessarily right or wrong. But some will lead to better maps—and theories—than others. Here we began with the conceptual maps provided by Mead and Marx. These were, to labor the metaphor a bit, overlaid and embellished. Now, in an attempt to refine the composite product, to make it a better guide to social reality, it is necessary to explore.

The purpose of this research is not, then, to formally test hypotheses, although this will be done implicitly, but to serve the perspective under construction by bringing it more into line with the social reality it is being used to interpret. This is an attempt to make it a better tool for understanding social reality and acting effectively toward it. Or, in terms of the metaphor again, the goal of this research is to improve a rough draft of a conceptual map.

This chapter has tried to bridge the theoretical work of chapters 1 and 2 and the empirical work reported in chapter 4. Perforce it has dealt with methodological issues—not merely methods—concerning how an empirical analysis might proceed based on the theoretical framework developed here. On this basis is was argued to be essential to investigate what people actually do and experience in the workplace in order to understand how work affects them psychologically. Methodological prescriptions and a set of questions for guiding such an investigation were then set forth. Finally, it was noted that the purpose of this study is not to conclusively demonstrate the truth or falsity of the natural labor perspective, but to preliminarily assess its validity and utility for analyzing the psychosocial effects of the capitalist labor process.

4

Exploration

The world is full of obvious things which nobody by any chance will ever see.
Arthur Conan Doyle

W hat follows is a report of findings regarding experiences of role taking, problem solving, means-ends comprehension, self-objectification and aesthetic pleasure in the capitalist workplace. But more than just displaying the data, this chapter will emphasize the ideas that emerge from the data. Only by this route can the conceptual map under revision be elaborated and refined rather than merely encumbered. And indeed, the data and ideas presented below demand a number of revisions, which will be undertaken in chapter 5. The study results reported below are thus not intended to verify the theoretical ideas developed in previous chapters, but to identify their strengths and weaknesses and provide an empirical foundation for their further development.

A SAMPLE OF PRODUCTIVE ACTIVITIES

It has been asserted that productive experiences of vastly different kinds arise in the capitalist workplace. Although it is hardly necessary to document the general claim that such different experiences occur, it is useful to document their occurrence among the subject population of this study, which comprised five distinct job groups: engineers, first-line supervisors, maintenance mechanics, production workers, and secretaries. The productive activities of people in these groups were explored in five capitalist firms; four of these were manufacturing firms, whose products included aircraft batteries, metal-casting machines, aluminum sheet stock, and irrigation equipment; one was a non-manufacturing, aerospace engineering firm.

The intent of this design (see also appendix B) was to obtain large variation with respect to levels of problem solving, role taking, self-objectification, and means-ends comprehension. Expectations were that engineers would experience these things to a much greater extent than, say, machine operators or assemblers, and that further interesting differences in these experiences would be observed across the other job groups. No difficulty arose in confirming these expectations; substantial differences in levels of problem-solving and role-taking demands, range and refinement of means-ends comprehension, opportunities for self-objectification, and actual aesthetic experience were evident. But before presenting these findings, some background description of the productive activities characterizing each job group is in order.

Although those in the engineering group claimed a variety of titles, their work was much the same from firm to firm. They performed most of the conceptual tasks underlying product design, production, and, in most cases, product application as well. In some cases their work was almost entirely conceptual, while in others it was both conceptual and physical or "hands on." At various times all of the engineers at the manufacturing firms engaged in making things of their own design. Sometimes these were complete products in themselves, although more often they were components of larger products or product systems. The range of tasks they performed is perhaps best described in their own language. The following is an abbreviated amalgamation of the responses given to the question, "What kinds of things do you do in your work?":

> I . . . solve problems on the (shop) floor; design tooling and machinery; work with machine shops; select equipment; layout facilities; troubleshoot equipment; design new products; work with customers and contractors; build prototypes; schedule and coordinate productions; draft (i.e., draw); compute; make sales presentations; write project reports; check other people's work for mistakes; read and occasionally do research; write users' manuals for our products.

As will be discussed later, these activities demanded considerable problem solving, role taking, and means-ends comprehension, offered opportunities for genuine self-objectification, and gave rise to aesthetic experience. The engineers represented a 'paradigm group' in these respects; all others could be measured against them in terms of the lesser problem solving, role taking, self-objectification, and means-ends comprehension they enjoyed.

The activities of maintenance mechanics were like those of the engineers in many respects. They too performed numerous conceptual tasks related to the production process, although seldom having to do with product design or application. In this sense most skilled maintenance mechanics were 'practical engineers' in their own right; they had to design things (for example, machine parts) as they worked to keep a production process functioning. In this way they did not merely maintain the process, but often contributed to piecemeal modification of its operation. Like the engineers, many maintenance mechanics had opportunities to put their ideas into practice; however, their work was in reverse proportion more physical than conceptual in comparison to the engineers. In their combined words:

> I...do everything from plumbing to electric; weld; repair and rebuild machinery; build offices; do pipefitting; machine parts; oil the machines; keep maintenance records; repair forklifts; tune the company's cars; help design production equipment.

The activities of maintenance mechanics also demanded problem solving and means-ends comprehension, provided opportunities for self-objectification, and gave rise to aesthetic experience. The role-taking demands mechanics experienced were different, however, from those experienced by engineers. In this respect mechanics were more like production workers than engineers.

First-line supervisors were difficult to pin down regarding what they actually did on their jobs. Most preferred to describe their work in terms of what they were *responsible for* rather than what they did. In part this seemed to be a reaction to common perceptions (on the shopfloor) that they did little more than "talk and fill out forms." But in one sense this was true; their physical activities were often limited to talking to people and filling out forms, punctuated with occasional material handling or equipment testing. While first-line supervisors did not design and make things as did engineers and mechanics, they did devise production plans, strategies for motivating people, ways of making job assignments, methods for monitoring production, and the like. As they described their activities:

> I...handle work orders and time cards; schedule work; contract

maintenance when necessary; fill out paper work; keep machinery running; train people; deal with people's gripes; listen to people's problems; hire and fire people; deal with the union; test equipment; watch people; assign jobs; requisition equipment and materials; monitor production; motivate people; estimate time requirements for jobs; ensure smooth running of the operation; keep track of time cards; distribute paychecks.

Supervisors' verb choices reflected the distinct character of their work, which demanded different kinds of problem solving, means-ends comprehension, and role taking than that of engineers or mechanics. Their opportunities for self-objectification and aesthetic experience also arose in different ways and under different circumstances than did those of other workers.

The work of secretaries represented a mixture of 'talking to people' (like supervisors) and 'making things' (more like production workers than engineers or mechanics). In addition to a core set of traditional secretarial duties, most performed diverse office chores specific to their firms or departments. They were, in this sense, the utility workers of the white-collar world. Though sometimes called upon to perform conceptual tasks, for the most part their work was physical (for example, typing) or routinely social (answering the phone). Descriptions of their activities were wideranging:

> I...make travel arrangements; type; manage the benefit plan; act as the credit union representative; place want ads in the paper; schedule vacations; listen to people's problems; handle insurance claims; make appointments for my boss; file; answer the phone; set up meetings; make coffee; do special projects; take dictation; work on the display writer; write and edit letters; deal with customers; set up retirement plans; take employment applications; do employee orientation; do monthly accounting reports; work on the computer; run the office; make my boss's life easier; answer questions; give out information; organize social events; keep peace in the office; work up charts; make copies; train other girls; keep track of credit cards; compile information; assemble reports.

These activities demanded a substantial amount of role taking, some problem solving, and occasionally provided opportunities for self-objectification. As such, secretarial work did give rise to aesthetic experience for some people.

Production workers performed the most limited range of tasks, which they tended to describe in very concrete terms:

I. . .run the buffer slitter; burn chips onto battery cells; fill up the machine and let it go; put the finishing hardware onto the batteries; assemble battery terminal hardware; solder connections; cut fiber blankets; test cells; pour epoxy sealant over the connections; pour molds in the oven and take them out when they're dry; cut aluminum plate; work on the furnace; sweep; drive a forklift; bring plate down to gauge; reclaim impure aluminum from the furnace; order parts and put them away; put decals on; wire-up terminal blocks.

Production workers typically engaged in activities that were highly structured for them, providing few opportunities for problem solving and generating minimal role-taking demands. Although their work demanded only limited means-ends comprehension, most had more extensive knowledge of the production process in which they participated (that is, they knew more than they needed to know to do their work). The opportunities production workers had for self-objectification were slight and of a limited type. Aesthetic experience in their work was rare.

Also, various other workers who were neither engineers, mechanics, supervisors, secretaries, nor production workers were interviewed on site. These included a distinct group whose activities were predominantly computer-oriented, involving by their descriptions "entering data; programming; supervising data entry people; evaluating programs; analyzing customers' (software) needs; testing programs; writing users' manuals." No attempt will be made to analyze the activities and experiences of these workers as a group. However, reference well be made to these activities and experiences when it is useful for illustrative or comparative purposes.

Overall, this sample of job groups and productive activities exhibited substantial variation with regard to role-taking and problem-solving experiences, range and refinement of means-ends comprehension, opportunities for self-objectification, and appearance of aesthetic experience. It was thus possible with this sample to identify the work experiences of interest as well as the contextual and personality variables giving rise to them. The following sections discuss these experience and the forms they took. Although for organizational purposes these experiences are discussed separately, each is but a facet of the whole. By virtue of the theoretical framework employed here, each of these sections is a partial reflection of all the others; they must ultimately be interpreted as a whole.

MEANS-ENDS COMPREHENSION IN PRODUCTIVE ACTIVITY

Exploration of means-ends comprehension began with people's perceptions of the products of their work. People were asked if they could see how their work contributed to a final product of some kind. It was found that those in different job groups perceived the products of their work in quite different ways. Two distinctions in types of perceived products were evident: one between material and operational products, and another between individual and collective products. Means-ends comprehension was most complete with regard to individuals' material products; almost all felt they could see how their work contributed to an immediate, material outcome of some kind. With regard to other types of products the range of means-ends comprehension varied considerably across job groups; people in these groups understood to greater or lesser degrees the consequences of their productive activities, both within and beyond the workplace. The bases for these observations are discussed below.

People in different job groups consistently identified certain kinds of products they felt were the results of their efforts in the workplace. Some of these were immediate and concrete, such as an engineer's drawing or a secretary's typed manuscript. Other were less tangible, especially from an outsider's perspective; for example, a secretary's claim that a "smooth-running office" was her final product. Although people themselves seldom offered any conceptual distinction between the types of products they generated, a distinctions between material and operational products was clearly suggested. Material products were defined as those physical objects directly or indirectly resulting from an individual's efforts. Operational products were defined as states-of-affairs (or preconditions for production) that people felt they created or sustained through their efforts.

Secretaries, supervisors, and mechanics saw both kinds of products resulting from their efforts. Secretaries perceived such things as typed documents, reports, and hand-drawn charts as their material products; "keeping peace in the office" or "making things easier for the boss" were their commonly cited operational products. Close parallels in product perception were found in other groups. Mechanics, for example, identified the machine parts or other hardware they sometimes made as their material products; they also perceived operational products in the form of a "department of smooth-running machines." Supervisors and foremen likewise perceived material products in the form of their department's or unit's quantitative output; their operational products were represented by the "smooth operations" they claimed to create in their units. In each instance people perceived a definite causal connection between their actions and these material or operational products.

Engineers made few references to operational products. In describing the consequences of their work they focused almost exclusively on material products, including those they produced individually and, more often, those of the firm. Indeed, they did have a variety of hard products to point to: machines, tools, drawings, prototypes, and so forth. The operational products a few engineers cited included, for example, "more efficient production lines" and "the profitability of the firm." In general, engineers were oriented to material products, which they saw as the direct results of their conceptual efforts.

Production workers did not refer to operational products at all. The products they perceived as reflecting their efforts were identified in terms of quantity of output (much like supervisors in this respect). Usually these were conceived in terms of a day's output of batteries, sprinkler heads, aluminum sheet, or whatever. There was no evidence that production workers perceived any operational products as resulting from their efforts.[1]

The distinction between material and operational products is only a preliminary one, however. Perhaps more important with regard to means-ends comprehension were distinctions between individual and collective products. As implied, individual products were the immediate results of an individual's personal efforts; these were always intermediate to the firm's collective product. And as further implied, collective products were those identified as the results of a firm's or a unit's collective efforts (references were sometimes to an internal department's final product and sometimes to the firm's final product). A crucial issue here was the connection people perceived between their individual and collective products. For some the connection was clear, for others it was not at all apparent.

Engineers, mechanics, and supervisors, for example, generally felt they played essential roles in production and that the link between their individual products and the firm's product was obvious. To paraphrase the comments of a number of mechanics on this point: 'if the machines aren't running, they [the company] aren't making anything'. Similarly, supervisors sometimes claimed that if they didn't 'keep their people working', nothing would get done. Engineers were both more confident in asserting their essential roles in production and less presumptuous in assessing their indispensability; they usually simply pointed out that they designed 'whatever this company makes'. It should be added that people's reports of seeing or feeling a connection between their work and a firm's final products were not taken as proof this connection was understood. This issue will be taken up again below.

Those workers who felt they did not play essential roles in production had more difficulty seeing how their work contributed to the firm's collective product. Some mechanics, for example, did not feel the viability of production rested on their shoulders. One mechanic, whose work consisted largely of fleet maintenance, saw little connection between his individual products (well-running cars) and the firm's collective product (aluminum-casting machines). His situation was much like that of most secretaries, who perceived their roles in production as adjunct or supporting. This made it difficult to see a connection between their individual products and the company's product. As one secretary described this:

> One definite difference [between work and home] is that I see the finished product there [at home] right away. Here [at work] I see a finished product, but not directly in line with the product ***** makes. I see maybe a letter I've composed; okay, fine, it looks great, it's neat, you know. But generally I can't relate that to how it helps our battery.

In this case the secretary did not see how her work contributed to the collective product of the firm. But for many, *feeling* a connection between personal and collective products did not hinge on cognitively understanding such a connection. As a secretary elsewhere said, "No. I don't see how my work contributes to making a missile, but I do know things happen down the line." And another, "there's satisfaction, like when you see a missile launch and knowing that somewhere down the line you contributed to it."

Interestingly, production workers seldom made any distinctions between their individual products and the firm's product. In part this might have been because production workers rarely conceived of anything as their individual products; as such, it would be impossible to conceive a relationship between distinct individual and collective products. Some distinctions were made, however, between their individual efforts and the result of the collective efforts of their department or assembly line. But this distinction was not extended to the firm's collective product or products.[2] With some workers, then, there were clear distinctions between individual and collective products, and clear or not-so-clear connections between them.

Summarized in table 4.1 are the points made so far regarding individual and collective products and means-ends comprehension.

Table 4.1   Means Ends Comprehension and Perceptions of Individual and
Collective Products

Individual Perceives Connection Between:

Own Efforts and Individual Products	- and between -	Individual and Collective Products
a. partial means-ends comprehension		a. full means-ends comprehension within production
b. link between individual and collective products may be felt, if not understood		b. felt and understood link between individual and collective products
c. associated with perception of adjunct or supporting role in production		c. associated with perception of essential role in production

This table represents only part of the story, however. Important differences in the range and refinement of means-ends comprehension were also observed. In light of the theoretical concerns of this study, it is important to consider these dimensions of means-ends comprehension both within and beyond the production process.

Among the subject population of this study means-ends comprehension with regard to immediate, individual products was nearly complete. Most people could see the immediate results of their work and understand how those results came about. This is as would be expected among adults of normal intelligence (it would indeed be unusual to find any adult of normal intelligence performing wholly incomprehensible tasks). Beyond this baseline of means-ends comprehension, however, consideration must be given to the range and refinement of people's understandings of their productive activities. In the present study both dimensions of means-ends comprehension varied from job group to job group and from individual to individual.

As a group, engineers exhibited the greatest range of means-ends comprehension (that is, they understood why particular things were done at almost any point in the production process). This is hardly surprising, as it was an engineer's job to understand and manipulate a production process from beginning to end. Maintenance mechanics, also because of the demands of their work, tended to have a comparably broad understanding of the production process. Supervisors, too, depending on their technical backgrounds, also generally had thorough knowledge of a production process.[3] The reference here is not to refined knowledge of production mechanics or chemistry, but to general understanding of means-ends connections within the process. Refinement is used to refer to the degree of an individual's understanding of how the mechanics or chemistry of production can be manipulated to yield desired outcomes. Engineers were the foremost group in this respect as well.

Range of means-ends comprehension was reflected in statements people made about seeing the final products of their work. When asked if they could see how their work contributed to a final product of some kind, various people responded:

> Yes, I can see the final drive assembly; I know what it goes into and what it does. (supervisor)

> Yes, I know what the final product looks like. (production worker)

> Yes, I can see the contribution of what I've designed; I even get feedback from users. (engineer)

The engineer's statement reflects the broadest range of means-ends comprehension; it extends from design considerations, through production, to customer use. The supervisor's statement reflects another level of means-ends comprehension: understanding how an intermediate product (a drive assembly) functions as part of a sprinkler system. But the production worker's understanding seemingly does not even extend this far; all he knows is what the final product looks like. Means-ends comprehension is thus not merely present or absent. It may be present, and quite adequate for an individual's purposes, without being very expansive.

The distinction between range and refinement was suggested when an electrician misunderstood the scope of the question about his ability to see how his work affected a final product. He interpreted the question as referring to finished aluminum rather than, as intended, the aluminum-casting machines built at the firm where he worked. To understand the connection between his work and finished aluminum, he said,

> You'd need to understand a whole process, including how a machine forms metal, to see the contribution of electrical maintenance to a finished product.

As the electrician pointed out, the process-as-a-whole may be more or less opaque depending on the depth of a person's technical knowledge. In the machine-building industry such knowledge would have to be extensive; one would have to understand everything from mining to electricity to metallurgy and physics. In other spheres of production means-ends comprehension of this degree of refinement would characterize the knowledge of the craftsman. In the large-scale industrial sphere upon which this study focused, this degree of knowledge was approached by engineers only.

As the above implies, means-ends comprehension can also extend beyond an immediate production process. Relevant here was the matter of comprehension of a product's use or function beyond the factory. Most people knew what the products they helped make were for, even if they didn't have complete understandings of how those products worked or who used them for what. Once more, engineers' means-ends comprehension beyond production was most extensive. They often began with customers' needs prior to production and sought feedback following production. This entailed refined understandings of how products were supposed to function and how they actually performed (or were used) beyond the factory walls. Beyond a general understanding of 'who buys our product and what they use it for', means-ends comprehension among other workers was limited. One supervisor expressed some frustration with this:

> In chopping wood the end result is you stay warm. You never see sometimes the end results at work. I put things together but I don't know what the end product is. I'm taken to a showcase and I'm shown it, but you never see the *total* end product.

The total end product of interest in this case was an airplane in which the firm's product functioned. This supervisor's desire was to extend his means-ends comprehension beyond the production process to ultimate use.

Means-ends comprehension beyond production must also logically include moral as well as technical ends. In this respect, however, there is little that can be said based on the present data. Or, more accurately, there is little the data can positively illustrate. In part this is because batteries, irrigation equipment, and metalcasting machines aroused few moral concerns for most workers. Only one production worker—at the aluminum casting plant—recalled thinking about "who was on the receiving end" of the ordnance manufactured at the plant during the Vietnam War.[4] At the aerospace engineering firm, which was heavily involved in weapons production, moral concerns were mentioned only

slightly more often. One secretary, who was otherwise quite happy with
her job, had some qualms about helping build nuclear missiles:

> People here put thoughts about the morality of building nuclear
> weapons out of their mind because of the money. I wish *****
> built something else. I'd *love* to work for them if they built
> something else.

Only two others interviewed at this firm expressed similar thoughts.
While most knew what they were helping to produce and how that product was intended to be used, means-ends comprehension was only forcibly extended to the consequences of actual use, or so it appeared.[5] In this
sense, then, the data are perhaps most revealing by virtue of what they
do not contain.

In sum, several things are suggested with regard to means-ends comprehension: (1) the ends people comprehend are not always observable
from a non-participant perspective (for example operational products);
(2) means-ends comprehension depends on the type of ends in question;
(3) it is necessary to distinguish between range and refinement of means-
ends comprehension; and (4) means-ends comprehension can refer to the
technical dynamics of a production process or to its moral dynamics
within a larger social system. In the present study most people were
found to conceive different types of products (material and operational;
individual and collective), to have nearly full means-ends comprehension
with regard to their immediate material products, and generally not to
exhibit concern for moral 'ends' arising beyond production. Variations in
these dimensions of means-ends comprehension were observed across
job groups and individuals. The contextual and personality variables
that appeared to account for some of this variation will be identified and
discussed separately below.

Before proceeding it should again be emphasized that from a Meadian perspective it makes little sense to analyze means-ends comprehension as an isolated variable when it is important only in relation to
considerations of role taking, problem solving, self-objectification, and
aesthetic experience. The observations reported in this section will thus
become fully meaningful only as the remainder of the chapter unfolds.
The need to consider means-ends comprehension as part of a complex set
of experiences in productive activity is underscored by the paradoxical
remark of a furnace operator: "Yes, I can see the finished product. But I
don't have to think to make it." To understand such experiences much remains to be considered in addition to means-ends comprehension.

SELF-OBJECTIFICATION IN PRODUCTIVE ACTIVITY

Inquiry into how people perceived the final products of their work was simultaneously an inquiry into self-objectification: when people perceived these products as their own, they experienced self-objectification. But here again empirical investigation suggests this experience takes at least two forms: marked and unmarked. Marked self-objectification was experienced when an individual perceived the results of his productive activities as reflecting his unique abilities or ideas. The objects thus perceived were specially 'marked', unmistakably reflecting a person's own way of producing. In contrast, unmarked self-objectification involved perceiving a reflection of one's uncreative efforts in some object or state of affairs; that is, the results of productive action were seen as reflecting physical rather than creative, conceptual efforts. The difference between unmarked and marked self-objectification was the difference, for example, between assembling a battery and designing one from scratch.

Most self-objectification observed in the present study was unmarked; people could see the results of their efforts, but seldom as reflecting any creative thinking on their part. Production workers experienced this kind of self-objectification in pointing to their quantitative output as a reflection of their efforts (a few cited quality of their products in this regard). First-line supervisors also experienced these unmarked forms of self-objectification, citing both quantity and quality of output as clear reflections of their efforts. Secretaries too had opportunities for this kind of self-objectification. Often this was expressed in terms of the satisfaction associated with finishing a job:

> I think my biggest satisfaction is when I complete a procedure revision and updating and all that. There's satisfaction there because that's sort of the final thing for me in the procedure [revision] process: that I've actually gotten it done. It's an accomplishment on the big, big projects to see that you've just typed 80 to 100 pages, that you've finally gotten it done.

Here the products being identified as embodiments of labor did not reflect the secretary's own creative thinking. They merely represented changed states of affairs, as was generally the case with all forms of unmarked self-objectification. The reward value of this objective performance feedback was nonetheless undeniable.[6]

Some people did have opportunities for marked self-objectification. Engineers had such opportunities when designing new products or production equipment. These tasks provided opportunities for them to "put their ideas into practice," to see them reflected in the shape and function of an object. Although it seemed they had more opportunities to do this than any other group, they did not have a monopoly on the experience. Mechanics could also put their ideas into practice when they effected repairs or built production equipment. Though the bulk of their work was routine, mechanics could often express their own inventive styles in construction or repair projects. Supervisors also sometimes felt they could see themselves reflected in their operational products; for example, one supervisor noted, "how it [the second shift] is run, is the characteristics of me." To emphasize the distinction: the referent experience here is more than just seeing the results of one's efforts, it is seeing them as specially marked by one's own ideas and abilities.

As the above implies, opportunities for marked self-objectification were differentially distributed across job groups. Engineers and mechanics had more such opportunities built into their work than did secretaries, who had more such opportunities (although quite limited) than production workers. There was some evidence that this resulted in different cognitive orientations to objects of production. Engineers and mechanics were more attuned, it seemed, to reflections of self and others in material objects than were people in other job groups. Mechanics, for example, claimed they could usually tell who did a particular job by looking at how it was done. Or as one engineer expressed the same principle: "A drawing is like a piece of art; you can look at it and tell how much a person enjoys his job." That different cognitive consequences might ensue from these different types of self-objectifying experiences would be theoretically expected. Seeing one's conceptual efforts reflected in material reality ought to produce a different kind of learning than seeing one's physical efforts so reflected.

One final issue regarding self-objectification deserving comment is the distinction between self-objectification *in* work and self-objectification *at* work. Data collection and the above discussion focused on the former: self-objectification in 'official' productive activities, those things people got paid to do. There are, however, other unofficial opportunities for this experience in the workplace; for example, in such things as decorating one's office, arranging objects in one's work space, and in affecting aspects of personal style. This sort of self-objectification is not unimportant and may significantly affect some aspects of job satisfaction. And in some realms of inquiry into mental health (for example, in the area of schizophrenia) this sort of mundane self-objectification might be very important indeed.[7] For present purposes, however, there is no choice but to treat it as a relatively inconsequential constant.

To summarize, then, two forms of self-objectification were identified: marked and unmarked. The former, involving a creative expression of self, was much less frequent than the latter, which involved an uncreative expression of physical effort. Opportunities for marked self-objectification appeared in all job groups; that is, almost all could experience some results of their work as direct reflections of their efforts. Only engineers and mechanics, however, regularly experienced marked self-objectification. In general, chances to engage in truly creative work were not absent among the subject population, but they were rare.

PROBLEM SOLVING IN PRODUCTIVE ACTIVITY

In anticipation it seemed that problem solving could be studied by asking about the problems people confronted in their work. In fact, things were not so simple. An unexpected problem arose: that of determining exactly what people were referring to when they spoke of "a problem." Most people claimed to solve at least some problems in their work. But often what they cited as problems were simply disliked activities or extraordinary tasks. These were not instances where routine action was disrupted; in fact, in dealing with most of these so-called problems, habit sufficed. In the Meadian sense, then, these were not problems at all. Identifying real problems required penetrating the rhetoric of problem solving in order to see what actually inhibited productive action in the workplace. Essentially, only two things appeared to do so: intractable physical matter and intractable people.

The difference between activities people described as problems and real problems can be illustrated with reference to secretarial work. Among the examples of problems secretaries cited as arising in their work were "looking up information when the boss needs it," "redistributing work when someone is sick," and "juggling calendars to set up meetings." While these activities sometimes involved real problems, they were not problems per se. Looking up information, for example, was not a problem if habit sufficed to locate the desired information. Redistributing work was also not a problem if an established procedure existed for doing so. The same principle applied to juggling calendars to set up meetings. Real problems arose only when habitualized procedures for performing these tasks proved inadequate. In other words, if the information a secretary sought was not where she expected it to be, or if people refused to abide by normal procedures for redistributing work, or if people refused to have their appointments rescheduled, then real problems arose that inhibited the smooth flow of action.

Interestingly, some engineers, supervisors, and mechanics also cited "looking up information" as an instance of problem solving. This merits closer consideration because it is symptomatic of the underlying semantic problem noted above. What kind of problem is looking up information? As stated, it is not a problem at all but an activity. Why then did people describe it as a problem to be solved? Typically because it was associated with some act that had been inhibited for a lack of information. Although this may seem obvious, it is an important point to make explicit: it was the inhibition of some other activity that created the need to look up information; the real problem arose in that other activity, not in looking up information (which was usually accomplished with no problems). For example, the act of making a phone call might be impeded by a lack of information, such as a phone number. Similarly, the act of calculating a flow rate might be inhibited by a lack of information regarding which formula to use in a particular case. In either event, the real problem arises when the initial act (phoning or calculating) is impeded. Real problems thus arose prior to what people tended to cite as 'the problem'. This disjunction between real problems and what people called problems appeared consistently when people responded to direct questions about problem solving in their work.

Another form of disjunction between real and rhetorical problems appeared among production workers. Machine operators and assemblers cited a variety of problems they had to deal with in their work, most involving defective parts or malfunctioning equipment. Such things could represent real problems or not, depending on how workers responded to them. For example, one machine operator cited "defects in the aluminum" as a problem he had to deal with in his work; however, he then added, "But you don't think of them as problems. It's more like initiative: if you see a problem [a defect in the metal] you can either ignore it or report it." This was another form of "a problem" that was not a real problem; action was not inhibited at all unless the operator chose to stop work to call attention to the defect. And even in this event, no problem solving on the part of the operator was required; whatever 'problem' might be pointed out, it was seldom the production worker's responsibility to do anything about it.

Machine operators and assemblers did sometimes confront and solve real problems in their work. When minor equipment malfunctions occurred or parts "didn't fit quite right," production workers often dealt with these matters on their own. Their action would be only momentarily impeded until they figured out how to proceed. But rarely did such problems call for any substantial judgment on the operator's part; in fact, it behooved the operator to call anything serious to the attention of his supervisor. In cases where serious malfunctions did occur, these represented genuine problems for the production worker in that his action was inhibited. Finding a way to proceed, however, was not within his purview. In this way people sometimes confronted real problems they were never required to solve. For production workers and others, dealing with a problem did not necessarily mean solving it.

What the above illustrates is that real problems were determined by an individual's perspective. A malfunctioning machine, for example, could represent a real problem from one perspective and a rhetorical problem from another. That is, a broken machine could be a real problem for the operator whose action was impeded; for the mechanic called on to fix the machine, there might not be any real problem. Thus when mechanics said they "solved problems all the time," they were usually referring to other people's problems. A real problem for a mechanic might arise if a machine malfunction defied diagnosis or repair. But if a machine could be repaired on the basis of habit (supposing, say, a recurrent malfunction), no real problem would appear from the mechanic's perspective.[8]

Engineers claimed to do a tremendous amount of problem solving in their work. This was expressed in various ways: "engineers have problems always," "problems come from all directions," and "if there were no problems there wouldn't be much of a job." The concrete things engineers referred to as problems were sometimes real and sometimes rhetorical. As noted previously, engineers often cited the non-problem of "looking up information" as a problem. They also cited such things as "finding parts," "dealing with customers," and "performing calculations." But again, these seldom involved any impeded activity; engineers usually accomplished all these things quite effectively by following established patterns. And no matter how annoying the activity, as long as the pattern sufficed to guide it to completion there was, strictly speaking, no problem.

This is not to suggest that few real problems were evident in the present study. Indeed, many things disrupted the smooth flow of work. Production workers confronted malfunctioning machines and defective parts that brought their work to a halt; mechanics sometimes could not determine how to get a machine running properly; supervisors could not get their subordinates to work together; secretaries could not get their word processors—or their bosses—to do what they wanted them to; and engineers did not always have established patterns to follow in designing new products to meet customer needs. It seemed clear, however, that actual problem solving occupied only a small portion of anyone's time, and certainly a much smaller portion of time than self-reports of problem solving superficially suggested. This is as would be expected: in the highly organized context of the workplace the bulk of everyone's activity is patterned. Organization itself implies that most problems of production and interaction have been 'solved'; that is, most action and interaction has been habitualized.

It was hoped this analysis would yield a typology of problems or a scheme for categorizing different kinds of problem-solving activities. Because of initial confusion between real and rhetorical problems it was at first difficult to see what underlay the seemingly diverse forms of problems people claimed to deal with in their work. This confusion made generating analytic categories itself problematic; no set of categories seemed to adequately distinguish and order the apparently different types of problems people claimed to solve. Preliminary attempts to categorize types of problems thus generated numerous labels: interpersonal problems, organizational problems, people problems, materials problems, functional problems, technical problems, communicative problems. But, as later realized, these preliminary categories were generated largely by misleading adjectives rather than theory.

From the Meadian perspective it seemed appropriate to try analyzing these apparently diverse types of problems in terms of what it was that fundamentally inhibited action, to try categorizing them based on the source of inhibition. In essence, it appeared that only two things impeded productive action in any case: physical matter (parts, tools, machines) that did not respond to manipulatory action as anticipated, and people who did not respond to symbolic action as anticipated.[9] Problems arising out of failed symbolic action were termed interpretive problems; those arising out of failed manipulatory action were termed technical problems. At root, no problem cited by any subject could not be so categorized.

People in all job groups confronted both kinds of problems. The engineer trying to manipulate various battery components to yield a certain level of performance confronted technical problems (presuming a solution was not obvious). The same engineer trying to assess a customer's battery needs confronted interpretive problems (again presuming such needs were not immediately obvious). The production worker confronted technical problems when his assembly materials did not fit together as they were supposed to. In trying to figure out what his supervisor expected of him, the same production worker confronted interpretive problems. The secretary trying to reorganize a filing system might confront a technical problem of space utilization. In trying to coordinate such a reorganization effort with a co-worker, she might confront an interpretive problem. Technical problems thus arose when inanimate objects did not respond as anticipated. These were problems of instrumental control, of getting objects to respond as desired, or of adjusting to their unanticipated potentialities. Interpretive problems arose out of attempts to coordinate action. These were problems of understanding, of forging common perspectives, of fitting lines of joint action.

Even though people in all groups had occasions to confront both technical and interpretive problems, the proportions of each varied from job group to job group. Secretaries, for example, had more interpretive problems to solve than did mechanics, whose problems were predominantly technical. Production workers generally had few technical or interpretive problems to solve. Supervisors confronted technical problems in two ways, with regard both to physical matter and to people. To the extent they attempted to manipulate and control subordinates as objects rather than understand them as subjects, they transformed interpretive problems into technical ones. This was not unique to supervisors, but characteristic of dominant-subordinate relationships. It should be noted, however, that not all supervisors approached interpretive problems as technical ones; many did attempt to understand their subordinates as subjects. Engineers, by virtue of the materials they were expected to manipulate, and the many people they were expected to satisfy, seemed to have more of both kinds of problems than people in any other job group. Thus while both technical and interpretive problems arose in all job groups, one or the other typically predominated; moreover, absolute levels of either type of problem also varied from group to group.

To recap, problem solving in productive activity proved to be more difficult to make sense of than anticipated because of a disjuncture between real problems in the Meadian sense and the numerous disliked activities people were prone to call problems. The latter were termed rhetorical problems to distinguish them from real problems, which arose only when productive activity was genuinely disrupted. When analyzed from a Meadian perspective it appeared that all real problems derived from either intractable physical matter or intractable people. Problems arising because of the former were termed technical problems; those arising out of the latter were termed interpretive problems. Although both types of problems arose in all job groups, the proportion and absolute frequency of each type varied from group to group.

ROLE TAKING IN PRODUCTIVE ACTIVITY

Role taking emerged as the most complex of the work experiences examined here. It was initially approached via direct questions about the need to "think about how other people will use or react to the results of your work." Other lines of questioning, however, also yielded valuable data on role taking. Inasmuch as all human social behavior is predicated on role taking, it was not surprising to find it universally implicated in the work experiences of collectively producing adults. Four ideas with regard to role taking in productive activity were suggested by the data. First, that role taking is experienced differently depending on its status-directionality; second, that role taking varies in the degree of differentiation it demands; third, that it arises out of diverse motives; and fourth, that role-taking abilities are multi-dimensional. Each of these ideas will be discussed in turn.

That role taking occurs between status equals and unequals in a heirarchial organization is obvious. That the role-taking experience is different depending on one's status relative to the other is not so obvious. It does seem to be the case, however, that when status unequals role-take in face-to-face interaction—or via objects—the experience is different for each. The role taking that occurs between status unequals will be discussed in terms of upward and downward role taking; that which occurs between status equals will be termed lateral role taking. The value of these distinctions does not lie in identifying status-directionality per se, but in suggesting how power relations affect the type of cognitive activity involved in role taking.

Upward role taking can be described most simply as 'taking the role of the boss', something everyone in the present study had to do quite often. This type of role taking occurred in face-to-face interaction, in written communication, and via objects of production (the latter mode of role taking is of primary interest here; in general, however, what applied to it applied to the other modes as well). Taking the role of the boss is what people typically referred to when they said they had to think about how someone might react to the results of their work. It was revealing that people keyed on the word "react" in the question instead of "use." This suggested that role taking in the context of asymmetric power relations was not experienced as a 'neutral' cognitive activity. It apparently had a powerful emotional component arising out of the impulses that motivated role taking. Upward role taking seldom arose out of concern for how a work product would be used; rather, it was motivated by concern for how a superior might react to a mistake or other evidence of poor performance (such reactions were invariably assumed to be negative). This was an important aspect of role-taking experience about which more will be said later.

Upward role taking implies downward role taking. In order to interact at all, status-superiors had to take the perspectives of their status-inferiors. First-line supervisors had to do this all the time vis-à-vis production workers. Those engineers and mechanics who occasionally supervised others also engaged in downward role taking. While they were seldom concerned with how subordinates would react to the results of their work, they were concerned with how subordinates would react to their supervisory styles, because extreme negative reactions could interfere with getting work done. Secretaries and production workers had few status-inferiors to interact with; as such, downward role taking was rarely part of their work experience.[10]

Upward and downward role taking would be less important if they could not be distinguished from lateral role taking. Most lateral role taking occurred in face-to-face interaction as co-workers simply talked to each other. But it also occurred via objects of production, and in especially interesting ways.

In lateral role taking individuals were not trying to anticipate and avoid negative reactions to their work; rather, they were trying to coordinate their efforts with those with whom were functionally interdependent. Mechanics, for example, sometimes had to do this when they repaired machines. As one mechanic pointed out, "You have to talk to the [machine] operator. If I don't fix it to the guy's liking, he bitches. I ran a machine so I know how it is." Various other interdependencies also gave rise to lateral role taking. One machinist noted that he, like other machinists, had to think about the assembler when making parts; it was important to keep in mind, he said, whether everything would fit together right for the assembler. Similarly, a warehouseman (a shipping dock worker) noted his concern with a truck driver's perspective when loading trucks: he had to distribute the load just right so the driver would not be ticketed when weighed. Thus, in contrast to vertical role taking, the motivating interest underlying lateral role taking was neither submission nor domination, but cooperation.

All lateral role taking did not necessarily occur between status equals within a single organization. Design engineers, for example, had to take the role of a machine operator in order to design a machine an operator could use. The operator's perspective was crucial, an engineer explained, because "if an operator doesn't like it [a casting machine], he'll make sure it doesn't work." Although engineers and machine operators were technically not status equals, in this case their functional interdependence required more lateral than downward role taking (via an object of production). Clearly, though, the engineer ultimately exercised more control over the operator's work than the imaginary operator did over the engineer's design. But this was not intentionally an act of domination.[11]

It is important to emphasize the different motives underlying upward, downward, and lateral role taking. Most upward role taking, it seemed, was motivated by fear of reprisal, of being caught making a mistake. Production workers thus took the role of the boss in order to "avoid the boss's bullshit," as one furnace operator put it. The logic of interaction here was plain enough: by taking time to think about what the boss might react negatively to, workers could avoid doing it and getting chewed out or fired. But this meant that upward role taking was experienced as an act of submission or, in essence, self-repression. The nearly universal negative experience of upward role taking was described matter-of-factly by a mechanic: "You always worry about what people are going to think about your work. Just like anybody, I suppose." Obviously, however, one seldom worries about others *liking* one's work; one worries about just the opposite. Part of the reason for this more or less perpetual worry was described succinctly by another mechanic, who said, "If the work is okay they [bosses] don't say anything. If it's bad they let you know."

Another important aspect of role-taking experience concerned its degree of differentiation; that is, the extent to which it involved taking a generalized role or a specific role. This aspect of role-taking experience was more powerfully affected by the practical rather than political demands of production. Differentiated role taking occurred when an individual had to take the role of a specific other in order to perform his work. Secretaries, who often had several bosses, had to do this when drawing charts, typing letters, and formatting manuscripts for particular persons. Although secretaries could often follow pre-established patterns in doing their work, they frequently had to tailor it to the demands of a particular individual. In contrast, mechanics seldom had to engage in differentiated role taking. While it sometimes helped to take the operator's perspective toward the machine (as described above), it was seldom necessary to take a particular operator's perspective. For the mechanic's purposes operators were functionally interchangeable; they represented a generalized rather than differentiated perspective; if the machine worked for one operator, it would work for another. Further along the continuum were production workers, who experienced no demands for differentiated role taking via the objects they produced. Their products were not tailored for any particular individual; they were fit to a predetermined pattern, always.

While the demands of an individual's work chiefly determined the degree of role-taking differentiation experienced, it seemed personality variables played an important part as well. First-line supervisors, for example, necessarily did a great deal of role taking in face-to-face interaction with their subordinates. But they varied tremendously in role-taking style. Some were more concerned with individual workers and interacting on a personal basis than others. Some seemed to deal with subordinates as interchangeable members of a category. In the latter case role taking was less differentiated; supervisors took the generalized 'role of the assembler', but not the role of any particular assembler. Thus while supervisors had to understand the generalized perspective of their subordinates, they did not have to understand individual perspectives. The approach any particular supervisor actually took seemed largely a matter of personal inclination.

The idea that role taking arises out of diverse motives has already been introduced. But it is in need of some qualification. As discussed, production workers were motivated to take their boss's perspective out of an interest in material survival; that is, out of an interest in keeping their jobs and maintaining their livelihoods. This interest was hardly limited to production workers, however. Indeed, material motives were at the root of most role taking in productive activity. Even downward role taking was motivated by an interest in material survival: if a supervisor could not effectively communicate with or motivate his subordinates, then his job too was in jeopardy. To say that material interest underlay this role taking would be banal, however, if other interests were not also apparent.

It should thus be pointed out that people who worked together were often friends who interacted in the interests of achieving mutual understanding, providing social support, and just having fun. Role taking necessarily occurred in these activities just as it did in official productive activities.[12] Role taking was also sometimes motivated by moral concerns: people expressed feelings of empathy for others who had somehow been treated unfairly (for example, in promotion or layoff decisions, job assignments, etc.). Such feelings, however, were rarely projected beyond the immediate sphere of production. As noted previously, only a single production worker in the metal-casting plant spoke of thinking about who was on the receiving end of a product (aluminum shell casings) that

had obvious moral implications. What role taking that did extend beyond production was motivated less by moral impulses than by material
ones. This was role taking evoked as part of a managerial control strategy.

In some cases role taking was encouraged expressly for motivational
purposes. For example, several first-line supervisors explained that they
encouraged their subordinates to look at the firm's product as would a
customer. At the battery manufacturing firm one supervisor described
his method: "I try to make people [assemblers] look at a battery like a
customer. I ask them, 'would you buy a battery like this?' " Apparently
this was a commonly used tactic to get production workers to exercise
more care in their work. It was essentially an attempt to get production
workers to engage in lateral instead of upward role taking. But because
this was prompted by management, it too became a form of submissive
role taking. Those production workers who said they took the customer's
perspective usually implied that their reason for doing so was worry that
a late-discovered error might come back to haunt them. In one sense,
then, this motivational strategy made even the customer the enemy.

There was some evidence, however, that engineers, mechanics, supervisors, and secretaries authentically motivated themselves by role
taking. Engineers were genuinely concerned that their products worked
as customers expected them to. For engineers, the admiration and appreciation they anticipated receiving for a good design was a source of motivation. Skilled mechanics approached their work in much the same way,
being motivated by the expectation that others would be able to see and
appreciate their work. Supervisors also sometimes took others' perspectives to give meaning to their work. One supervisor described his concern for quality as motivated by "thinking about some poor sonofabitch
out there with a battery that won't work." Secretaries also reported that
they tried to "keep their standards up" by imagining how others perceived their work. As representatives of their departments some secretaries felt they were "always on stage" and that they had to be ever aware
of "how other people interpret what we do." For secretaries, this kind of
role taking was a source of motivation for taking care in work and self-
presentation.

Perhaps the most critical questions to ask about role taking of this kind
are, whose role is being taken by whom? and, which perspective evokes
what kind of concern in whom? In Meadian terms, what is involved here
is the individual selecting an attitude out of a generalized other, an attitude that serves to motivate his own behavior in particular ways. This is
an internal search for a socially appropriate and functional motive

within the conglomeration of motives that the generalized other comprises. This view of the role-taking process once more points up the importance of distinguishing ability and propensity in this respect. Some assemblers might, for example, be perfectly able to take the role of the customer, but not be inclined to do so, even under the urging of their supervisors. Conversely, no individual can take a perspective he is not familiar with, no matter what the external coercion. Thus a mechanic might be motivated to do careful work because he imagines his coworkers will respect him for it; he may be unable, however, to motivate himself by adopting a customer's perspective if he has no idea who the customer is and no familiarity with that perspective. The customer's perspective in such an instance would not be incorporated in the mechanic's generalized other; nor, therefore, could it be a source of motivation for the mechanic's behavior.

Finally, role taking was also identified as a multi-dimensional cognitive activity. That is, role taking was not an either-or proposition. It occurred along different dimensions reflecting different cognitive abilities and types of social knowledge. These dimensions can be thought of in terms of range, depth, and accuracy. The latter is perhaps the most familiar.[13] It refers to an individual's ability to accurately judge the attitudes of another and anticipate another's responses in a particular situation. Accuracy is partly dependent on familiarity with the other's role, but more importantly depends on ability to read communicative cues. The present study did not expressly examine role-taking accuracy. It is mentioned here to distinguish it from the other dimensions of role taking with which it has sometimes been confused. It was an interest primarily in role-taking range (intellectual flexibility) that led to distinguishing these dimensions of role-taking ability.

Role-taking range refers to the number of alternative perspectives an individual can adopt. It was clear in the present study that the work of those in different job groups demanded different degrees of role-taking range. At one extreme were the engineers, who had to look at their projects from a customer's perspective, a production perspective, a sales perspective, and a service perspective (these among others). At the other extreme were production workers, who usually had to take only two perspectives: that of other workers and that of their supervisor. Mechanics, supervisors, and secretaries shared a middle ground in that they had to take multiple perspectives, but not as many as engineers nor as few as production workers. It should be added that range and accuracy can vary independently: an individual can be familiar with many different perspectives without being an accurate situational role taker. Or he could be an accurate situational role taker without being familiar with a wide range of perspectives. Role-taking range can also be thought of as the number of perspectives incorporated within a person's generalized other.

Role-taking depth refers to more than just being able to adopt alternative perspectives. It refers to the degree of intimate understanding a person possesses with regard to any particular alternative perspective. Mechanics, for example, might exhibit considerable role-taking range but not depth. In other words, they might have vague ideas of how salespeople, secretaries, and managers look at things, without having deep understandings of any of these perspectives. In this same sense salespeople, secretaries, and managers might have vague ideas of how mechanics look at some things, but not have intimate understandings of the mechanic's perspective. This is limited role-taking depth. As a general rule it seemed that most people were intimately familiar with only a few alternative perspectives, usually ones they had experienced themselves, and superficially familiar with a much larger number.

In sum, role taking in productive activity is a complex experience affected by status-directionality, demands for differentiation, and underlying motives. And as an ability, it also varies along dimensions of accuracy, range, and depth. What this suggests, preliminarily, is that role-taking experience is unlikely to have simple, singular consequences. More likely its consequences will vary depending on status-directionality, differentiation, and motivation. Further, if role-taking abilities are proposed to be consequences of role-taking activity, they need to be conceived in more specific terms, with reference to specific dimensions of ability. Merely speaking of role-taking ability in general terms might be inadequate. In chapter 5 the implications of these aspects of role-taking experience for cognitive development will be further explored.

AESTHETIC EXPERIENCE IN THE CAPITALIST WORKPLACE

It was not anticipated that instances of aesthetic experience would be described as such. The attempt to document its occurrence was thus indirect; reports of 'specially satisfying experiences' that might prove to be aesthetic in the Meadian sense were sought. This strategy was productive, for in describing their most satisfying work experiences people described what were readily interpretable as aesthetic moments. The first step below will be to document this. Then three related ideas will be discussed: the importance of projects, aesthetic experience as a source of motivation, and alternative sources of satisfaction in productive activity.

Aesthetic experience was evident in every job group, except that of production workers (who are discussed separately below). In other job groups aesthetic experience was reported when people had opportunities to put their ideas into practice, to see the results of their work, and to take an appreciative attitude toward those results. Engineers were again the paradigm group in each respect. They reported special satisfaction in designing things to meet special needs, solving problems ("getting things to work right"), and doing "hands-on" engineering (building prototypes). For the most part only engineers could describe their satisfaction in these terms:

> I guess the most enjoyable experience I have is when I'm working on something that I start from scratch. And it's kind of my own design, and then I complete it and it works—does what it's supposed to. That's my biggest reward.

Other engineers identified sources of special satisfaction in similar terms, many emphasizing the importance of *seeing* a product work. Another engineer, who cited this experience as the reason he went into engineering, put it simply: "A good portion of my pay is in the work itself."

Engineers did not, however, have a monopoly on aesthetic experience. Others had opportunities to put their ideas into practice and see them 'work'. An electrician, who occasionally designed electrical controls for casting machines, was one such example. In one case he

> built a gear drive for a wire feeder. It was one unit designed to replace three. I fought for the idea for four years. It works beautifully; everybody thinks it's great. After four years it was an especially satisfying accomplishment. It works and customers are happy. That's all you need.

His description of this experience highlights the importance not only of seeing the results of one's work, but of being able to adopt some perspective that values those results. In this case the electrician could value his invention from several perspectives, namely, customers', co-workers', managers'. The importance of perspective is further emphasized in a statement by a shop superintendent, a machinist by trade, who described aesthetic experience in machining in all but those words:

> A good man always gets a lot of satisfaction out of what he creates. In other words, when he lays a job [a finished piece of work] on the floor, in a good time, and it looks good—the finishes are good and he knows it's to size—that's probably worth more to a good man than the money.

These examples may imply that aesthetic experience was always associated with opportunities for marked self-objectification (that is, these
people felt they were making things that reflected their unique ideas or
abilities). But apparently this was not essential for aesthetic experience.
Recognizing one's essential contribution to a finished product seemed to
be sufficient, as it was for at least one mechanic:

> Whenever you got a job to do and it went smoothly and you put
> it out of that door and you know that you did it to be best of
> your ability. . .I felt proud. You know, I really felt good about it.
> Because from a bunch of parts. . .you got the engineer's thoughts
> on paper and you built this machine that he wanted. And it
> worked and it was a good machine. It looked good and you knew
> that it was right. To me that's a good feeling.

But as noted previously, mechanics also had opportunities to put their
ideas into practice. For some this was the key to the aesthetic experience
they found in their work. One mechanic spoke representatively when he
said:

> Yes [I enjoy my work]. I like being able to work with my hands
> *and* mind; being able to look back [at a finished job] and say,
> 'that's good'.

Clearly, an important part of aesthetic experience for mechanics and
engineers was making things and seeing them work. This is as would be
expected; seeing an object of one's own making in operation—seeing it
work *right*—represents consummation of a productive act. It also implies
achievement of usability, which confirms an appreciative perspective experientially. Some expressly cited this as a source of special satisfaction.
As one computer programmer explained why she enjoyed her work: "I
think it's because you can see something useful. . .knowing what you've
done is being used." This would seem to underscore the importance of
role taking as a source of special satisfaction in itself.

Secretaries reported deriving special satisfaction from taking on and
completing "little projects." These were sets of tasks unusual in that they
were aimed toward clearly defined endpoints. For secretaries these kinds
of activities stood out amidst the continuous flow of events (phone calls,
conversations) that filled the bulk of their days. The discrete products involved were often charts or typed reports of some kind. As one secretary
described the satisfaction she derived from this:

> I like the technical end. I like to type view-graphs and different
> things my boss has written. I can see the finished product; it
> looks nice. A lot of secretaries like to look at what they've typed.

There was also evidence that secretaries derived aesthetic pleasure from the work process itself. For example, another secretary cited "doing graphs" as a particularly satisfying activity, emphasizing the satisfaction she got from "thinking about how nice they'll look when projected on a screen" as she was actually drawing them. Here again, as with the mechanic assembling the engineer's machine, marked self-objectification did not appear to be essential for aesthetic experience. What was more important was taking responsibility for a finished product that could be seen to 'work right' or 'look right'. This was, in other words, unmarked self-objectification.

First-line supervisors did not report deriving special satisfaction from making things, at least not in the direct sense that engineers, mechanics, and secretaries did. Supervisors commonly reported that their most satisfying work experiences arose when they could "see things running smoothly" and "everyone working together." Some also cited "setting goals and meeting them" as a special source of satisfaction. As discussed earlier, these things were the operational products supervisors perceived as resulting from their efforts. As such, it seems reasonable to suppose that supervisors derived some aesthetic pleasure from taking responsibility for these products, although this is hard to document based solely on what supervisors said. In one case a foreman who was also a machinist reported special satisfaction in "seeing good parts go through the shop," "seeing a finished machine work properly," and "getting out in the field to see how the product behaves." Clearly this particular foreman felt responsible for the discrete material product (a casting machine) coming out of his department. If this was aesthetic experience, it was much the same as that described above by the other former machinist. In this case the foreman retained a machinist's perspective on the finished product; he felt it was very much a reflection of his efforts.[14]

Production workers did not describe any special satisfaction arising from their work that could be interpreted as aesthetic experience. This is not to say they reported no satisfaction arising in their work; some did. But the things they reported had more to do with social relations on the job and making time pass quickly than with work itself. Although this observation does not support a conclusion that these sources of satisfaction compensated for a denial of aesthetic experience, it does suggest that some things may become more salient sources of satisfaction in the absence of others, as is further discussed below.

In documenting instances of aesthetic experience it became apparent that the opportunity to do projects of one's own was especially important. This was typically exemplified by engineers and mechanics. But perhaps because most of their work came in the form of projects, engineers and mechanics less often made special reference to this fact. It was secretaries, whose work only occasionally involved small projects, who brought the importance of project activity into sharp relief. It is not just this observation that is most interesting, however. Rather, it is the structure of projects, for this is what engenders aesthetic experience. When asked what kinds of projects she most enjoyed, one secretary responded:

> When it's something. . .ok, there's a goal and a time limit, ok, *this* is what I'm working towards and I set my steps all along the way: I have to do this, this, this, and this and accomplish them all and everything falls together the way it's supposed to. And it's something that's, you know, a short time frame that I can see the results of. I think that's part of it too. I feel like I've really accomplished something and I feel good about it.

There is a special satisfaction in finishing the project, in consummating the act, as this secretary reports. But the project is also satisfying because it comprises numerous sub-tasks, each of which can provide aesthetic experience as it is completed within the meta-act represented by the whole project. This secretary's statement nicely supports the proposition that productive activities allowing consummation of intermediate acts prior to consummation of a meta-act should yield the greatest aesthetic pleasure.

The importance of projects suggests why supervisors and production workers reported little in the way of aesthetic experience. The work of both was mostly continuous; there were few projects with clear beginnings and ends. Thus while supervisors could take satisfaction in "setting goals and meeting them," production workers could seldom do even this. They had no projects of their own that allowed them to imagine a goal and set out a series of intermediate steps leading to its achievement. And even when 'goals were met' by a production unit, representing project activity of a sort, production workers could not take direct responsibility for the accomplishment in the same way a secretary could when she constructed a chart or some other discrete material product.

It thus appeared that production workers were more dependent on other sources of satisfaction in their work. One of these was a feeling of special competence at whatever they did. Most production workers cited at least one activity or set of tasks they felt they performed better than anyone. They were not unique in this; most engineers and mechanics also cited some specialty jobs they felt they were particularly good at and from which they derived special satisfaction. For production workers, however, what was important was not just that they were good at some-thing, but that they were at least as good as anyone else.[15] This was the prime source of satisfaction for one machine operator:

> I feel that I do my job as well as anybody who's ever done that job has done it. Not that I feel I'm better than anyone else, but I feel I'm as good as the best they've ever had on that job. And I've had people I work with compliment me about the work I've done. It's usually the people who have to deal with the metal after it goes through the slitters. They would rather deal with the processing of metal that I've run, in most cases, as opposed to one of the other operators. It's gratifying to me to know that they think I might do a little better job than the next guy.

Similar feelings were expressed by other machine operators and some as-semblers. At the most this suggests that where little or no aesthetic expe-rience is possible, people may come to focus on other sources of pleasure in their work. For many production workers these sources seemed to have more relevance for maintaining self-esteem than for self-objectification or aesthetic experience.

Aesthetic experience also appeared as a source of motivation for some workers. For engineers, mechanics, and some secretaries, this was especially important, as suggested already. In fact, there was some evi-dence that engineers demanded this experience be part of their work. At the aerospace firm (where nothing was actually manufactured) the lack of opportunities for aesthetic experience was described, although not in so many words, as problematic for maintaining engineers' morale. The personnel manager first mentioned this in an early orientation interview, as did an executive secretary some time later. The secretary's comments were recorded:

> A lot of your engineers who have been accustomed to working on a product that they can go out and see built eventually and say, 'this is mine'...it's difficult for them to come in here [i.e., join the firm] where basically their end product is paper. They can see the missile yes, but it isn't theirs because it was built by someone else. And they don't feel that kind of kinship. We've lost a lot of good engineers because of that. They want to be able to *see* it. At the end of five years they want to see that baby fly in the air and say, 'see that little bolt down there on the bottom by the left-hand side? I designed that'.

According to this secretary, when some engineers could not derive aesthetic pleasure from their work they chose to leave the firm. Although this is a second-hand report, it is entirely consistent with what was learned by talking directly to engineers. At the manufacturing firms engineers took aesthetic experience for granted as a natural part of engineering itself; it was that portion of their pay "in the work itself."

As at the aerospace firm, managers elsewhere recognized the motivational value of aesthetic experience. In the early days of the casting machine firm its founder staged events for the unstated purpose of fostering aesthetic experience. One foreman who had participated in those events recalled:

> When we completed a job, Joe [the owner] would take and have a big dinner and show us movies of the installation. It really gave you a sense of pride and happiness to see what you together had created and that it went in and was working good and the customer was satisfied with it. You were really looking forward to the next project.

The owner was himself an engineer, machinist, and inventor by trade. It seems obvious he was not only familiar with aesthetic experience, but also knew what a powerful motivator it could be. According to the foreman quoted above, the experience was quite real and indeed motivating.

To review, it seems clear first of all that aesthetic experience does arise in the capitalist workplace, and not only for salaried engineers but also for wage-earning mechanics, machinists, and secretaries.[16] And while the data do not support a conclusion that production workers never had aesthetic experience, they provide no evidence for it. What seemed to account for this was the structure of productive activity rather than how the activity was formally rewarded. Aesthetic experience was possible when people had opportunities to put their ideas into practice, to see them embodied in something that 'worked right' or 'looked right', and to take responsibility for it. It did not appear necessary for aesthetic pleasure that people experience marked self-objectification; all that was necessary was a feeling of responsibility for a product or project outcome. It was also crucial that people were able to adopt an appreciative perspective with regard to the product. In many cases all these things came together in the form of projects. Finally, aesthetic moments were not only known as sources of pleasure and motivation to those who experienced them, but also to managers who tacitly knew they could be induced to motivate people.

CORROBORATING EVIDENCE OF AESTHETIC EXPERIENCE IN
THE CAPITALIST WORKPLACE

During on-site interviews people were asked to identify things they did in their jobs that they especially liked. The purpose of this was much the same as in asking about sources of special satisfaction: it was hoped that people would cite activities involving aesthetic experience. Indeed it seemed they did, along with other things. This section will briefly present some additional evidence regarding aesthetic experience in the capitalist workplace derived from questions about specially-liked activities. This evidence is summarized in two parts. The first identifies activities people reported special liking for that could be linked to aesthetic experience. The second identifies activities or conditions people also reported special liking for, but which appeared to be associated with other social-psychological processes.

Summarized in table 4.2 are some of the things people indicated they especially liked doing as part of their jobs. These are things that seemed to be directly pertinent to aesthetic experience. In some cases people cited very specific activities, in others they cited general types of activities. In this table specific activities have be assimilated to general categories (for example, designing batteries is incorporated into designing things). Also indicated are those groups within which these sources of enjoyment were most often cited. Finally, the cognitive experience relevant to aesthetic experience is also suggested.

The expectation that at least some of the things people had special liking for would be related to aesthetic experience seems to have been met. It should be emphasized that these activities or categories were not suggested to people who then indicated whether they enjoyed them or not; people cited these spontaneously, with no cueing. This fact should lend support to the proposition that aesthetic experience arouses a positive affective response to the activities in which it arises. Of course, this presumes aesthetic experience to be implicated in these activities, a presumption that seems eminently warranted if not absolutely verifiable.

Production workers, it will be noted, appear only once in table 4.2 (a few reporting special liking for occasions when their group work went smoothly). But none of the other activities associated with aesthetic experience were cited by production workers. Indeed, only among production workers did a substantial proportion (31%) indicate there were *no* parts of their work they especially liked. This lends further support to the

Table 4.2   Most-Liked Work Activities Associated with Aesthetic Experience

What People Liked	Typically Cited By	Cognitive Experience
Making usable products	Engineers Secretaries	Role taking Means-ends comprehension
Helping people, teaching people	Secretaries Supervisors	Role taking Problem solving
Working with others, especially in small groups	Engineers Machine Operators (who worked in teams)	Role taking
Seeing finished products, seeing them work properly	Engineers Mechanics Secretaries Supervisors	Self-objectification Means-ends comprehension Consummation of the act
Doing work that makes sense	Secretaries	Means-ends comprehension
Designing things, putting own ideas into practice	Engineers Mechanics	Self-objectification
Troubleshooting, getting things to work right	Mechanics Engineers	Problem solving
Setting goals and reaching them	Supervisors Engineers	Consummation of the act
Learning new things, variety	Mechanics Secretaries	Problem solving
Projects	Secretaries Engineers Mechanics	Consummation of intermediate acts within meta-act

claim that, at least among the production workers studied here, aesthetic experience was rare. Again, however, this is not to say production workers found no satisfaction in their work. As discussed in the previous section, some did enjoy certain things, but these were not aspects of productive activities per se. Rather, these were aspects of the conditions under which productive activity occurred. These are summarized in table 4.3, which also suggests the operative social-psychological process in each case.

Table 4.3 Most-Liked Work Conditions Associated with Other Social-Psychological Processes

What People Liked	Typically Cited By	Operative Social-Psychological Process
Being left alone by the boss	Production Workers	Maintenance of self-esteem Avoidance of conflict
Having control over own work	Engineers Mechanics Supervisors	Self-esteem enhancement via sense of efficacy
Doing specialty work, using special skills or knowledge	Engineers Mechanics Production Workers	Affirming job-related identity Self-esteem enhancement via sense of efficacy
Keeping busy	Production Workers Secretaries Mechanics	Avoidance of conflict

Such things as autonomy, control, opportunities to work in one's area of special competence, and "keeping busy" seemed to be important to people in all job groups (though not everyone made special reference to each of them).[17] While some of these conditions, such as autonomy and control, may facilitate aesthetic experience, it seems they also evoke pleasure in their own right or via other social-psychological processes. Autonomy, for example, permits an individual to take responsibility for his work and thus potentially experience self-objectification. It may also, however, contribute to self-esteem by engendering a sense of efficacy and be experienced as pleasureful for this reason. The same process would seem to underlie 'working in one's specialty area'; such opportunities might provide aesthetic experience, but the efficacy-based self-esteem they generate may be a more important basis for satisfaction.

Comparing aesthetic experience to self-esteem enhancement as root sources of satisfaction in work is, however, somewhat like comparing potatoes to potato bugs; both can be found in close association in the same contexts, but they are two quite different things. The purpose of discussing these alternative sources of pleasure in work is to acknowledge that however important aesthetic experience in productive activity may be, other psychologically consequential experiences also arise in the workplace. All such things remain easier to disentangle theoretically than empirically.

Finally, it should be apparent that opportunities to engage in these specially-liked activities, or to experience specially-liked work conditions, varied from job group to job group. It also seems clear that these opportunities covaried with the occurrences of the aesthetic experience documented in the previous section. The evidence presented both here and in the previous section thus suggests aesthetic experience can be seen as distributed differentially across job groups. The issue, then, is not whether aesthetic experience can arise in the capitalist workplace—it does—but what accounts for its distribution. A number of contextual and personality variables were identified as important in this respect.

CONTEXTUAL AND PERSONALITY VARIABLES AFFECTING POSSIBILITIES FOR AESTHETIC EXPERIENCE

A second major aim of this study was to identify the conditions under which aesthetic experience arose. Two sets of variables were identified as affecting possibilities for this experience. One set includes variables associated with the organization of work—these are termed contextual variables. Another set includes variables associated with workers' dispositions and capacities—these are termed personality variables. The set of contextual variables comprises: (1) vertical integration; (2) plant size; (3) project activity; (4) project size; and (5) product standardization. The personality variables identified as important for engendering aesthetic experience are: (1) motivation to understand the production process; (2) motivation for self-objectification; (3) task competence; and (4) ability to adopt an appreciative perspective. Contextual variables will be discussed first.

Vertical integration refers to the scope of a production process found within a single plant.[18] In a vertically integrated plant raw materials are fully transformed into finished products. To the extent such transformations are less complete, a plant would be said to be less vertically integrated. Three of the plants in the present study were vertically integrated to a significant degree. At the battery plant, lead ingots, base chemicals, and other raw materials were transformed into complete, finished batteries. At the machine-building firm, unformed steel and other metals were transformed into complete aluminum casting machines. At the irrigation equipment plant, plastic chips were melted, molded, and eventually transformed into functional sprinkler parts. None of these firms were totally vertically integrated, however. Each made use of parts and materials produced elsewhere. But each could be said to have brought unformed raw materials in one end of the plant and sent usable products out the other. Of course, this notion of vertical integration cannot be similarly applied to the non-manufacturing aerospace firm.[19]

As a contextual variable, vertical integration is important because of its consequences for means-ends comprehension and self-objectification. In a vertically integrated plant it is easier for people to see and learn about a production process. Employees at the battery plant, for example, could literally see raw materials being transformed into batteries. At this firm, according to assemblers and their supervisors, most people understood the process fairly well. Most assemblers in fact worked at a variety of jobs at different stages in the process. This experience allowed them to learn how batteries were made and how their work contributed to a final product. Even if they did not have a deep understanding of the process, they understood where it began, how it proceeded, and where it ended—at least within the plant. Much the same was true at the machine-building plant and the irrigation equipment plant. Employees could see the production process in operation as well as the collective products it yielded. This seemed to enhance means-end comprehension and appreciation for the use value of the firm's product.

In contrast, the aluminum casting plant was much less vertically integrated. Pure aluminum and aluminum scrap were melted, cast, and rolled into sheet stock, which was the firm's final product. This stock was then sold to other manufacturers to be turned into all manner of things (mostly aluminum siding for mobile homes). But as it left the factory it still required further transformation before it would take shape as a recognizable, usable object of any kind. It was not the case that workers did not understand the in-plant production process; nor were they ignorant of how the aluminum would be used. However, they could not readily look at a roll of sheet aluminum and take the role of its user. No production workers at this plant cited the sheet aluminum as a finished product they could look at and take pleasure in imagining how it would be used.

The latter observation raised the issue of just whose aesthetic experience is affected by vertical integration. One group that seemed to be affected was that of engineers. At the three vertically integrated plants engineers frequently noted their liking for working where they could see finished products. Others said they liked "having everything under one roof." A few mentioned having worked at less vertically integrated firms and enjoying it less. For engineers, then, working in a plant which produced a recognizable product out of an expansive production process was especially satisfying. This corresponded, it seemed, to increased opportunities for aesthetic experience.

It is difficult to say how vertical integration affected those in other job groups. Few others were as oriented to a firm's final product—and the whole production process—as were engineers. In principle, though, it would seem that vertical integration might increase everyone's *chances* for aesthetic experience just by making means-ends comprehension easier and final products more visible. What actually happens in this regard would depend on many other things.

One of these other things, closely related to vertical integration, is plant size. Among the firms in the present study vertical integration was inversely related to plant size, the smaller firms being more vertically integrated. Again this seemed to enhance means-ends comprehension. It also made it easier for any employee to see a finished product, just by virtue of plant geography. As for whose aesthetic experience was actually affected by this, again it is difficult to say. This must largely be inferred from various comments made about the satisfaction inherent in being able to see finished products. While this seemed to apply to everyone to some extent, it was perhaps most applicable to engineers. At most, then, it can be said that plant size appeared to affect means-ends comprehension (that is, with regard to the firm's product) and the possibility of deriving satisfaction from seeing the firm's finished product.

As discussed earlier, project activity also facilitates aesthetic experience. Projects allow people to imagine ends, make plans for achieving them, and to consummate many intermediate acts prior to consummation of the meta-act (that is, the project as a whole). Those who have opportunities to engage in project activity definitely have more opportunities for aesthetic experience than those who do not. What varied in the present study was the prevalence of project activity in the work of people in different job groups. Engineers and mechanics engaged in quite a bit of project activity, secretaries and supervisors engaged in some, and production workers very little. Possibilities for aesthetic experience seemed to vary accordingly.

Autonomy and control must also be mentioned in conjunction with project activity. By themselves, autonomy and control cannot give rise to aesthetic experience; what is crucial is the structure of the activity with regard to which an individual has autonomy and control. With regard to project activity, autonomy and control take on special importance because they allow people to take responsibility for the outcomes of their projects, to claim the results as their own. Autonomy and control in project activity also mean an individual has to think about the structure and outcome of a project for himself rather than simply follow instructions. Thus, as general principles, project activity can establish possibilities for aesthetic experience, which autonomy and control further enhance.

The size of the project is also important in this regard. Most of those who engaged in any project activity preferred small projects to large ones (when citing activities they especially liked); they felt it easier to perceive a contribution to a small project than to a large one. This was most pronounced in the aerospace firm where some projects involved hundreds of people. In the large projects, people (primarily software engineers) felt their efforts were 'diluted'. In other words, the size of the project made self-objectification more difficult. With smaller projects individuals more often participated from beginning to end—from conception to execution through to completion. On many large projects, although they did have opportunities eventually to see a final product, more people participated on a partial basis only. For some this inhibited means-end comprehension, undermined feelings of self-objectification, and thus diminished their aesthetic experience.

It seems likely there is a point at which any project becomes too big for optimal aesthetic experience. Thus while most engineers enjoyed project activity and working with others, many felt their satisfaction diminish as projects grew beyond the scope of their control, participation, or understanding. Other workers who engaged in project activity, such as mechanics and secretaries, seldom participated in projects of such scope. For the most part their projects were small ones, limited to themselves or a handful of others. For them project size was less often a variable affecting their aesthetic experience. And for those not engaged in project activity at all, project size was of course irrelevant.

Another important contextual variable is degree of product standardization. This is much the same as task routinization, except the focus is on the outcome of the productive act. When products are standardized people have little need to think about a user's special needs; in fact, they sometimes have little need to think at all (recall the furnace operator's statement). When production is standardized people have to think only of how well a product fits a predetermined pattern. This was the case for most production workers, whose products could almost always be judged either acceptable or unacceptable according to an objective standard. It was only when products did not have to take a standard form that people had to think about what they would produce and how they would produce it. This was the case for engineers, mechanics, and (sometimes) secretaries when they took on tasks for which predetermined goals had not been rigidly defined.

Product standardization varied within narrow limits. This is as would be expected in a highly-organized manufacturing firm (as opposed to, say, an artists' commune). One secretary pointed out these limitations in her own work:

> We have a manual on how to do just about everything: a standard practices manual, a controller's manual. . . . There are certain ways you have to do things; there's usually a procedure for everything. There's very little opportunity to invent procedures on your own. Maybe just the way you run your own little office, that's up to you: whatever works best for your group.

In this case product standardization was directly tied to work formalization; rules were set forth to prescribe almost everything a secretary might do. People in other job groups had to contend with similar rules. Such rules were never exhaustive, however; small spheres of autonomy remained for secretaries and others. Within these spheres people could derive aesthetic experience from activities that demanded connections between conception and execution and aroused felt connections between efforts and results.

Product standardization obviously was relevant to only those whose work involved some product variability. As discussed, this applied chiefly to engineers, mechanics, and secretaries. Supervisors occasionally produced non-standard products, but most were like their subordinates; they seldom had to devise new means of achieving new ends. Possibilities for aesthetic experience were thereby limited. The general principle here is that any from of product standardization operated to decrease possibilities for aesthetic experience. Low standardization, conversely, created needs for imaginarily linking new means to new ends and thereby increased possibilities for aesthetic experience to arise.

These contextual variables should be seen as establishing possibilities for aesthetic experience. It is inappropriate, based on the present analysis, to see them as determining variables. All that can properly be said is that they create conditions predisposing to aesthetic experience. While each can operate independently in this respect, additive effects are also possible. In principle, therefore, possibilities for aesthetic experience should be greatest in small, highly vertically integrated plants where people make non-standard products through small-scale project activity. Although these would be optimal conditions for aesthetic experience, its actual occurrence could not be predicted without also knowing about the producers involved. As observed in this study, there are important personality variables that must be considered.

To focus exclusively on the characteristics of the context within which aesthetic experience arises is to focus on half the picture. The work context alone cannot give rise to anything in the absence of a subject—a human being with certain perceptual, symbolic, and manipulatory capacities. Although the importance of technical mastery as a personal trait was acknowledged earlier, it seems that other equally important personality variables were overlooked. These variables have to do with an individual's motivation to employ his mental and physical capacities in certain ways. Like the contextual variables discussed above, these personality variables also affected possibilities for aesthetic experience. One of these was an individual's motivation to understand the activity in which he was engaged.

This motivation to understand refers to an individual's desire to establish means-ends connections, to comprehend the production process in which he participates. Among engineers this desire seemed especially strong; many expressed a dislike for working on projects they did not fully understand. Few seemed content to work without such understanding. As one engineer described himself: "My personality is to look at the whole picture, even though I might be just a cog in a project." Like many of his co-workers, this engineer wanted to understand the projects to which he contributed. To the extent such desires led to fuller means-ends comprehension, possibilities for aesthetic experience were increased. It seemed, however, that such desires were less strong among those in other job groups. Secretaries and production workers, for example, were much less interested in "looking at the whole picture." To the extent such feelings inhibited pursuit of means-ends comprehension, possibilities for aesthetic experience were diminished.

It should be interjected at this point that while a motivation to understand is identified as a personality variable, its roots in the objective conditions of work are not at all denied. Clearly, the work of secretaries and production workers seldom demanded looking at the whole picture in the way an engineer's might; as such, their motivation to understand a production process might be quickly extinguished. At the same time, the demands and rewards of an engineer's work might fuel this motivation. Obviously, then, the objective conditions an individual faces in his work will affect the development and expression of these personality variables. Indeed, another way to look at the difference between the engineer and the assembler in this regard is to see the assembler as having adapted himself to alienated labor and the engineer as resisting it at every turn. It also seems that the engineer may strive for means-ends comprehension because his work contains the potential for aesthetic experience. For the assembler this potential may not exist, making any struggle for means-ends comprehension less rewarding. Notwithstanding the structural sources of these differences in motivation, it seems that even within job groups this motivation varied, and with it possibilities for aesthetic experience.

An individual's motivation for self-objectification also affects his possibilities for aesthetic experience. Again, however, such a motivation might be rewarded or stifled by conditions beyond the individual's control. But presuming the existence of some opportunities for self-objectification, an individual's motivation to seek this experience could affect possibilities for aesthetic pleasure. Among, engineers, for example, there were clear differences in drives to put ideas into effect; some struggled harder to do this than others. When engineers competed to see whose ideas would be put into effect, those who fought more vigorously for their ideas were more likely to experience self-objectification. In the most general terms, this motivation can be described as a desire to do things one's own way. When individuals in any job group were more aggressive in this sense, their possibilities for aesthetic experience were usually enhanced.

Task competence is a personality variable which also enhances possibilities for aesthetic experience. This refers to an individual's technical mastery in some realm of productive activity. Such mastery affects possibilities for aesthetic experience in at least three ways. First, it means individuals possess the understanding of means-ends relationships necessary for aesthetic experience in any activity. Second, those who possess a high degree of technical mastery are more likely to have autonomy and control in their work and be allowed to carry out projects independently. They are, in other words, more likely to be given work that contains the potential for aesthetic experience. And third, competent individuals are also more likely to prevail in any struggle over whose ideas will be put into effect. To experience self-objectification requires resources that are rationed out carefully in the capitalist workplace; competent individuals are usually more likely to acquire or command these resources.[20]

This type of mastery is described in terms of task competence because it was typically observed to be task specific; that is, people were skilled and knowledgeable with regard to some things and not others. They had autonomy and control in some activities and not others. And they were more or less likely to put their ideas into effect in some arenas than others. Thus it was not 'general competence' that ensured aesthetic experience, but competence in an activity with potential for aesthetic experience (potential that derived from a configuration of contextual variables). Quite simply, though, those who possessed special competence in some activity had more possibilities for aesthetic experience than those who did not.

The ability to adopt an appreciative perspective is also essential for aesthetic experience. If an individual can not adopt some valuing attitude toward a finished product, he can not experience it aesthetically. The ability to do this was observed to vary in a few cases; some could see value in a particular object while others couldn't. This was most evident in the aerospace firm. While most employees could adopt appreciative attitudes toward the weapons the firm helped build, a few could not. In various other instances individuals cited things they produced in which they could see no value. One secretary said this of the monthly accounting reports she typed. They were valueless to her because she couldn't imagine anyone doing anything with them or even reading them. She could not, in other words, take a perspective within which the reports had any use value. This illustrates the general principle that possibilities for aesthetic experience decrease when a person's generalized other does not include an appreciative attitude that can be taken toward any given individual or collective product.

These personality variables should also be viewed as establishing possibilities for aesthetic experience. They no more determine aesthetic experience than do contextual variables. Also like contextual variables, these too can be seen as having independent and additive effects. In general, then, possibilities for aesthetic experience should be greatest for those with strong motivations for means-ends comprehension and self-objectification, high task competence, and abilities to adopt appreciative perspectives toward their work products. But just as contextual variables are insufficient for aesthetic experience, so are these personality variables; both sets of variables must ultimately be considered in relation to one another, not independently.

It is thus necessary to recognize that neither contextual nor personality variables alone can account for aesthetic experience arising in the capitalist workplace. Opportunities for aesthetic experience in any workplace arise only out of the conjunction between contextual and personality variables. While the objective features of a work situation establish some possibilities and rule out others, what actually occurs is a result of the relationship between individual capacities and the possibilities latent in the situation. Aesthetic experience must therefore be understood as arising not out of a simple subject/object relationship, but out of a whole web of material and social relations. These principles can be further illustrated by considering aesthetic experience as it arises outside the capitalist workplace.

AESTHETIC EXPERIENCE OUTSIDE THE WORKPLACE

In off-site interviews people were asked about their hobbies and crafts and how these activities compared to what they did at work. It was hoped that this line of questioning would yield useful information about the nature of aesthetic experience itself. A peripheral interest was in identifying any relationships that might exist between opportunities for aesthetic experience inside and outside the workplace. It was found, first of all, that many people engaged in no hobby or craft work they could sensibly compare to their workplace activities. Second, people made a variety of mundane, but interesting, comparisons between hobbies and work. And third, people made comparisons that clearly suggested they had aesthetic experience in one realm and not the other. In general, what was learned about aesthetic experience outside the workplace confirmed what was learned about it in the workplace.

Most (73%) of those interviewed off site engaged in some kind of hobby or craft work. However, this includes only those activities wherein individuals actually worked with their hands to make things. Some claimed such things as "skiing" and "softball" as hobbies, but these could seldom be sensibly compared to workplace activities.[21] There was also a marked sex-typing of hobby and craft activities, men tending toward the mechanical (racing cars, machining, building) and women toward the non-mechanical (crocheting, sewing, writing poetry). This also created problems in asking people to compare their hobbies to their work. Many women felt there were simply no meaningful comparisons they could make between, for example, secretarial work at the office and their hobby work at home. For men comparisons were less difficult since their hobbies often reflected the mechanical activities they engaged in work.

People made a variety of mundane comparisons between their hobbies and work. These spoke only to the more superficial differences between the two. They were nonetheless interesting in that they highlighted some of the important differences between the two contexts. Among the comparisons made in this vein were: "at home there's no time pressure, no deadlines"; "at home you can learn from your mistakes [without catching hell]"; "at home you have to think about the job because there's no one there to tell you what to do"; and "work at home is more physical than mental." Although some of these comparisons may be relevant to aesthetic experience (such as having to think for one's self at home), they do not really tell much about the differentiation in subjective experience between the two types of activity. By pressing people to describe how they approached hobby work differently from their paid work, and how the satisfaction derived from the two froms of activity was different, more interesting data were obtained.

Perhaps most interesting in this respect was that even upon reflection some people reported no difference in the two experiences. This was frequently the case among engineers and mechanics, many of whom said they approached their hobbies in much the same way as their work but with less intensity. A foreman, a former machinist, made this comparison:

> No. I would probably say that I approach it [work at home] in the same way. I would say the difference in it being that at home if I create something I'm creating it to satisfy myself, where when you do something here at work you're not only creating it to satisfy yourself with a sense of pride, but you also have to satisfy other people within the company. That's probably the only difference.

For this person aesthetic experience apparently arose both at work and at home. While there was definitely more creative freedom involved in craftwork at home, this didn't make for any substantial differences in approach or type of satisfaction. An engineer expressed a similar outlook in response to a question about whether the satisfaction from his job was the same as the satisfaction he got from building things around the house:

> Yeah. I think so. Especially if it's totally my own project. I get a lot of satisfaction out of doing something and saying, 'I did it'. I take a lot of pride in my work. I try to do it real well. I don't like to do something that doesn't look good. If I do something I'm usually very proud to say I did it. And it's perfect. If it's not, I take it apart and redo it.

Here again craftwork at home was experienced much like engineering on the job. It would also seem that aesthetic experience, or at least self-objectification, arose in both realms of activity. Finally, a supervisor implicitly described the aesthetic experience underlying feelings of satisfaction at work and elsewhere:

I think they're pretty much the same. If you do a job and think you've done it well and get satisfaction from standing back and saying, 'hey, I had a hand in that', you know, I think it's basically the same, no matter whether it's at home or on the job or doing it for a neighbor or whatever.

It would seem therefore that people who had opportunities for aesthetic experience at work could create such opportunities for themselves at home. Moreover, they were aware of the similarity of the experience in dissimilar contexts. Others, who had few opportunities for aesthetic experience at work, were equally aware of the differences in their experiences at work and at home.

Those people who had few or no opportunities for aesthetic experience at work but had such opportunities at home were most interesting theoretically. A few such people were found among those interviewed off site. Unlike those quoted above, these people subjectively experienced their productive activities at work and at home quite differently. A machine operator distinguished the experiences available to him in the two contexts thus:

Most of the work with wood [at home] is on my own time and it's for me. As opposed to what I'm doing at *****. I think that probably working with wood you could express yourself a little more than doing anything with the aluminum I work with. For instance, if you're making furniture—if you're making it for yourself—then what you make is a reflection of you. If somebody else likes your work then it's gratifying, to me anyhow. What I do at work just isn't all that gratifying to me.

What seems to be at stake here is the difference between opportunities for marked self-objectification at home (in woodworking) and no such opportunities at work (in operating a machine). In this instance it would appear there is an implicit awareness of the possibility for aesthetic experience in one realm of activity and not the other. As discussed earlier, the structure of activity was also an important contributor to this. Projects were every bit as important outside work as in it. This was the principal basis for one secretary's comparison:

I don't really have projects at *****. To me, like wallpapering a room and finishing it, gives me a sense of, 'gee, I did this—it's finished and I like it'. My job at ***** is not that way because I don't have finished projects. It's just [typing] correspondence.

In these latter cases people had few or no opportunities for aesthetic experience in their jobs, but did have such opportunities in their craftwork.

What is most significant, however, is that they distinguished their experiences on precisely this basis.

In talking about various other off-work activities they engaged in, people occasionally made implicit reference to aesthetic experience. These statements were valuable for providing further data on the nature of the experience itself. In one case a maintenance mechanic talked about the different kinds of craftwork he did:

> I think I enjoy fixing instruments better [than any other form of craftwork], but I've lost track of it to a lot of other things because I'm so busy. You know, if I just had something that I would want to do on my own, where I had the money and the time to sit and do it, I would probably just do [i.e., work with] instruments alone. I enjoy tuning instruments because it's self-satisfaction. I get more self-satisfaction out of that than I think I do anything because it's cleaner and you can appreciate it when you're done. It's like my bike [motorcycle]: I appreciate it because when I go down the road I know it's gonna be all right.

The expressed preference for working with musical instruments seems to derive from the intensity of aesthetic experience it provides. In general, it would be hard to get a more direct description of aesthetic experience in common language. Also nicely illustrated here is the importance of taking an appreciative perspective toward the products of one's work. Furthermore, the link between such a perspective and taking the role of a user is also evident. For this mechanic, aesthetic experience arose in actually or imaginarily using a self-repaired musical instrument or, in this case, a custom-built Harley Davidson motorcycle.

Finally, it also seemed that aesthetic experience could be enhanced when appreciative perspectives were confirmed or reinforced by others. This involves others reaffirming the value of one's work and its status as a true reflection of one's self. One of the engineers interviewed off site also designed and built swimming pools as an independent contractor. In addition to its financial rewards, this activity provided great satisfaction in

> The end results on how it [a pool] looks. If it looks nice, then great, you can pat yourself on the back. If it looks like shit, well, you aren't going to take anyone over and show it to them.

This would seem to once again indirectly confirm the importance of role taking. Not only is role taking necessary in the sense of being able to adopt an appreciative perspective, but its immediacy can also enhance aesthetic experience.[22] In this particular case, however, it seems likely that self-esteem deriving from reflected appraisals (of the engineer's work) may be an equally important source of good or bad feelings about a job. Aesthetic experience is undoubtedly of major importance, but it is not the sole source of 'self-satisfaction' in productive activity.

DOCUMENTATION OF PSYCHOLOGICAL CONSEQUENCES

The qualitative analysis reported above revealed a great deal about the complexity of problem solving, role taking, self-objectification, and means-ends comprehension. The quantitative analysis summarized here (see also appendix C) does not, indeed cannot, attempt to cope with the complexity of these experiences as described above. However, by accepting a degree of simplification—as necessary in any analysis of this kind— it can offer something a qualitative analysis cannot: objective documentation of the consequences of these experiences. Their distinct purposes notwithstanding, it seems reasonable to briefly consider the consistency of the two approaches where their findings overlap.[23]

By way of inconsistency, observed differences in means-ends comprehension and control across job groups were not reflected in the survey data. Fieldwork data suggest some explanations for this. In the case of means-ends comprehension it seems the subtle differences in this experience, involving different types of products, range and depth of comprehension, simply were not tapped by questionnaire items. Measured differences in this experience across occupational and class categories were thus not as expected. On a superficial level, however, the measure of means-ends comprehension did seem to be valid.[24] In correlating strongly and positively with work enjoyment the scale behaved exactly as predicted (regardless of aggregate class or occupational differences, individuals who scored high on means-ends comprehension also tended to score high on work enjoyment). In the case of control, self-reports are considerably out of synch with observations. This appears attributable in large part to a self-enhancement bias arising whenever personal control is in question (Langer, 1983). Such a bias appeared consistently in on-site interviews; the questionnaire items intended to measure control apparently failed to penetrate it.[25] Because of this the control measure was only weakly related to class and occupation, and showed no significant relation to any psychological outcome variable.

For the most part, however, where there was any basis for comparison the quantitative data were consistent with the qualitative. Specifically, observed variations in problem solving, role taking, and routinization across job groups were also reflected in the survey data.

While this does not necessarily establish the validity of either analysis, the consistency between the two is certainly evidence in favor of their validity. On the other hand, if the survey data had shown, say, production workers scoring highest on problem-solving and role-taking demands, then serious doubts about both analyses would have been warranted. Where inconsistencies did appear, knowledge gained during fieldwork could be used to make sense of them straightforwardly without straining the credibility of the data.

A retrospective comment should be made here about the timing of these two study phases. Dealing with five different research sites unfortunately necessitated carrying out fieldwork and surveys concurrently. Ideally, the surveys would have followed the fieldwork at a greater distance, so that questionnaire and scale construction would have been directly informed by fieldwork. It might also have suggested other aspects of work experience, such as project activity, that could have been tapped with the questionnaire. Future survey work based on the natural labor perspective must take into account the aspects of work experience, contextual and personality variables, and measurement problems identified in this effort. But again, such survey work should be preceded by fieldwork to develop an appropriate degree of contextual understanding.

The purpose of the survey work done in the present study was to document a two-stage connection between the capitalist labor process and its psychological effects. In this respect the data were largely supportive of theoretical arguments, if in some cases only modestly. The relationships appearing in the survey data are summarized in table 4.4 As shown in the table, most theorized relationships appeared as expected; the two-stage link between the capitalist labor process and psychological functioning—via the structuring of work experience—was thus established. This further illustrates several important links between social structure and personality posited by the natural labor theory.

In addition to the connections shown here, analysis also revealed that education had a significant effect on intellectual flexibility and an effect on reification nearly as strong as role-taking demands. It also showed that gender had the greatest effect on role-taking propensity when work experiences were controlled. None of these findings poses any threat, however, to the social-psychological component of the natural labor perspective. That education increases intellectual flexibility is hardly surprising; nor it is surprising that eduction decreases reification.[26] And with regard to 'being a male' diminishing role-taking propensity, there is a substantial body of theory and research suggesting that differences in male and female socialization patterns contribute to making

Table 4.4 Summary of Survey Findings[a]

Relationship	Eta[b]	F	Expected Pattern Observed	Relationship	Expected	Observed[c]
Class position and:				Routinization and:		
Routinization	.43	18.59**	yes	RTPROP[d]	−	−.11
				REIFCN	+	.16**
				INTFLX	−	−.22**
				WENJOY	−	−.25**
Control	.12	1.17	no	Control and:		
				RTPROP	+	.12
				REIFCN	−	−.05
				INTFLX	+	.05
				WENJOY	+	.06
Means-ends comprehension	.22	3.98*	no	Means-ends comprehension and:		
				RTPROP	+	.06
				REIFCN	−	−.06
				INTFLX	+	−.02
				WENJOY	+	.30**
Role taking	.50	26.84**	yes	Role taking and:		
				RTPROP	+	.14*
				REIFCN	−	−.20**
				INTFLX	+	.19**
				WENJOY	+	.23**
Problem solving	.48	24.82**	yes	Problem solving and:		
				RTPROP	+	.08
				REIFCN	−	−.17*
				INTFLX	+	.18*
				WENJOY	+	.19**

[a]See appendix C for a more complete analysis of the survey data.

[b]Eta is the square root of the proportion of variance in the dependent variable accounted for by the independent variable. Its interpretation is analogous to that of the Pearson product-moment correlation coefficient, although eta can refer to linear or non-linear relationships. It derives here from a one-way analysis of variance.

[c]Pearson product-moment correlation coefficient.

[d]RTPROP = role-taking propensity; REIFCN = reification; INTFLX = intellectual flexibility; WENJOY = work enjoyment. See appendix B for information on scale construction.

women more empathic and adept at role taking than men.[27] All this simply points up the fact that experiences in contexts other than the workplace are consequential for psychological functioning, a fact not disputed by the natural labor perspective, and one it can well accommodate.[28]

What then are the substantive implications of these date for revising the natural labor perspective? They are in fact few. This phase of the study was expressly deductive, intended not to generate new ideas but to confirm the logical entailments of 'old' ones. If these had not been confirmed, much revision—or rationalization—would have been necessary. The modest contribution of the survey data lies, then, in providing supplemental evidence of the psychosocial consequences of the work experiences of concern from the natural labor perspective. Moreover, they have served as a reminder that the workplace is not the only place where social structure shapes experience and, in turn, psychological functioning.

5

Reassessment

We need to rid ourselves of any concepts which keep us from seeing that the essential problems of men at work are the same whether they do their work in the laboratories of some famous institution or in the messiest vat room of a pickle factory.

Everett C. Hughes in *The Sociological Eye*

Drawing on both sets of data the following general conclusions can be put forth: (1) the work experiences predisposing to aesthetic experience are complex, multi-dimensional, and not adequately described by the theoretical framework set forth in chapters one and two; (2) aesthetic experience can and does arise within the capitalist labor process; (3) aesthetic experience itself, both inside and outside of the capitalist workplace, is much as Mead described it; (4) to understand the occurrence of aesthetic experience it is necessary to understand the person-environment relationship; (5) the work experiences predisposing to aesthetic experience appear to be cognitively and affectively consequential as predicted; and (6) these psychologically consequential work experiences are systematically related to class position as predicted. Each of these conclusions will be discussed briefly in turn.

REVIEW OF THE DATA

First, the work experiences predisposing to aesthetic experience were found to be much more than a yes-or-no proposition. People did not sim-

125

ply have or not have a grasp of *the* means-ends relationship; they under-stood the connections between their work and its consequences with varying degrees of range (span of comprehension) and refinement (depth of comprehension). Further, they perceived a variety of material and op-erational products as following from their efforts. Self-objectification was also found to be more than a yes-or-no proposition. People did not have to create unique objects to experience this; they had only to per-ceive some valued transformation of nature attributable to their agency in the workplace. Regarding problem solving the data say too little, largely because of the unanticipated difficulties that arose in asking direct questions about problem solving. Even so, a basic distinction between technical and interpretive problems was established. Much more was learned about role-taking, which was found to vary depending on status-directionality, underlying motives, and degree of differentiation; more-over, role-taking ability was suggested to vary along dimensions of range, depth, and accuracy. In sum, the data suggest more attention must be given to determining how the discovered complexities in these work experiences might have varying cognitive and affective consequences.

Second, aesthetic experience was found to arise within the capitalist labor process. Some people were found to possess considerable means-ends comprehension, to have opportunities for self-objectification, and to experience role-taking and problem-solving demands in their work. Aesthetic experience was thus entirely possible and, in fact, quite evi-dent. When people could put their ideas into practice and take responsi-bility for the results—presuming other necessary conditions—they experienced aesthetic pleasure in their work. Most often this occurred in project activity where intermediate and distant goals were clearly defined and where individuals had autonomy and control in working to achieve them. Opportunities for this kind of experience varied across occupa-tional and class categories. Those in the working class had the fewest such opportunities, as documented through both fieldwork and survey data analysis.

Third, aesthetic experience was found to occur in much the way Mead described it. In productive activity aesthetic experience arose when individuals could see relationships between their activity and its conse-quences. But more importantly, aesthetic experience depended on being able to adopt an appreciative perspective toward an object, finished or unfinished, in actuality or in imagination. In actual productive activity aesthetic experience was most common where individuals had to reflect on means-ends relationships in working toward valued ends—as in plan-ning and executing sequential steps in a project. Aesthetic experience was also found to be a powerful motivator; it was an experience individuals sought and management sometimes intentionally induced. However, it was also found that other social-psychological processes affected work enjoyment, especially among those who had the fewest opportunities for aesthetic experience. In general the data suggest Mead's theory of aesthetic experience is firmly grounded in the reality of productive activity as people experience it, if only occasionally in the capitalist workplace.

Fourth, it was found that consideration of contextual variables alone was inadequate to understand the occurrence of aesthetic experience. Features of the work context were nonetheless important; degree of vertical integration, plant size, extent of project activity, project size, and degree of product standardization all seemed to affect possibilities for aesthetic experience. But these conditions did not determine aesthetic experience, which arose only out of a complex web of material and social relations partly defined by the characteristics of the acting subject. Among these characteristics were motivation to seek means-ends comprehension, task competence, motivation to seek self-objectification, and ability to adopt an appreciative perspective toward a product. The data thus underscored a point made earlier: aesthetic experience arises out of a conjunction between contextual and personality characteristics. By implication, the cognitive and affective consequences of the capitalist labor process can be understood only by examining the person-environment relationship.

Fifth, the work experiences predisposing to aesthetic experience were found to be significantly related to the theorized outcome variables intellectual flexibility, reification, work enjoyment, and propensity to role-take. Although not all theoretically expected relationships appeared in the survey data, nothing unexpected appeared either. The survey data were generally consistent with theoretical expectations in showing these work experiences to be associated with hypothesized psychological outcomes. The survey data also showed that other variables, such as sex and education, were significantly related to psychological functioning. These findings support the validity of the Meadian social-psychological perspective upon which arguments about the psychological consequences of productive activity have been based. However, they also point to the need to consider other contexts where similar psychologically consequential experiences arise.

Sixth, and perhaps most important for the Marxian aspect of this analysis, the work experiences found to be consequential for psychological functioning were also found to vary systematically across class categories. Those in the working class experienced significantly less problem solving and role taking and, conversely, significantly more routinization. Semi-autonomous employees, supervisors, and managers all experienced more problem solving and role taking and less routinization. This was precisely as the Marxian analysis of the capitalist labor process predicted. Logically, then, working class position in the capitalist labor process should be associated with decreased work enjoyment, intellectual flexibility, and propensity to role-take; and, conversely, with increased reification.[1] Based on this reasoning, the data thus affirm a two-stage link between the capitalist labor process and psychological functioning.

Overall, the data speak well for the natural labor perspective, but not unequivocally. Empirical analysis revealed unanticipated complexities and failed to reveal some expected relationships. These messages must be heeded along with those directly supportive of the perspective as originally formulated. And they are no less valuable, for they point out what must be done to improve the perspective. But before tackling the matter of revision directly, another matter judiciously avoided to this point must be addressed. The question must be answered: is there natural labor in the capitalist workplace?

NATURAL LABOR IN THE CAPITALIST WORKPLACE

Whether or not aesthetic experience arises in the capitalist workplace is no longer in question. It does. But aesthetic experience is not natural labor, although it is a necessary element of it. To repeat the definition advanced earlier: aesthetic experience is the subjective moment of natural labor; the creative advance of nature is its objective moment. A creative advance of nature, it should be recalled, involves an improved relationship between an organism and its environment such that life-sustaining impulses are more readily satisfied. On this basis, and the basis of the data, can it then be said that natural labor occurs within the capitalist labor process? The answer is a qualified yes.

It was suggested in earlier chapters that, in more concrete terms, a creative advance of nature in human productive activity might take the form of a newly developed skill, a new idea, a new tool or a new product. If any of these contributed to sustaining the life of a producer or to more readily satisfying his impulses, then a creative advance of nature could be said to have occurred. It is undeniable that new skills, ideas, tools, and products periodically emerge out of the capitalist labor process. There was indeed evidence of such things in the work experience of many persons interviewed in this study.[2] People did develop new ideas, skills, tools, and products in their work; and they did adapt themselves and their work environments in ways that allowed more ready satisfaction of their impulses. Such things would seem to constitute creative advances of nature.

To stand by the theoretical definitions guiding this study, it must be said that when such creative advances of nature occurred in conjunction with aesthetic experience, so then did natural labor. It can no longer be held, therefore, that the capitalist labor process absolutely precludes natural labor.

It should be clear that this observation in no way undermines or contradicts the premises of the natural labor perspective. The position here has been that the imperatives of capitalism shape the organization of work, which in turn enables and constrains certain kinds of productive activities and productive experiences for different classes of producers. Thus even within the capitalist labor process, it was argued, one must look at productive activities—what people actually do with their hands and minds—to find natural or alienated labor. In this analysis a rigid Marxist conception of all labor under capitalism as alienated was rejected. This does not deny, however, the alienation of labor qua *value*; it denies only that the psychological effects of this expropriation process can be understood solely in structural terms.[3] Thus to conclude that natural labor can occur within the capitalist labor process is not cause for rejecting any basic Marxian premises about the functioning of capitalism. That functioning is unchanged by the fact that Meadian social psychology permits one to see the capitalist labor process today as more complex and equivocal in its psychological effects than it was in Marx's time.

It should be added that while natural labor may arise within the capitalist labor process, this in no way diminishes the critical force of the Marxian/Meadian analysis. This force must still be directed against three facts of capitalist production. First, even though natural labor can arise in the capitalist workplace, it is grossly 'maldistributed'. As previous analyses have shown, the majority of all producers (those in the working class) have few or no opportunities for such experience. Second, the capitalist labor process puts ultimate constraints on natural labor, even for those who have the opportunity to engage in it. Because the capitalist production system has already been organized to satisfy the impulses of the capitalist class, any adaptation within it will be limited to what is ultimately functional for capital. In other words, the producer's capacity to transform his environment to make it more responsive to his needs will always be limited; 'nature' will be allowed to 'advance' only so long as it simultaneously advances capital. And third, as implied above, it is simply not the goal of the capitalist labor process to facilitate natural labor.

Its goal is capital accumulation. Over and above the destructive effects this has on individual producers, one could argue that from a global perspective capitalism has ceased to serve the survival interests of most human beings. That is to say, capitalism, because of its tendencies toward environmental destruction, may hold little adaptive value for most people on the planet. But that is another issue.

In sum, even though natural labor may occur within the capitalist labor process, this is not its goal. If natural labor occurs within it, it is largely accidental, an inevitable by-product of self-conscious human productive activity. But by letting us see that natural labor can occur at all within the capitalist labor process, the natural labor perspective complicates things considerably. Categorical critiques of capitalism because of its alleged psychological effects must now become qualified critiques, though not necessarily any less damning. To put it another way, the natural labor perspective forces us to look more carefully at what is adaptive or non-adaptive, beneficial or destructive, in *any* labor process. But before pursuing its further critical and sociological implications, it is appropriate now to return to the perspective itself to try putting it in better order based on what has been learned through this study. Exploring the praxical implications of the perspective will be the objective of the final chapter.

ADDITIONS AND ADJUSTMENTS TO THE PERSPECTIVE

One goal of the empirical analyses carried out here has been to bring the natural labor perspective more in line with the reality of the capitalist labor process. In terms of a metaphor used earlier, the goal has been to elaborate a rough draft of a conceptual map. As it turned out, the map proved to be a fairly good guide to the territory of interest. What is appropriate here, then, is not so much revision as elaboration. To pursue this in some systematic fashion I will consider in turn each major aspect of productive experience upon which attention was focused in this study.

Perhaps it is best to begin where there is most to say. Role taking is at the heart of the natural labor perspective, at least its social-psychological dimension, and it was about role taking that most was learned. The early treatment of role taking was overly simplistic. Role taking was initially treated as a unidimensional cognitive activity, something people either did or didn't do in production. Empirical investigation showed the matter to be more complex. People do not merely role-take or not; they are more or less always role taking. What is important is whose roles they are taking and how. These matters have been discussed in terms of status-directionality, underlying motivation, degrees of differentiation, range, depth, and accuracy.

What seems to be needed is a more systematic way to analyze role taking in productive activity, a way that takes this complexity into account. One way to approach this is via notions of "role-set complexity." This suggests it is important to consider the constellation of role relationships individuals have by virtue of their status in a production system. The value of this lies chiefly in structurally representing patterns of role taking. This sociograms in figure 5.1 suggest how this idea might be applied to some of the patterns of role taking observed in this study.

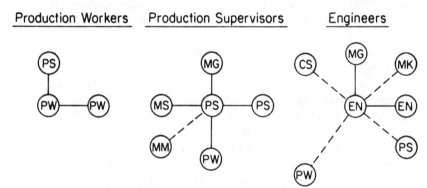

Production Workers   Production Supervisors   Engineers

Figure 5.1   Variability of Role-Set Complexity in Production
PS = production supervisor; PW = production worker; MS-maintenance
    supervisor;
EN = engineer; MM = maintenance mechanic; MG = manager; MK = marketing
    manager; CS = customer

The connecting lines in figure 5.1 are meant to indicate upward, downward, and lateral role taking. The vertical axis represents a status dimension in the capitalist workplace. Thus in the first drawing, production supervisors are shown having higher status than production workers, who must upwardly role-take with respect to their supervisors and laterally role-take with respect to their co-workers. They experience no downward role taking.

In the case of production workers the sociogram shows they have only two status levels to deal with (usually) in their workplace activities. In contrast, the next sociogram shows supervisors having three status levels to deal with. The situation for engineers is even more complex.

Angled lines represent relations across intermediate status levels. Broken lines represent informal relationships characterized by unofficial status differentials.

What a schematic analysis like this shows is role-set complexity in two dimensions. Lateral role taking requires an individual to take another perspective, but one that probably does not differ substantially from his own—at least within capitalist relations of production. Vertical role taking requires an individual to take perspectives more likely to differ from his own. Role taking across status levels would thus be seen as more cognitively demanding in that less can safely be assumed in communication; meanings must be elaborated and made explicit (cf. Bernstein, 1973; Gans, 1962). The more complex an individual's role set along both dimensions, the greater the overall cognitive demands involved in role taking.

Some have argued that it is precisely this kind of role-set complexity, with its attendant cognitive demands, that engenders intellectual flexibility. Rose Coser (1975), for example, emphasizes that individuals with complex role sets are more likely to be confronted with incompatible expectations, which require reflection, innovation, and flexibility to resolve. In this view intellectual flexibility is a result of the complex role-taking demands associated with particular status positions; hence, intellectual flexibility is an internal cognitive reflection of social structure. It is thus not only the content of thought that reflects social structure but, as the present analysis has also proposed, the form of thought as well. Other theorists have likewise emphasized complex role-taking demands as the wellspring of similar intellectual abilities (see Swanson, 1974; Kagan, 1972; Sieber, 1974).

Analyzing role-set complexity in this way makes a great deal of sense from the natural labor perspective. The theoretical suppositions linking role-set complexity to intellectual flexibility are, in fact, partly Meadian (symbolic interactionist) in origin. Using schematics of the sort in figure 5.1 is one way to give more structure to the study of role taking in productive activity. But it has some crucial limitations. As the empirical analyses here have shown, role taking is more complex than any line between two circles can indicate. While it may be helpful to use such sociograms to objectively represent role *relationships*, they are not quite adequate to represent role-taking *experiences*. Such sociographic representations fail to distinguish dimensions of role taking, fail to suggest that these dimensions might have differential consequences, and fail to connect role sets to the capitalist labor process in any systematic way. [4] So, then, some view of role taking that takes these matters into account is called for. Such a view is suggested in table 5.1.

Table 5.1   Social Structure Linked to Psychological Consequences via
Problem-Solving and Role-Taking Experiences

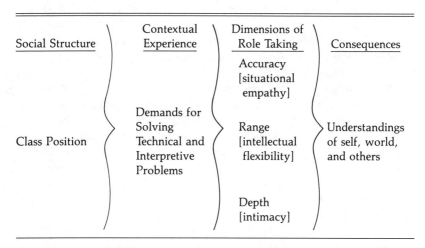

What this table suggests is that role taking must be seen as a multi-dimensional cognitive activity—shaped by contextual demands—that can produce differential psychological consequences. Two points of elaboration are necessary here. First, the "demands for solving technical and interpretive problems" giving rise to needs for role taking, should be construed in the broadest possible terms. In other words, any and all interaction with objects and people involves 'problems' until functional habits are established; these necessitate role taking at some early stage. Second, while range, accuracy, and depth are shown leading to "understandings of self, world, and others," it should be clear that these dimensions of role taking might vary in relevance for understanding one's self, the world, or others. Accuracy, for example, would probably be more relevant for understanding others than for understanding the material world. Admittedly, then, this representation could be elaborated further. But even at this point it is useful for illustrating connections between social structure, situational experience, and psychological outcomes.

Finally, the issue of role-taking ability versus role-taking propensity must be addressed once more. While the conceptual distinction between the two has already been made clear, what remains uncertain is whether both are affected by the same things. It seems they are not.

As the diagram above suggests, problem-solving demands will affect particular dimensions of role-taking ability. Problem-solving experiences can make people more accurate role takers, make them develop a wider range of adoptable perspectives, and lead to intimate understandings of other perspectives. Thus role taking can be considered an improvable ability. It should also be kept in mind, however, that all self-conscious humans role-take as a concomitant of language use. Role-taking ability must therefore always be seen in relative terms. Defining someone as a 'highly accurate' role-taker, for example, can only be done relative to someone less accurate. Among self-conscious humans there is no 'absolute zero' against which role-taking can be assessed.[5]

While role-taking abilities can be considered cognitive skills developed through exercise, so to speak, role-taking propensity cannot. It must be considered a disposition only. As such, it is probably affected by much more than demands for problem solving or role taking. It is quite possible for an individual to possess role-taking abilities he is not disposed to use under certain conditions. What affects ability and what affects propensity must therefore be distinct, though not necessarily unrelated. In the capitalist workplace those in the working class often experienced role taking as an act of submission, because most of their role taking was upward. It is thus conceivable that a decreased propensity to role-take on their part reflects resistance to relations of domination rather than any differences in ability.

Other theorists have also noted the possible effects of social structural conditions on role-taking propensity, if not in so many words. Simmel (1950), for example, discussed the "blasé attitude" that arises as insulation against the otherwise overwhelming emotional and perceptual demands of urban life. But it is not only potential overstimulation that calls forth defensive reserve with respect to role taking. According to Simmel, social relations premised on market relations are also responsible for a pervasive distrust and "inconsiderate hardness" among modern citydwellers. In this view a diminished propensity to role-take is seen as an adaption to a milieu wherein one typically assumes people are treating each other as means to ends. Certainly occupying a working-class position within capitalist relations of production makes such an orientation adaptive, quite regardless of urban density. The point again, however, is that role-taking propensity may not reflect true role-taking ability. It may reflect a resistance to domination, a general orientation to life in mass society, or a defense against entanglement in the exploitive social relationships common in all spheres of life under capitalism. At best, then, the natural labor perspective can be qualified to acknowledge this issue, which can be resolved only through further research.[6]

As with role taking, the initial view taken of means-ends comprehension was too simplistic. It appears that in any complex productive activity there are more means and ends involved than immediately apparent. People conceive all sorts of ends as following from their manipulatory activities, ends which may be non-material and perceivable only from certain perspectives. But in itself this discovery does not warrant any substantial revisions in the natural labor perspective. It is sufficient to recognize that people experience themselves as agents in many ways within the production process; this implies comprehension of diverse means-ends relationships. Even so, this does not diminish the importance of considering range and refinement of means-ends comprehension—two worthwhile additions to the natural labor perspective.

There is, however, one way in which the view of means-ends comprehension requires some adjustment. It was initially hypothesized that, along with problem solving and role taking, means-ends comprehension would associate positively with intellectual flexibility and propensity to role-take, and negatively with reification. This proposition was based on the assumption that both problem solving and role taking depend on means-ends comprehension; hence, these cognitive experiences must be concomitant. However, the survey data showed means-ends comprehension to be unrelated to any of the cognitive variables (although it was strongly related to the affective outcome variable). There is an obvious explanation for this: means-ends comprehension is based on habit (memory). In other words, an individual can develop means-ends comprehension in an activity which, once mastered, ceases to demand much, if any, problem solving. In the same way it is possible to develop means-ends comprehension in an activity that demands little or no continued role taking. Thus while problem solving and role taking necessitate means-ends comprehension, once established, means-ends comprehension can exist independently of problem-solving or role-taking demands. But again this requires no substantial revision of the natural labor perspective, just some qualification.

With regard to problem solving, it is unfortunate the data provide so little basis for revisions or qualifications. They do say, however, that problem solving is not a unidimensional experience.

Like role taking and means-ends comprehension, problem solving is experienced in several different ways. But this was entirely expected. What was not expected was difficulty in documenting these varieties of problem-solving experience. The empirical analysis undertaken here was able to distinguish only two basic types of problem solving. Nonetheless, the distinction between technical and interpretive problems is an important one; different cognitive activities would seem to be involved in trying to solve them. And these would seem to have different cognitive consequences. But such speculation provides no solid basis for modifying any aspect of the natural labor perspective. At present, then, this matter remains unresolved.

With regard to self-objectification, the natural labor perspective must be adjusted to acknowledge that this experience does not depend on 'creative expression of the I'. As argued with reference to means-ends comprehension, people see all kinds of effects they produce as attributable to their own agency. Even where these effects represent uncreative physical efforts it seems that some very satisfying self-objectification occurs. But to reemphasize the Marxian component of this analysis, it is important to point out that such experiences of self-objectification fall far short of what is possible. The effects people produce in the capitalist workplace are not truly their own; they belong to the capitalist; the individual cannot do with them as he pleases. Nor do such effects represent the full range of an individual's capacities. There thus remains alienation, in Marx's sense of failure, despite self-objectification. That people enjoy the limited opportunities they have for self-objectification within the capitalist labor process is not surprising. As the Meadian analysis explicates, it is an inherently satisfying experience in any morally acceptable context of action. And the capitalist labor process might, in some cases, provide opportunities for self-objectification that do not exist in other spheres of life. (Where else can most people participate in building multimillion-dollar precision machines?) Because the natural labor perspective does not see labor as either 'alienated or not', acknowledging the existence of these experiences within the capitalist labor process is not problematic. No revisions are necessary on this count.

As noted previously in this chapter, there seems to be no reason to revise the Meadian interpretation of aesthetic experience. There is only the need to recognize, as Mead undoubtedly did, that aesthetic experience is a function of the relationship between a self-conscious organism and various features of its environment. And it is this relationship that must be the focal point of analysis, not merely the organism or the environment, not merely the worker or the workplace. But this point serves more as a reminder of the need to properly and carefully apply the Meadian framework than as a basis for revising it.

Nor at this point does there seem to be any basis for revising the Marxian/Meadian interpretation of natural labor. In fact, the data demonstrated the usefulness of the natural labor concept precisely as intended: in showing that a labor process does not necessarily determine the experiential character of all the productive activities occurring within it. The concept also showed how within any labor process—even one precluding natural labor for the majority—some such labor can arise, making it impossible to predict with mechanical certainty the psychological consequences that will follow from it. But this not to say the natural labor concept is fully elaborated at this point. There are indeed some important unresolved issues having to do with the ends toward which it arises. These issues will be taken up in the last section of this chapter.

Finally, the data point up the limitations of a traditional materialist focus solely on the sphere of production. Certainly there is no doubt regarding the substantial effects of work and class position on psychological functioning. But other experiences in other spheres of life must also be taken into account to fully understand how social structure affects psychological functioning. However, as argued earlier, this is only a further challenge for the natural labor perspective, not a repudiation of it. The Meadian analysis can be applied to understanding how certain cognitive activities in any context may affect psychological functioning. And further, the Marxian analysis can be extended to other institutional spheres; education, for example, is closely tied to the capitalist labor process (Bowles and Gintis, 1976; Wrigley, 1982). What this calls for ultimately is, continued refinement of the perspective via further application to the sphere of production, and extension to other spheres of life in capitalist society.

The following section will explore how the natural labor perspective can be integrated with analyses of other work experiences related to the functioning of capitalism. Subsequent sections will explore the implications of the perspective for contributing to alienation theory and research, for formulating a critical theory of social structure and personality, and for studying the political economy of cognitive development.

Toward a Critical Social Psychology of Work

The mainstream sub-disciplines of industrial sociology and industrial psychology are interested in managing conditions within the confines of a capitalist system of production. When researchers in these sub-disciplines study how work affects workers, it is usually to determine how the most severe psychological manifestations of alienated labor can be alleviated. Of course, these manifestations are of interest largely because they can interfere with the accumulation of capital. Thus out of these uncritical traditions come recommendations for palliatives

such as "work humanization," "job enrichment," and "quality circles."
The ultimate goals of these traditions are to preserve the capitalist labor
process and, wherever possible, make it more efficient.

The goals and interests of a critical social psychology of work run
directly counter to these. Its interests are in understanding how the capitalist labor process limits and distorts the potential human development
of workers. Its goal is not to preserve such a system but to transform it
and eventually create a system of production that fully meets human material needs and maximizes development of human potential. These goals
and interests have been implicit in the Marxian/Meadian analysis. But as
has been acknowledged at several points, this analysis is but a first step
in acting on these interests and achieving these goals. A logical next step
is to develop a fuller view of how working for capitalism affects people,
with special consideration for how this bears on the project of transforming capitalism; *ergo*, a critical social psychology of work.

There is neither room nor reason to undertake here to develop such
a social psychology. But it is worthwhile to outline the assumptions upon
which it might be founded and to suggest how the natural labor perspective might be a part of it. As I see it (see also Bramel and Friend, 1981), a
critical social psychology of work would proceed from the following assumptions: (1) under capitalism there is a fundamental conflict of interests between workers and management; (2) alienated labor is
dehumanized labor; (3) under capitalism work is organized so as to constitute a constant threat to workers' self-esteem; and (4) a distinction
must be made between the spheres of necessity and freedom to realisti-
cally assess possibilities for workplace transformation. Each of these
points will be given brief treatment below.

The assumption of conflicting interests between management (acting
for capital) and workers is often challenged on grounds that both workers and managers share material interests in the survival of the firm. This
is the familiar profits-are-necessary-for-jobs apologia. While it is true
that in any single firm struggling for survival in a competitive economy
workers and managers share interests in its survival, the form their interests take once survival is ensured remain in conflict. In other words, the
goal of profit maximization is always in conflict with the goal of wage
maximization in any viable capitalist firm. And as noted earlier, one need
not subscribe to the labor theory of value to recognize this—any successful MBA trained in neoclassical economics is equally aware of it. But it is
also important to recognize how profit imperatives create further overt
conflicts between managers and workers. These conflicts are expressed in
authority relations in the workplace, bureaucratic forms of organization,

and day-to-day struggles for control on the shopfloor (see also Burawoy, 1981). A critical social psychology of work must recognize the structural conflicts underlying the organization of work under capitalism, else it cannot explain the shape of the workplace within which social-psychological processes operate. To conjure a dramaturgical metaphor: to explain the stage it is necessary to explain the theater as well.

To recognize that alienated labor is dehumanized labor requires that the concept of natural labor be a part of the theoretical equipment of a critical social psychology of work. In accord with arguments set forth in early chapters, this assumption can be restated in positive terms: natural labor is to be the standard against which actual labor is compared. The critical standard thus becomes what is humanly possible, not what is 'reasonable' within the parameters of capitalism. In this way a critical social psychology of work arms itself with concepts for both the immanent and transcendant criticism of work under capitalism. Indeed, it is only with a concept of natural labor that a critical social psychology can be more than critical; a concept of natural labor allows it to be a force for positive reconstruction.

The assumption that the workplace is organized so as to continually threaten workers' self-esteem carries with it implicit recognition that a variety of social-psychological processes must be taken into account to understand how work affect workers. As discussed in chapter 4, not all the significant psychological effects of the capitalist labor process can be understood in terms of aesthetic experience. In addition to processes affecting psychological functioning and feelings toward work, are those affecting interpersonal functioning, feelings toward others, values, and self-conceptions. All such matters are within the purview of a critical social psychology of work, for they are all relevant to the project of collectively transforming the capitalist labor process. Self-esteem is emphasized here because of its centrality to understanding behavior from a Meadian perspective, and because its connection to the organization of work under capitalism can be straightforwardly demonstrated (see, for example, Staples, et al., 1984). Making connections between the structure of capitalism and these social-psychological processes is in part what distinguishes a critical social psychology of work from mainstream sociology of work.

Finally, the assumption that the spheres of necessity and freedom must be distinguished is based on an interest in transforming the capitalist workplace into a human workplace. This interest is best served by realistic assessment of what is possible in late twentieth century industrial society. In the struggle for natural labor it would be naive to assume all industrial production, or even a large part of it, could be transformed into anything resembling craftwork. In the sphere of necessity, which sustains the material basis of any society, natural labor will never take the form of artisan craftwork. However, even in the sphere of necessity there can be worker self-determination, problem solving, role taking, means-ends comprehension, self-objectification, aesthetic experience, and natural labor. But these experiences will always be degrees less than what is possible in the sphere of freedom, where individuals are not constrained by the demands of large-scale industrial production. A critical social psychology of work cannot ignore the reality of industrial mass society. Only by being fully aware of where it begins can any social change project be aware of where it is going.

These last remarks should suggest that a critical social psychology of work can be more than a basis for criticizing the capitalist labor process. Its critical force can be applied to any labor process—and it must, for no stage of transformation should be immune to criticism. What people do in their productive activities must always be evaluated relative to what they could do. In this way a critical theory of work can continue to be a force for change even after capitalism is transformed beyond recognition. In more specific terms, Michael Burawoy asserts that Marxists and others sharing hopes for a socialist transformation of the capitalist labor process cannot afford to ignore serious questions about what labor will become under socialism:

> No serious study of the capitalist labor process can avoid an equally serious study of the socialist labor process; the understanding of the first demands an understanding of the second (1981:113).

A critical social psychology of work based on the natural labor perspective offers one basis for developing such studies. More than that, however, it offers a basis for transforming the objects of study.

CONTRIBUTIONS TO ALIENATION THEORY AND RESEARCH

No attempt has been made to locate this study in the sociological field of "alienation studies." In fact, as argued in chapter 1, the premises of this study are at odds with many of those underlying mainstream alienation studies. In recent years, however, attempts have been made to define an area of "alienation theory and research" encompassing both

Marxist and non-Marxist work on the topic (Geyer and Schweitzer, 1976, 1981). While it might be argued that it is a mistake to define these two schools of alienation as constituting a sociological sub-field, there are some reasons for taking it seriously. The most pertinent reason for doing so is that both Marxists and non-Marxists in this area are struggling with a common sociological problem: how to explain the relationship between objective social conditions and 'subjective alienation'.

Marxists have been interested in this for many of the same reasons motivating this study: principally, to show how capitalism affects the individual. Non-Marxists have been, in recent years, somewhat more concerned with linking their psychological studies of alienation to larger features of social structure, although not necessarily to the imperatives of capitalism. Underlying both interests seems to be a desire to mount empirical studies of alienation in a classic sociological tradition linking the individual to society (cf. Kohn, 1976:111). Marxists have hitherto been hindered in this by their own theoretical prejudices, which precluded treating alienation on a social-psychological level. Non-Marxists have been hindered by their lack of structural theories of society that could be coherently linked to 'subjective alienation'. This overarching sociological concern for the society/individual relationship has thus led to calls for merging structural and subjective perspectives on alienation (Schweitzer, 1981; Fischer, 1976; Plasek, 1974; Twining, 1980).

The results so far have not been especially promising (see Schweitzer, 1981, for a review). Although some theoretical work (for example, Hays, 1976; Markovic, 1981) and a rare bit of empirical work (Archibald, et al., 1981) has pursued inclusive structural/subjective analyses, the results have been extremely weak on one or the other level of analysis. Often operating with ill-fitting structural and social-psychological theories these analyses have been ill-equipped to see how the objective and subjective moments of alienation relate to each other. This situation was in part the impetus for pursuing the Marxian/Meadian synthesis.

The natural labor perspective solves the problem of how to relate objective social conditions to 'subjective alienation'. It should be obvious, however, that it does so by rejecting some of the assumptions upon which this objective/subjective bifurcation is based. From the natural labor perspective it makes no sense to speak of objective alienation as opposed to subjective alienation. Rather, we must speak of alienated labor as a form of activity existing only in a particular form of subject/object relationship. Then, if we wish, we can speak of its subjective dimension, as was analyzed in terms of Mead's philosophy of the act and theory of aesthetic experience. Further, if we wish, we can speak of the psychological effects of alienated labor. But these effects can now be described in terms of specific cognitive and affective consequences. For all practical purposes, the confounding term alienation as referring to an individual condition, could be discarded.

So if "alienation theory and research" is granted legitimacy as an area of sociological study, the natural labor perspective can indeed make a contribution to it by resolving the objective versus subjective issue. Of course, this presumes a willingness to adopt the natural labor perspective, wherein there simply is no such issue. But such willingness can hardly be taken for granted, especially as attempts are made to institutionalize the study of alienation and get busy with normal science.[7] If the natural labor perspective must be located in some institutionalized area of sociology, it is perhaps better that it be one more honestly characterizing its scientific interests, which are in social structure and personality.

Contributions To The Study Of Social Structure And Personality

Sociologically, development of the natural labor perspective is a means to yet another end: making sense of how stable patterns of practical and symbolic activity (social structure) affect psychosocial development and functioning. Here, Marx's concept of alienated labor served as a vehicle for linking the imperatives of capitalism to work experiences, while Mead's social psychology served to link these experiences to personality. Sociologists and cultural anthropologists have long sought to establish such connections. The latter have dealt mainly in theories of culture and personality or, sometimes, "national character." The former have, especially in recent years, focused more narrowly on specific aspects of social structure in relation to specific aspects of personality (see House, 1981). Since the concern here is for an explicitly sociological understanding of social structure and personality, contributions of the natural labor perspective will be considered in light of currently predominant sociological models of social structure and personality.

One way to illustrate what the natural labor perspective tries to do with regard to social structure and personality is offered in figure 5.2. The idea is simply that of structural forces shaping interaction contexts, which shape experiences, which have psychological consequences. A 'nested' model such as this is essentially what House (1981) argues is necessary for an adequate theory of social structure and personality. Ac-

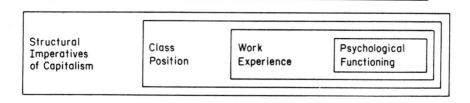

Figure 5.2 Representation of Social Structure and Personality Relationship in the Sphere of Production

cording to House, any such theory must take into account and somehow link components of social structure, proximate social experiences and stimuli and the psychological processes arising in response to these experiences and stimuli. The natural labor perspective can be compared to currently predominant perspectives on social structure and personality against these criteria of adequacy. Table 5.2 uses a modified version of House's framework to compare the natural labor perspective to those of Kohn and Schooler (1983) and Inkeles and Smith (1974).

Table 5.2 itself should need little elaboration. It simply displays the major elements of each of these perspectives, moving from social structure to individual experience to psychological processes and outcomes. Differences in the first two columns of the table reflect the Marxist and non-Marxist origins of the three perspectives. Differences in the three rightmost columns reflect differences in social-psychological and psychological theories. As shown, the natural labor perspective more explicitly identifies the individual experiences consequential for psychological functioning than does the Kohn and Schooler perspective, which is relatively more explicit in this regard than the Inkeles and Smith perspective. With regard to psychological processes, the natural labor perspective is again more explicit than Kohn and Schooler's, which relies on the "learning-generalization" thesis discussed earlier. The Inkeles and Smith perspective is quite unelaborated in this respect, although Inkeles (1983) has made significant efforts to remedy this deficiency. As for psychological consequences, both the natural labor and Kohnian perspectives theorize specific consequences following from individual experiences; the Inkeles and Smith perspective postulates the multi-dimensional consequence of "modernity" as following from experiences in dealing with modern institutions.

There is no need here to reiterate the criticisms of the Kohn and Schooler perspective made earlier, nor to embark on a critique of the less sophisticated Inkeles and Smith perspective. Some general characteriza-

Table 5.2   Alternative Sociological Perspectives on Social Structure and Personality

	Structural Determinants of Status-Specific Experiences	Most Important Social Status	Most Important Individual Experiences	Emphasized Psychological Processes	Theorized Psychological Consequences
Natural Labor	Imperatives of capitalism	Class position	Problem solving Role taking Means-ends comprehension Self-objectification	Development of cognitive skills through solving technical and interpretive problems Learning about self, world, and others via self-objectification	Reified consciousness Propensity to role-take Intellectual flexibility Work enjoyment
Kohn and Schooler	Division of labor in industrial society	Occupation	Self-direction in substantively complex work	Learning-generalization	Values for self-direction Ideational flexibility Orientations to self and world[a]
Inkeles and Smith	Industrialization	Unspecified within culture	Exposure to modern institutions (factories, schools, etc.)	Individual learns to accommodate to demands of modern institutions	Modernity[b]

[a]These orientations include such things as fatalism, trustfulness, anxiety, self-esteem, authoritarianism, conservatism, idea-conformity, standards of morality, distress, and subjective alienation.

[b]Psychological modernity includes a hodge-podge of values, attitudes, aspirations, information, and behavior. For elaboration see Inkeles and Smith (1974) and Inkeles (1983).

tions will suffice to illustrate what the natural labor perspective can contribute to this area of sociology. First, it can be said that the Inkeles and Smith perspective is largely limited in applicability to cross-cultural analyses of social structure and personality; specifically, to comparisons between traditional and modern societies. Theoretically it posits only a general social learning process associated with a shift from traditional to modern forms of social organization. While this is a useful scheme for looking at some of the psychological consequences of modernization, it is not especially useful for analyzing social structure and personality within a modern industrial society.

The Kohn and Schooler perspective is much more useful in this respect. It posits a series of plausible connections between social structure and experience suitable for analyzing modern industrial societies. But, as argued earlier, it breaks down in its simplistic treatment of psychological processing; it does not illuminate very well what psychologically consequential experiences underlie self-direction in substantively complex activity, nor how these experiences actually yield particular psychological outcomes. But no matter how poorly these connections may be made at a theoretical level, there is considerable empirical evidence to support contentions that some such connections must exist; however, the natural labor perspective may well be better at explaining them. Since the Kohn and Schooler perspective is a more sophisticated version of Inkeles and Smith's, it can be used as the basis for comparative evaluation of the natural labor framework.

In general, the natural labor perspective more than meets House's requirements for a theory of social structure and personality. It identifies components of social structure, describes how they function to shape individual experiences, and how these experiences affect people psychologically. The Kohn and Schooler perspective tries to do the same. But unlike the Kohn and Schooler perspective, the natural labor perspective does not merely assume a static social structural condition (the division of labor); it begins with an analysis of system dynamics in order to explain how certain structural conditions—class relations in production— are created. In this sense it identifies the human interests and relations of power that create and sustain social structures and shape individual experiences. This is something the Kohn and Schooler perspective does not try to do. In other words, the natural labor perspective takes less for granted on a structural level and moreover attempts to explain the structural conditions it brings into question.

At the level of individual experience the natural labor and Kohnian perspectives are not so divergent as may appear. Undoubtedly, self-direction in substantively complex work must involve some problem solving, role taking, means-ends comprehension, and self-objectification. In this sense the two perspectives are concerned with many of the same experiences. But it is worthwhile to explore these experiences more carefully, to elucidate them more completely, if the goal is to link them to particular psychological outcomes. The Kohn and Schooler perspective does not do this and thus remains weak in linking experiences to psychological outcomes. The natural labor perspective penetrates substantive complexity and self-direction to get at a more fundamental set of experiences. It can thus identify more clearly the specific experiences shaped by social structure and can more firmly link them to psychological consequences. Since it has been shown that such experiences vary independently across class categories, it seems undeniably advantageous to be aware of them and of their differential psychological consequences.

It also seems appropriate to evaluate these perspectives in terms of their generalizability. The Kohn and Schooler perspective can, in principle, be applied to other social statuses (for example, sex) and other experiential contexts (family, school). It could thus be generalized to account for links between self-direction, substantive complexity, and psychological functioning in life spheres other than the workplace. But in so doing it becomes less able to account for social structure on the one hand, while retaining its limitations with regard to explaining psychological functioning on the other. Although it has not been attempted here, the natural labor perspective could also be applied to other life spheres, such as family and school. In this it would lose none of its explanatory power on a social-psychological level, nor unlike the Kohn and Schooler perspective, would it lose its grip on social structure. As suggested earlier, the Marxian analysis of capitalism can be extended to other institutions of capitalist society, making it possible to link other contextual experiences to the functioning of capitalism (although this is not to say the Marxian labor process analysis applies to all capitalist institutions; clearly it does not). Pursuing a fuller theory of social structure and personality from a Marxist perspective is, however, a task to be taken up elsewhere.

In comparing these perspectives on social structure and personality it is important to bear in mind the different interests underlying them. The Inkeles and Smith perspective seems oriented to demonstrating how Western industrialization can produce the psychologically desirable consequence of "modern thinking." The Kohn and Schooler perspective, though less obviously biased toward demonstrating the virtues of capitalist development, serves almost as well to divert attention from the structure of capitalism. By focusing solely on occupation the Kohn and

Schooler perspective implies the irrelevance of class position, which can shape work experience quite independently of occupation.[8] In giving primacy to class position the natural labor perspective makes clear its own underlying interests. It thus does not address itself to associations between random aspects of industrial society and personality, but deals explicitly and critically with the demonstrable effects of the capitalist labor process on individuals. However, unlike other critical approaches to the same problem, the natural labor perspective provides a basis for more than normative criticism; it provides a basis for empirically researching specific connections between capitalism and individual personality. Moreover, it also provides a basis for reconstruction: a model of natural labor to strive for.

Whether one accepts its Marxist orientation or not, the perspective developed here can contribute to the study of social structure and personality via the Meadian analysis of work experience and its psychological consequences. If its Marxist orientation is accepted, however, it can constitute a critical theory of social structure and personality itself. Such a theory can contribute to understanding connections between social structure and personality, to researching those connections, and, potentially, to establishing new ones.

PROPOSAL FOR A POLITICAL ECONOMY OF COGNITIVE DEVELOPMENT

Another way to characterize the interests of the natural labor perspective is in terms of the political economy of cognitive development. This suggests a somewhat narrower focus on certain aspects of psychological functioning than does a critical theory of social structure and personality. Rather than dealing with a full range of personality variables potentially connectable to the imperatives of capitalism, a political economy of cognitive development would focus on such things as reasoning abilities, knowledge acquisition, and problem-solving skills, as they are affected by the functioning of the capitalist economy. Somewhat more broadly, however, it would not limit itself to the study of work, but would consider how other life spheres in which cognitive development occurs are also affected by economic imperatives. At present there is no well developed field such as this. The natural labor perspective suggests some direction for its possible development.

To point these out it is necessary to focus more specifically for a moment on cognitive development. Figure 5.3 is intended to represent stages

of cognitive development among the adult population in a modern capitalist society. The relative thickness of various parts of the triangle are intended to suggest proportions of the adult population at various stages of
development. It is intended to suggest, in other words, an unequal distribution of cognitive abilities in capitalist society.

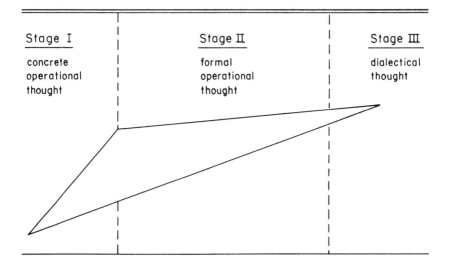

Figure 5.3   Distribution of Cognitive Abilities in Capitalist Society (speculative)

This model excludes stages of early childhood cognitive development. But it does suggest that many adults do not develop much beyond
what are normally considered childhood stages. Thus in Stage I here, individuals would be capable of such things as concrete logical reasoning,
hierarchial classification, grasping transitive relations, logical addition
and multiplication of classes and quantities, and conservation of number,
length, and mass. In Piagetian terms (for reference) this is the stage of
concrete operational thought. In Meadian terms, individuals at this stage
would be capable of reciprocal role taking, solving technical problems
when manipulating concrete objects, and, concomitantly, grasping diverse means-ends relationships but with limited range and refinement.

Only in Stage II do individuals become capable of triadic or abstract
role taking; that is, capable of imagining how other perspectives relate

independently of their own. This capability makes possible what Piaget called formal operational thought: the ability to apply mental operations to abstract situations. At this stage of cognitive development individuals are able to imaginarily construct logical possibilities independent of concrete reality, to recognize the observed as only a sub-set of the possible, to isolate variables and imaginarily 'hold other thing constant', to understand hypotheticals and probabilities. Although this is usually thought of as the stage attained by most normal adults, some research suggests nearly 50% of the adult population never attains it (see Kohlberg and Gilligan, 1972). For those who do attain it, it is at this stage that much domain-specific knowledge is accumulated and hypothetico-deductive problem-solving strategies are mastered.

In Stage III individuals develop the ability to think dialectically. This involves the ability to rethink domain assumptions, to explicitly grasp relational ontologies, to recognize the incommensurability of perspectives, and to move back and forth between incommensurable perspectives to forge new ones (cf. Basseches, 1983; Riegel, 1979). This implies the ability not only to take multiple perspectives within a paradigm, but to adopt perspectives across paradigms. There is no Piagetian equivalent for this stage.[9] In Meadian terms, this stage involves consciousness of sociality (that is, of being in two perspectives at once) and recognition of the relative but objective reality of perspectives.

Accepting that such stages of cognitive development correspond to what can actually be found in the real world, it is appropriate to ask what they might have to do with capitalism. The link between these stages and capitalism can be made via the natural labor perspective. In line with the basic premises of the perspective, the argument is simply this: each stage of cognitive development is achieved only via confrontation with and solution of certain kinds of problems, social structural conditions shaping an individual's opportunities for having these problem-solving experiences. The importance of the capitalist workplace as a context in which these experiences may or may not occur has been demonstrated. But other contexts are undoubtedly important also. A political economy of cognitive development would seek to link these other contexts, and problem-solving experiences within them, to the functioning of the capitalist economy.

The requirements for a theory to guide this field of inquiry must be as rigorous as those for any theory of social structure and personality. A model of political economy, presumably Marxist, able to account for situational experiences, would have to be wedded to a model of cognitive development prescribing the consequences expected to follow from those experiences. This could be derived from a specialized application of the natural labor perspective in which the concept of class would again figure prominently. For example, class position might be shown to affect the differential problem-solving experiences individuals have in family and school contexts. (In this respect it is important to remember that what individuals *don't* get a chance to do is just as consequential as what they do get a chance to do.) If these experiences, or lack of them, could be linked first to cognitive development, and then to class position, then the unequal distribution of various stages of cognitive development could be explained, partially, with reference to the political-economic order.[10]

An analysis of the political economy of cognitive development is only proposed here for two reasons; one, because it requires a fuller theory of capitalist *society* to account for how capitalism shapes institutions other than the workplace; and two, because it would also require a fuller theory of cognitive development (beginning with childhood) than has been presented here with reference to adult work experience. Both are possible, however; and both could be pursued productively drawing on the natural labor perspective.[11]

Working from the natural labor perspective there is, finally, no way to understand cognitive development in capitalist society but in political-economic terms. Indeed, if cognitive development is going to be understood in *sociological* terms at all, this understanding must take the functioning of capitalism into account; there is simply no other way to adequately explain the unequal distribution of experiences contributing to cognitive growth within capitalist society. A political-economic view of cognitive development would thus see alienation as failure-relative-to-potential not just in the workplace, but in all spheres of life under capitalism, with its pervasive class-based inequities.

UNRESOLVED ISSUES

This chapter has sought to draw out the implications of the data for the natural labor perspective. In this effort some loose ends have been tied up and a few new ropes cast. There remain, however, a few untied knots as well. Some of these unresolved issues owe to the limitations of the data, some to limitations of the theory. In order to suggest directions for future theoretical and empirical work, four of these issues will be discussed: (1) the nature of problem-solving experiences and their cognitive effects; (2) the possibility of threshold effects with regard to cognitive development; (3) the ends of natural labor; and (4) the behaviors following from the psychological effects of natural and alienated labor.

The qualitative phase of this study identified two basic types of problems people must solve in the workplace: technical and interpretive. The survey data showed problem-solving demands in work to be associated with intellectual flexibility, work enjoyment, and (de)reification. These findings are interesting and important, but tell us much less than needs to be known about the psychological consequences of problem-solving experiences. Clearly there is a need to further explore the kinds of thinking demanded to solve different kinds of problems. And there is a need to know if these different kinds of thinking lead to different cognitive outcomes. With this knowledge it may then be possible to determine whether different types of thinking are associated with the problem-solving demands of different class positions. It seems reasonable to suspect that demands for inductive, deductive, analogical, and dialectical thinking may be associated with social structural position. If so, we may be able to see even more clearly how social structure influences cognitive development. But more focused psychological and social-psychological research will be necessary to make these determinations. Such research might well serve as the empirical foundation for a political economy of cognitive development.

A related and equally unresolved issue is that of possible threshold effects in the course of cognitive development. This refers to just how problem-solving and other experiences produce psychological outcomes. The implicit assumption here has been that such outcomes are the cumulative products of problem-solving experiences. In other words, theorized psychological outcomes were assumed to be affected in a cumulative, linear fashion by problem solving experiences. This may not be the case, however. It may be, rather, that particular kinds of problem-solving experiences are much more consequential than others, producing significant changes very quickly. The same principle might also apply to self-objectification. It may be that special instances of self-objectification produce great leaps in understandings of self and world. Experience, to put it another way, may not simply 'add up' to produce incremental psychological changes; it may produce dramatic changes under some circumstances and none under others. Further research will be necessary to explore the possibility that key experiences are responsible for a large part of an individual's cognitive growth. A critical theory of social structure and personality would of course be interested in relating opportunities for these key experiences to an individual's class position.

These matters could be addressed within the natural labor framework. As pointed out earlier, no revisions of the framework are necessary to accommodate a more thorough study of problem solving; nor are any necessary to deal with the possibility of threshold effects. To do so, more empirical work is necessary. Other issues, however, cannot be resolved solely with more and better data. These issues strain the present capacity of the natural labor framework and demand further theoretical work. One such issue concerns the ends of natural labor.

Theoretically, natural labor does not require strong moral commitment to particular ends. As long as ends arouse no moral revulsion, it was argued, aesthetic experience and natural labor are possible. If this is so, and the data suggest it is, one is called to look carefully at the ends of natural labor; most importantly, to see from whence they arise. This is an important matter for a theoretical perspective critical of capitalism and hopeful for social change. Clearly some tension is created by recognizing that, in principle, building nuclear weapons can involve natural labor as surely as building a hospital or a school. If this is so, then it seems natural labor itself, without some set of guiding values, is not sufficient to overcome the dehumanization of labor under capitalism. The issue of guiding values will be reconsidered at the end of the next chapter. The unresolved sociological issue here is, where do the impulses that are satisfied in dehumanized labor come from?

One possible answer to this question is that such impulses don't come from anywhere, because they don't really exist. In other words, the impulses to build instruments of torture, nuclear weapons, napalm, nerve gas, and so forth, do not really exist in those who actually build them. All that really exist for most producers are impulses to materially survive, these being satisfied through wage labor carried on oblivious to the particular products involved. Such an answer is partially correct. But it ignores a larger unpleasant reality. It seems undeniable that aesthetic experience can and does arise in the production of objects whose only values are in human destruction. Some impulses are being satisfied in this productive activity, and they are not all oriented merely to material survival.

The Meadian perspective does not provide a ready answer to the question of where such anti-human impulses come from. From a strictly social behaviorist standpoint it could be argued that initially humans have impulses only for material survival. As individuals mature, these impulses are given concrete expression depending on the possibilities for material survival provided by the environments in which they find themselves. Thus in a capitalist society most people's impulses to satisfy their biological and social needs are answered to only by cash obtainable via wage labor. The individual is thus conditioned to a particular mode of productive activity by a social system that renders moral judgment about products not only irrelevant but maladaptive.

That is one explanation. Another views anti-human impulses as arising out of competition for valued resources. It may be the case, in other words, that one human community answers to an impulse, present in another human community, to remove an obstacle to the flow of resources it deems essential to its survival. In such a case members of one community attempt a creative advance of nature—as determined from their perspective—at the expense of members of another community. The questions around which judgments of morality thus revolve are, how inclusively is the community defined in any given case? and, from whose perspective is the universal good to be determined? I shall return to these considerations of morality later. For the moment the point is simply that if the destructive or adaptive character of any impulse or set of impulses is perspectivally determined, then the very labelling of some impulses as anti-human is problematic. Perhaps the best that can be done, analytically, is to explore how answers to the questions posed above are socially produced and how individuals come to accept them. The natural labor perspective further demands, however, that we explore how or whether the social conditions that produce particular answers also produce individuals able to challenge and reformulate them.

But, as argued earlier, these matters cannot be accounted for without a full historical analysis of capitalist society. It remains a challenge, then, for the natural labor perspective to incorporate such an analysis and attempt to account for the origins of impulses antithetical to human life and development—as defined based on the value premises of the perspective itself. Only by so doing can it be an adequate guide to social change.

A final unresolved issue concerns the behaviors following from the psychological effects of natural and alienated labor. Psychological consequences are surely important in themselves, but even more so because they affect what people do. Exactly what people do or don't do because of these consequences remains to be determined. Even at this point, however, a sense of urgency calls for some speculation. It seems likely that certain moral and political behaviors must be affected by role-taking propensity, intellectual flexibility, and reification. Consideration of these matters leads quickly from sociological to ethical theory.

In the Meadian view, moral behavior is founded on role taking; that is, on imagining how one's words and deeds will impinge on the well-being of others. Without role taking such behavior is impossible, as it is for animals. But as noted above, with respect to self-conscious humans this ability is not in question, at least not at a fundamental level. What is in question is the propensity to role-take and, therefore, the propensity to act in morally responsible ways. If a lack of role-taking demands in work can diminish an individual's propensity to role-take, this might diminish his propensity to take the well-being of others into account before acting.

There is, however, another obvious way in which capitalism powerfully represses concern for the well-being of others. The ever present threat of a loss of livelihood promotes not only conformity in the workplace, but also, it seems, a generalized amorality upon which conformity depends. It is thus not only a lack of role taking in production that may lead to a diminished propensity to role-take, but also the social relations of capitalist production which permit an employer to deprive an individual of the means of survival should moral concerns come to inhibit job performance. Under such conditions, self-repression of moral concerns and the role taking that evokes them, actually takes on adaptive value for the individual. One can argue, then, that the relations of economic bondage upon which capitalism operates tend to extinguish role-taking propensity independently of the effects of productive activity per se. Capitalist relations of production, in other words, begin to undermine moral and intellectual freedom as soon as people must enter into them. From a Meadian perspective such a social formation must be judged inherently immoral, as it tends to destroy the prerequisite foundation for morally responsible behavior.

Of course, moral behavior is always situationally influenced and only partially determined by personality dispositions. Certainly future research into the behavioral consequences of forms of labor must take these other factors into account. The Meadian analysis nonetheless provides at present a valuable inroad to the sociological understanding of moral behavior and how it might be influenced by the imperatives of capitalism.

Political behavior is likely to be affected by the tendency to hold a reified view of the world and by intellectual flexibility. Seeing the world as made up of powerful self-animating social forces can undermine a sense of political efficacy, a prerequisite for political action. Those holding a reified view of the world would thus seem to be less likely to try to change it (cf. Olsen, 1968). And by the same token, those with less intellectual flexibility, those less able or willing to adopt alternative perspectives, may be less open to considering why and how the social world might be changed. This could also inhibit effective political action. But again, political behavior no more than moral behavior can be understood solely in terms of personality dispositions. The natural labor perspective would have to be elaborated to take these other factors into account. Nevertheless, future research could easily address itself to examination of these behaviors as expected consequences of the psychological effects of productive activity.

If these speculations about behavioral consequences are correct, and there is reason to believe they are, then it is arguable that alienated labor serves largely to create humans who are less and less able to transform social reality.[12] This runs counter to the traditional Marxist position that sees great promise for change in the frustrations produced by alienated labor. But the contrary implications of the natural labor perspective are clear. If intellectual flexibility and role-taking propensity are essential for rational collective action, and if de-reification is essential to seeing possibilities for reconstructing social reality, then any labor process restricting development of these cognitive abilities constitutes a powerful force for its own perpetuation. The behaviors following from the psychological effects of alienated labor would thus be more likely to lead to stagnation than to revolutionary change. As suggested before, under capitalism nature advances only when it simultaneously advances capital.

Obviously, though, the capitalist labor process does not reproduce itself perfectly; it does not survive without crises and some adaptation of its own. But if change occurs, it is likely the result of natural labor cropping up unintentionally.[13] As discussed in chapter 3, it is via natural labor that people learn about themselves, others, the world, and possibilities for change. If the values underlying the natural labor critique of capitalism are accepted, there is but one path to resolving the issue of stagnation versus change. If alienated labor restricts possibilities for change by restricting human development, then the crucial issue becomes how to create and sustain natural labor, and thus human growth. But at this point we are no longer dealing solely with a sociological issue. We have arrived at an inescapable ethical one: how shall we live? In the final chapter I will explore the implications of this study for answering that question. And for acting on the answer.

6

Praxis

For if any be a hearer of the word, and not a doer, he is like unto a man beholding his natural face in a glass. For he beholdeth himself, and goeth his way, and forgetteth what manner of man he was.

Epistle of James, I:23/24

In this book I have attempted to solve a number of social scientific problems concerning relationships between the capitalist labor process and psychological functioning. If these are indeed problems in the Meadian sense, their solutions must be means to other ends; there must be some meta-act yet to be consummated. As implied throughout, the meta-act subsuming this intermediate project is the transformation of capitalism. Given the explicitly critical and transformative interests of the natural labor perspective, it is appropriate finally to consider the courses of action the present analysis suggests.

THE META-ACT OF TRANSFORMING CAPITALISM

A mapmaking metaphor has been used to describe the interests of this study. It was said that, like a map, the natural labor perspective could provide a guide to a territory of interest. And it has. But like all metaphors, no matter how useful, this one too is imperfect. It is, first of all, overly passive; it implies that a social theory can be constructed as a veridical representation of human experience and left at that, static. It

157

also implies that social theories have no more effect on social reality than maps do on geographic reality. Both propositions are false. Social theories are more than neutral representations of social realities or autonomous human experience; they are products of those realities and can, when acted upon by self-conscious humans, change the very realities and experience which gave them rise. A conceptual map thus not only represents a territory, it helps reproduce or alter it. It inevitably becomes a dynamic part of the world it represents.

From a Marxist perspective there are two primary functions to be served by the theorizing undertaken here (cf. Szymanski, 1977). One of these is to help people understand the shortcomings of particular social formations. The social formation of interest has been the capitalist labor process, its shortcomings being found chiefly in its limiting effects on psychological development and functioning. The natural labor perspective has made visible the links between the capitalist labor process and these destructive effects. In this it has served a critical function. The second function of such theorizing is to suggest optimal futures to strive for. In the case of the natural labor perspective, what is suggested is an optimal form of labor to strive for. In doing this the perspective can serve a reconstructive function.

Empirical research such as that undertaken here also has specific functions from a Marxist perspective. In itself such research is not transformative; it generates no force for change. But even in generating descriptive information it is valuable; it tells us about the situation in need of changing and, though sometimes redundantly, documents and justifies the need for change. Perhaps more importantly, however, it serves as a check on unrestrained theorizing. Without such a check, theory developed from a Marxist perspective, or any other, is apt to be of little use in dealing with the nuts and bolts of everyday human experience. Such fanciful theory can still be used to interpret the world, but it is unlikely to be very useful in trying to change it.

But this amounts to little more than post factum justification at this point; these functions were assumed from the start. Indeed, without them there would have been no point in starting at all. More important at this juncture are the promises of the natural labor perspective: what it tells us, what it can be used for. The pertinent question for this chapter is thus, what do this study and its theoretical foundations tell us about pursuing the project of transforming capitalism?

It seems there are at least three things it tells us. One, that the consequences of the capitalist labor process can undermine the revolutionary potential of the working class. Frustration born of alienated labor may be a spark for social change, but alone is not enough to accomplish it. Two, that there is a need to strive to overcome the limitations on psychological functioning imposed by the capitalist labor process (and all capitalist institutions). If the working class is to play a central role in the transformation of capitalism—and it must—then the transformers themselves must be transformed. The natural labor perspective suggests some directions for this. And three, that natural labor as a part of an optimal future to strive for is by no means utopian. If it can exist in small pockets within the capitalist labor process, it can be made pervasive in a socialist labor process free of domination.[1]

All this is rather abstract, however. The struggle now is to get down to a more concrete level. While it is neither possible nor desirable here to offer a Blueprint for a New Society, it is possible and desirable to suggest where to go from here. This is to identify the implications for praxis—for joining theory and action—that follow from the natural labor perspective and what it has revealed about the psychological consequences of the capitalist labor process.

THE ABOLITION OF ALIENATED LABOR

Our first concern is with labor within the sphere of necessity. The goal is to abolish alienated labor within this sphere. This means abolishing productive activities that demand no problem solving or role taking, do not foster means-ends comprehension, provide no opportunities for self-objectification and, because of all this, preclude aesthetic experience and inhibit the creative advance of nature. However, this is not a call for reorganizing productive activity within the framework of capitalism. It is a call for abolishing capitalism in particular, and, in general, all domination in productive activity.

The project of abolishing alienated labor is already underway in some socialist countries and in some enterprises within capitalist countries.[2] The movement of most interest in this respect is that for workers' control of production. This is not equivalent to "participatory management" or schemes for worker ownership that do not involve genuine control.[3] Workers' control means just that: those who produce determine what and how they shall produce. As a movement, the ultimate goal of workers' control is not merely control of particular firms or industries, but of the entire economy. The goal, to make it explicit, is the abolition of capitalism. But, as André Gorz argues, there must be an even more far-reaching goal:

> ...neither the workers' councils, nor the factory or shop committees, nor the workers' power they stand for can prevail unless the political power of capitalism is broken, unless the capitalist state itself is overthrown and the capitalist relations of production and division of labor are abolished. The struggle for workers' control must either develop an all-out attack against all forms of hierarchy, against all forms of monopolization of power and of knowledge, against all forms of domination and bureaucracy, or else whatever power the workers have won in action within the factories will be broken and rendered meaningless in a very short time (1982:410).

Workers' control is thus not an end in itself but an intermediate project to be accomplished on the way to a total transformation of capitalist society. From the natural labor perspective this is a vitally important step. It is so because its main result is that it changes people (see, for example, Schlesinger and Bart, 1982; Russell, 1982; Blau and Alba, 1982; Wells, 1981). It develops abilities and skills and awareness of even greater capacities; it enhances a sense of efficacy; and it leads to realization of possibilities for social change. Opportunities to develop these capacities and understandings are precisely what alienated labor denies. Workers' control, by virtue of the demands for role taking and problem solving it provides, produces human beings capable of abolishing capitalism. As a first step toward overcoming the psychological retardation caused by alienated labor, workers' control is essential. It would be unwise to try by-passing it in the revolutionary process.

The above does not, however, constitute a naive embrace of the so-called theory of escalation, which sees workers' control of production as automatically and inevitably leading to a full flowering of socialist consciousness. As Greenberg (1983) has argued, the political consequences of workplace democracy vary depending on the economic and political contexts in which it appears. In capitalist societies such as the United States, it is entirely possible for workers' control to become "workers' capitalism" since market forces can create irresistible pressures toward enterprise egoism and narrow profit concerns. There may thus be no spillover effects of democratic, egalitarian, or cooperative orientations beyond the firm. While this may indeed occur under certain circumstances, it does not negate the point that the *personal* transformations often attendant to workers' control are prerequisite for larger social transformations. The catalyst for the latter, in the presence of the former, is education in socialist values, without which the meta-act cannot proceed, as will be argued again below.

As discussed in the section outlining a critical social psychology of work, realistic consideration of possibilities for transforming the workplace demand the distinction be made between the spheres of necessity and freedom. It is thus important to recognize that workers' control in the sphere of necessity is not synonymous with an end to all unpleasant or repetitive productive activity. That is to say, workers' control per se does not signal an automatic change in the mode of production that sustains the material basis of society. But what it must bring with it if it is to lead to a complete transformation of capitalism is, drastic change in how people experience large-scale industrial production.

Thus while workers' control of production should seek elimination of menial work wherever possible, where this is not possible, such work should not be *career* work for anyone.[4] It should be rotated or shared work that does not lead to the chronic underdevelopment of the capacities of any class or group of producers. Along these same lines, workers' control in the sphere of necessity should bring with it expanded training and comprehensive education for all who want it. Barriers between mental and manual labor should also be broken down. And, of course, the means and ends of production should be determined collectively and so experienced as the responsibility of those who produce.

Actual strategies and tactics for attaining the intermediate goal of workers' control have been discussed in detail elsewhere (for example, Vanek, 1975; Lindenfeld and Rothschild-Whitt, 1982; Zwerdling, 1980). As such, there is no need to do so here. The crucial point in the present context it that, of the strategies for abolishing alienated labor that might be pursued, workers' control is likely to be the most effective in light of what the natural labor perspective tells us about the psychological effects of work. It tells us, to reiterate, that the effects of alienated labor retard both individual growth and social change. But it also tells us what kinds of experiences might reverse these effects and encourage growth and change.[5] These therapeutic experiences are those likely to be associated with genuine workers' control of production. This is one direction in which to pursue the prerequisite goal of 'transforming the transformers' on the road to transforming a society.

But this is only half the project of social transformation compelled by the natural labor perspective. Here we have dealt with the sphere of necessity and the possibilities for maximizing workers' control, initiative, responsibility, and creativity within it. This amounts to a struggle for natural labor within the sphere of necessity—a struggle that can be won only up to a point. As argued earlier, natural labor in the sphere of necessity will always be limited; it will always be less than enough to fully develop human capacities, to permit the furthest advance of nature. The other half of the transformative project is, then, the institution of natural labor in the sphere of freedom.

THE INSTITUTION OF NATURAL LABOR

As argued above, natural labor can be instituted in the sphere of necessity. In large-scale productive enterprises this would come about through progressively greater workers' control, which would lead to a reorganization of productive activity so as to maximize possibilities for aesthetic experience and the creative advance of nature. In small-scale productive enterprises—still within the sphere of necessity—natural labor could be encouraged via increased vertical integration, expanded project activity, and, to the extent possible, less standardized production.[6] This presumes of course that the person in the 'person-environment relationship' is not ignored, that education and training to develop capacities for engaging in natural labor are part of any such reorganization of production. The attempt to institute natural labor within the sphere of freedom must proceed somewhat differently, however.

The emphasis on the sphere of freedom as opposed to the sphere of necessity is based on an implied premise that should be made explicit: necessary labor (labor for survival) is not the goal of human existence. Although work and self-objectification are man's 'species-callings', so to speak, necessary work and self-objectification are not. The human struggle, as Marx described it in *Capital*, is not to make necessary labor an end in itself, but a means to achieving free and creative labor. As discussed in chapter 1, the human struggle is always to minimize the sphere of necessity, wherein possibilities for natural labor are limited, and maximize the sphere of freedom. So while workers' control of the sphere of necessity must aim to incorporate natural labor within it to the extent possible, it must ultimately aim to shrink the sphere of necessity to the extent possible. Only via workers' control will the productivity gains that would make this possible be converted into paid free-time for workers instead of profits or unemployment.

The sphere of freedom is, then, the sphere of activity within which people are not constrained by the organizational imperatives of large-scale collective production. It is the sphere within which they can autonomously (if they wish) pursue their own productive and developmental interests. Within this sphere they can pursue satisfaction of their own creative impulses, completion of their own self-conceived and self-directed projects. This is not to advocate everyone becoming an artist; rather, it is to assert everyone's right of self-production, which means two things: the right of access to the materials, tools, and knowledge necessary to produce subsistence or exchange objects for one's self, and the right to produce one's self as a human being through engaging in natural labor. Instituting natural labor in the sphere of freedom thus depends, first, on shrinking the sphere of necessity, and, second, on acknowledging the right of self-production.

It should be clear that 'expanding the sphere of freedom' does not mean 'expanding idle time'. Outside the sphere of necessity individuals should have the choice to remain idle if they so desire. But that must be a choice and not a sole option. To institute natural labor in the sphere of freedom the right of self-production must be translated into the right of access to tools, materials, and knowledge. This is essential to make free time productive time. As Gorz makes this point:

> More than upon free time, the expansion of the sphere of
> autonomy depends upon a freely available supply of convivial
> tools that allow individuals to do or make anything whose
> aesthetic or use-value is enhanced by doing it oneself. Repair and
> do-it-yourself workshops in blocks of flats, neighborhood centers
> or rural communities should enable everyone to make or invent
> things they wish. Similarly, libraries, places to make music or
> movies, 'free' radio and television stations, open spaces for
> communication, circulation and exchange, and so on need to be
> accessible to everyone (1980:87).

This is obviously not a policy prescription for a capitalist society but for a socialist one. It is a highly pertinent prescription for the transformative project suggested by the natural labor perspective. It demands, quite simply, that people have the opportunity to exercise their capacities for marked self-objectification, for creating and solving problems of their own, for engaging in natural labor, and, therefore, for becoming fully human.

Arguing for attenuation of the sphere of necessity, expansion of the sphere of autonomy, and the right of self-production, runs counter to some traditional Marxist notions concerning the goals of social transformation. Traditionally Marxists have emphasized work in the sphere of necessity. The natural labor perspective reverses this emphasis. There is of course no less concern for workers' control in the sphere of necessity, but there is recognition that it is not the sphere within which full human capacities can be realized. That can happen only within the sphere of

freedom. To recognize this is to legitimize demands for individual autonomy and control, something traditional socialist thought has resisted.
From the natural labor perspective, however, individual autonomy and
control cannot be denied. Without such autonomy and control aesthetic
experience will ultimately be diminished and the creative advance of nature impeded.[7] Nevertheless, this is not an argument for renegade autonomy or rejection of community, as is discussed below.

In sum, the implications for praxis suggested here, in the project to
institute natural labor, are these: workers' control of the sphere of necessity must aim to contract that sphere and expand the sphere of freedom;
the right to self-production must be the foundation upon which the
sphere of freedom is expanded; and individual autonomy and control in
the sphere of freedom must not be compromised. Abolishing alienated
labor and instituting natural labor are the major intermediate projects
within the meta-act of transforming capitalism. But there remains a major problem: how to generate the impulses that will initiate and sustain
these projects. For this something more than theoretical prescription is
required.

THE NEED FOR A SOCIALIST PEDAGOGY

Neither the abolition of alienated labor nor the institution of natural
labor will come about spontaneously. Both projects require the conscious, collective efforts of those sharing interests in consummating the
meta-act of transforming capitalism. As noted above, both projects are
well underway in various places: in some socialist countries and in some
worker-controlled enterprises in capitalist countries. Although such
things are highly relevant, the concern here is not for what has happened
or is happening in socialist countries.[8] Nor is the concern for what is happening in the relative handful of worker-controlled firms in the U.S.
Rather, the concern is for the overwhelming majority of the U.S. working class and the lack of revolutionary tendencies to be found within it.

Historically, Marxists have romanticized the working class. Marx
himself was guilty of this, but only because he could not envision the tremendous power capitalist institutions would develop over workers in the
late twentieth century. Instead of bringing together skilled workers able
to recognize their class interests and the dispensability of capitalists, capitalism has produced a mass of unskilled workers disempowered by the
division of labor, divided by labor market status, racism, and sexism,

and unable to recognize their shared class interests. As capitalism has matured we have not seen a progressive increase in working-class consciousness but, since the 1930s, its withering.[9] Moreover, the problem of class consciousness not withstanding, we have also seen a deterioration of the transformative capacity of the working class. Those in the working class may still have the potential to be the gravediggers of capitalism, but it seems unlikely they will take up shovels soon.

In recognition of these problems some Marxist theorists have refocused their attention on the "new working class" (Mallet, 1963; Gorz, 1967). In brief, these theorists have argued that the revolutionary impulses of the traditional blue-collar working class have been tempered by the material standards made possible by modern imperialist capitalism. Also the capacity of the traditional working class to carry off a successful revolution has been eroded by the division of mental and manual labor. Because of this, the potential for revolution in modern capitalist countries has to be found outside the traditional working class. This potential can now be found in the new working class, the class of skilled technical and mental workers whose work is being progressively proletarianized. These workers, it is argued, have both the capability and the motivation to resist capitalist encroachment on their work and, with proper inspiration, might turn their efforts toward overthrowing capitalism. The historical evidence lends equivocal support to these arguments about the new working class.[10]

From the natural labor perspective these arguments are certainly plausible, if somewhat simplistic. As noted previously, it has always been the most skilled among the working class, those most likely to engage in natural labor, who have been quickest to challenge capitalist control of the labor process. The corollary to this also seems undeniable: those among the working class least likely to engage in natural labor are least likely to challenge capitalist control. Impressions garnered during the present study support this. Those workers most likely to engage in natural labor (engineers, trade-skilled foreman, and mechanics) most often expressed resistance to managerial control and, in some cases, disdain for the whole system of capitalist production.[11] Even so, this is only to recognize an understandable shift in the locus of working-class revolutionary potential. It is not to describe what must be done to realize that potential.

The question remains, then, how can the working class, or particular segments of it, be educated and motivated to begin the intermediate projects necessary to fully transform capitalism? At an abstract level traditional answers to this question have suggested the following sequence of action: a socialist consciousness must be instilled among the working class so internal divisions can be overcome; a sense of working-class power or efficacy must be fostered; and then, concrete alternatives to capitalism, toward which the unified working class can begin working, must be set forth. From the natural labor perspective it seems this sequence is backwards. A successful socialist pedagogy must begin with impeded impulses, for there is nowhere else revolutionary action can originate.

If there is any hope for action we must first assume some impulses for change are present; or, to put it differently, we must assume some impulses are not being satisfied by existing social conditions. Only if such impulses are present can action be initiated. It seems an eminently safe assumption that such impulses are present, that the capitalist labor process generates frustration among workers (cf. Zipp, et al., 1984). But it makes no sense to assume these impulses can be satisfied by creating a socialist consciousness in workers, at least not immediately. What makes sense is supposing that workers can understand how certain concrete actions might satisfy their blocked impulses. This it to propose, as a first step, formulating concrete alternatives to the labor process that frustrates workers. This is to devise an endpoint for a transformative act, to create something that can answer to a latent impulse.

The traditional sequence of arousing working class action is thus reversed from the start. Action does not await formation of a longed-for socialist consciousness, but begins—as it must—with impulses present in the worker. The second step in this process remains the same, however. Action can proceed only if there is a sense of efficacy, a sense that action can succeed.[12] This is to encourage belief that behavior can be reorganized such that previously frustrated impulses can be satisfied. It is to encourage belief in the possibility of a creative advance of nature— something that is easier to do among those who have experienced it than among those who have not. The emergence of a socialist consciousness, one that is de-reified and exhibits intellectual flexibility, may follow from the experiences attendant to this sort of transformative project. But a socialist consciousness can no more precede such experience than any form of consciousness can precede experience. A socialist consciousness must therefore be seen as the outcome rather than prerequisite of the project of transforming capitalist society.

Unfortunately, if we are considering implications for praxis there remains a problem with this. Such prescriptions may be theoretically sound guides to action but they still do not tell us what to do; they suggest only strategies, not tactics. The question of how, under prevailing historical circumstances in the U.S., the working class can be educated remains unanswered. The education in question, as implied above, has to do with conveying understandings of possibilities for change, instilling a sense of efficacy, and fostering class consciousness. The unanswered question is, in other words, how can these things actually be accomplished?

To answer this question it is necessary to descend from theoretical to practical discourse. If we are interested in influencing the "strategic choices of class actors," to use Erik Olin Wright's phrase, we must make decisions about doing it, not just pronouncements about how it should be done. The idea of a socialist pedagogy based on collective conceptualization of alternative futures, creation of new social formations, problem solving, critical thought, and so on, still floats above the real problem from the Marxist social scientist's perspective. This real problem is, how to launch the pedagogical project of transforming the transformers. Do we use broadcast media? Popular books? Alternative schools? Political campaigns? Or do we abandon the U.S. and work to strengthen socialist revolutions underway in less-developed countries? These are questions of what ought to be done tomorrow, not what might be done someday.

These are hard questions. To a large extent they must be answered by individuals for themselves. It is, in other words, a matter of individual problem solving in the face of impeded revolutionary action. But this situation in itself is not discouraging, difficult though it may be for many people to resolve. What is discouraging is the systematic failure of Marxists to collectively recognize the need for a socialist pedagogy and a plan for implementing it. To proceed without such a pedagogy, either individually or collectively, is to proceed with the hope for a teleological unfolding of history that will bring revolution with it. Such wishful thinking conveniently absolves one of responsibility for acting; as such, it is a form of in-house academic Marxist ideology.[13] This is not only morally negligent but, from the natural labor perspective, ultimately hopeless. Social reality may change by sheer drift, as nature may change by haphazard mutation; however, we are by no means drifting toward a socialist future—nor, perhaps, toward any future at all. Survival, and a true creative advance of nature, now seem to depend on awakening the capacity for natural labor that has been stifled among a large portion of the human race.

The final question, then, is, what is the role of social scientists in the project of transforming capitalism as outlined here? In a sense we have been considering this all along; elaborating, refining, and using a socialist pedagogy is the overarching objective for a critical social science. But there are other particulars worth mentioning: there is value in theoretical work that points up the shortcomings of existing social formations and suggests new forms of life to strive for; there is also value in empirical research that documents the human wastefulness of capitalist production and tests the validity and utility of important theoretical propositions; and there is value in teaching to and writing for presocialist audiences about all these things. What must be avoided, however, is the tendency to make this work an end in itself, to lose sight of the meta-act of transforming capitalism. When this happens critical intellectual work loses its reason for being; it may continue to provide aesthetic experience but it will not lead to a creative advance of nature.

THE ENDS OF NATURAL LABOR RECONSIDERED

The issue of the ends of natural labor was raised in the previous chapter, where it remained unresolved. Natural labor, it was suggested, might appear even though its ends were seemingly destructive. If this can be, there remains a grievous contradiction to contend with. The contradiction is this: natural labor has been argued to be the ideal from of human productive activity; but what moral force can be mustered to sustain this argument if natural labor can be anti-human and destructive? If this contradiction cannot be resolved it would be perfectly reasonable to argue in favor of alienated labor so long as it was not outright destructive. It would be better, perhaps, to have alienated laborers build cars than natural laborers build bombs.

This issue can be reframed as a question: is natural labor, with no regard for its specific ends, a morally defensible end in itself? An answer to this question depends on further clarifying the definition of natural labor. If natural labor were synonymous with labor that provided aesthetic experience, the answer would have to be no. This is so because aesthetic experience could arise in the work of a dedicated assassin as surely as in the work of a dedicated physician, given the appropriate circumstances. Because it admits of no moral distinctions, aesthetic experience alone cannot morally justify any particular activity. But natural labor, as it has been conceptualized, requires more than aesthetic experience; it requires a creative advance of nature. Determining exactly what constitutes a creative advance of nature is the key to resolving the contradiction identified above.

Previously offered definitions of a creative advance of nature emphasized the adaptation of individual organisms (or, in the present context, individual producers). But seemingly this provides no basis for moral judgment either; whatever from of production is adaptive for one individual must be acknowledged as potentially an instance of natural labor. Clearly, however, what is adaptive for one individual can be maladaptive for another. Thus we seem to be led again to the conclusion that natural labor can be destructive, as long as it is adaptive from *some* perspective. This conclusion is wrong, however, because it ignores the principle of sociality implicit in the Marxian/Meadian concept of natural labor.

The referent principle of sociality here is not the strictly Meadian one (referring to being in two perspectives at once). It is, rather, the principle of social interdependence upon which human existence and survival are predicated. This principle asserts that no person survives or exists *as a human* independently of others.[14] Embodied in this principle is a moral imperative of mutual responsibility—an obligation for every self-conscious human to take the roles of the others upon whom he depends for satisfaction of his material and social needs, and of those who likewise depend upon him. All morally responsible behavior springs from an awareness of the principle of sociality and a willingness to act in accord with it. Among the world of self-conscious humans, then, no true creative advance of nature, of the human social world, can occur irrespective of this principle. Apart from this principle there can be no natural labor.

It must follow, then, that anti-human, destructive labor can never be natural labor. No productive activity that proceeds oblivious to the moral imperative of the principle of sociality can result in a true creative advance of nature. This is not to say, however, that all productive activity must advance the survival interests of *all* human beings or it cannot be termed natural labor. Certainly much natural labor might be very limited in scope, of consequence to only a few. The point is that no productive activity that jeopardizes the survival or development interests of others can be considered natural labor, even if aesthetic experience arises within it. This means that in natural labor means-ends comprehension must extend not only to the use of some product, but to its full range of foreseeable consequences for human survival and well-being. To put it another way, natural labor must always be responsible to the largest community for which it may possibly have consequences.

This represents a Meadian reformulation of the familiar theme that a crucial element of a socialist consciousness is a sense of responsibility to the whole human community. In practical terms this must entail elimination of nationalist, racist, and sexist attitudes—all of which tend to support destructively exclusive definitions of the human community. Along with the struggle to abolish the social structural conditions inhibiting role taking, what must be fostered, then, are internationalist, non-racist, non-sexist orientations. Another goal of a socialist pedagogy is thus to redefine the human community in universal terms, making this definition a part of the taken-for-granted reality of all producers. Establishing such a definition as part of the generalized consciousness of a particular community would preclude the possibility of any intentionally destructive natural labor arising within it.

By offering a more elaborate definition of natural labor these arguments may resolve the apparent contradiction between the ends of natural labor and natural labor as an end in itself. It is now consistent to argue for natural labor as an end in itself because its ends, by definition, must always be morally responsible ones. But there is still a problem here, for it has not been determined from whose perspective the ultimate moral responsibility of a productive act shall be determined. At this point, however, there are no theoretically derivable answers, only inescapable choices.

There is no scientific method for dealing with this problem. No sociological theory can dictate choices between forms of life. To support a choice of the natural labor vision one can only point to the bedrock of values upon which it rests. And these values speak to the maximization of human potential for rational social life free from domination. All else is derivative from this. Consider another expression of the principles advanced here:

> Fully authentic human creativity is constrained by the moment of sociality as well as by the other moments of praxis. This constraint precludes creativity in designing poison gases, in designing instruments of torture, and in pursuing scientific means of circumventing the self-system. This constraint also precludes the evasion of reciprocity as might result from the situational abandoning of social identities and the cynical performance of roles (Welsh, 1983:15).

There is no theoretical justification for such a position, yet it must be taken. This project has done the same: the natural labor perspective is committed *a priori* to these same expressed values. Without such a commitment there would have been no point in developing the perspective, nor in using it to oppose alienated labor. Thus the real dilemma here turns on an irreducibly ethical, not theoretical, question: how shall we live? The foregoing is my attempt to answer it.

The issue of how natural labor can involve individual autonomy and control without rejecting community has also been resolved here. I have argued that from the natural labor perspective there is no possibility for any truly human productive activity without community; there is, simply, no self-conscious productive activity of any kind without community. Nor can there be any morally responsible productive activity— hence no natural labor—apart from a community within which moral responsibility is defined. In the natural labor view, community must always precede individual autonomy and control, as it is the basis from which these things develop. All natural labor arising in autonomous productive activity thus depends on community; indeed, natural labor cannot exist apart from community.

This project itself represents a struggle for natural labor. It has yielded an individual product, but only in the most immediate sense— obviously enough it could not have been conceived or realized apart from the community of its author. While its execution has evoked aesthetic experience, its objective character as an instance of natural labor depends on its contribution to a creative advance of nature as discussed above. By virtue of the personal capacities this project has developed, a creative advance of nature can be said to have occurred; but again, only in the most immediate sense. Whether it can contribute to a true creative advance of communal nature remains to be seen. If it can, it will not be by leading directly to consummation of the meta-act discussed in this chapter. Rather, it will be by further documenting the need for this meta-act to be consummated and by suggesting how it might proceed past this currently problematic period in human history.

Appendixes

Appendix A: Act Structures in Natural and Alienated Labor

The constitution of the act was said to be the bedrock of social reality underlying alienated labor. Further, this reality was said to be accessible only via the subject who constructs the act in the face of simultaneously enabling and constraining structural conditions. This requirement for examining the constitution of productive acts from the standpoint of the subject also applies to natural labor. It was suggested in the text that productive acts can be initiated by a variety of impulses, for example, to acquire wages or to create objects with immediate use values. The impulses productive acts can potentially satisfy, it was also suggested, are constrained by the organization of concrete productive activities. These matters can also be addressed in terms of act structures in natural and alienated labor. Figure A.1 schematically represents several possible act structures that can be distinguished as natural or alienated.

Three types of productive acts are shown as forms of natural labor. They are distinguished by the different impulses out of which they arise. Natural labor may, to take the first example, be oriented to satisfying an impulse to produce an object for its immediate use value. This is

Labor Process		Productive Activity
Natural Labor	Subsistence (direct)	$I_{(obj)}[i\text{-}m\text{-}c/i\text{-}m\text{-}c/i\text{-}m\text{-}c] \; C_{(uv)}^{i} \cdots\cdots\cdots ;$
	Exchange (indirect subsistence)	$I_{(obj)}[i\text{-}m\text{-}c/i\text{-}m\text{-}c/i\text{-}m\text{-}c] \; C_{(ev)} \longrightarrow C_{(uv)}^{i} \cdots\cdots\cdots ;\cdots\cdots ;$
	Expressive	$I_{(res)}[i\text{-}m\text{-}c/i\text{-}m\text{-}c/i\text{-}m\text{-}c] \; C_{(cv)}^{i} \cdots\cdots\cdots ;$
Alienated Labor	Exchange (non-capitalist)	$I_{(obj)}[i\text{-}m/i\text{-}m/i\text{-}m] \; C_{(ev\text{-}o)} \longrightarrow C_{(uv)}^{i} \cdots\cdots ;\cdots\cdots ;$
	Exchange (capitalist)	$I_{(obj)}[i\text{-}m/i\text{-}m/i\text{-}m] \; C_{(ev\text{-}p)} \longrightarrow C_{(uv)}^{i} \cdots\cdots ;\cdots\cdots ;$ $\boxed{I_{(obj)}[i\text{-}m/i\text{-}m/i\text{-}m] \; C_{(uv)}}$

Figure A.1—Act Structures in Natural and Alienated Labor

i = impulse; m = manipulation; c = consummation; uv = use value; ev = exchange value; cv = communicative value; obj = object; res = response production for material survival or direct subsistence. The impulse in this case is to realize the consummatory value of an object immediately upon completion of the transformative act. In figure A.1 this object-oriented impulse is indicated as $I_{(obj)}$.

In the actual process of producing this object a series of intermediate acts must be performed. These are shown in brackets in a repeating impulse, manipulation, consummation pattern (perception is omitted for brevity). Taken together these intermediate acts (i-m-c) make up what is referred to in the text as a meta-act. As each of these intermediate acts is completed, the pleasure of final consummation $[C_{(uv)}]$ is imported into the productive process. It is also imported into the manipulatory phase of each of these acts. Aesthetic experience thus pervades productive acts constituted in this form. We can again refer to the hypothetical knifemaker to illustrate this. First, we must assume that the impulse upon which he acts is oriented to producing a tool for his own immediate use. To produce the knife he must proceed through many intermediate steps: selecting materials, shaping a blade, shaping a handle, assembling these parts, polishing, and so on until the knife is ready to use. Each of these intermediate steps constitutes an act in itself. Cumulatively these acts result in a finished object with immediate use value. Its use is the consummation of the meta-act $[C_{(uv)}]$.

As shown in figure A.1 it is also possible for natural labor to be oriented to production for exchange rather than immediate consumption for subsistence. In this case the meta-act again subsumes a series of intermediate productive acts. From the standpoint of the producer these intermediate acts result in a finished product with immediate exchange value $[C_{(ev)}]$ and potential use value. The impulse that initiates the knifemaker's productive act in this case is not a need for a knife; rather, the act originates in an impulse oriented to achieving the consummatory value of an object that can be acquired in exchange for a knife. It is in the use of this object, acquired through exchange, that consummation of the meta-act occurs.

The final form of natural labor illustrated in figure A.1 is suggested to originate in an impulse for self-expression. An act of this type, which may be representative of pure artistic endeavors, is included to contrast with those forms of natural labor oriented to subsistence. Once subsistence is ensured, it becomes possible to act on impulses oriented to achieving other types of consummatory values (in the sphere of freedom). The consummatory value of an act originating in an impulse for self-objectification is posited to be communicative value $[C_{(cv)}]$. This is consistent with the Meadian view that art objects serve to forge common perspectives between their producers and those who view or otherwise 'use' them. The important distinction here is that, while natural labor can arise out of a communicative interest or impulse, this possibility is precluded by alienated labor.

Two forms of alienated labor are shown in figure A.1. They are most importantly distinguished from natural productive acts in that no consummation occurs in the intermediate productive process. The impulse out of which these forms of productive acts arise is for the attainment of use values of objects acquired via exchange. But unlike natural productive acts oriented to exchange, producers here are not free to organize their productive activities in a way that allows for experiencing consummation in the intermediate productive process. These forms of productive acts can be consummated only via procurement of wages $[C_{(ev)}]$ and ultimately consummated in the use of objects acquired with wages $[C_{(uv)}]$. Capitalist and non-capitalist forms of wage-oriented production are distinguished to show how productive acts may be similarly constituted regardless of the equity of exchange that follows them. In the capitalist version of alienated labor the producer's $C_{(ev)}$ becomes $C_{(ev-p)}$, or, exchange value minus profit, the surplus value that accrues to the capitalist.

The act structures diagrammed in figure A.1 are for heuristic purposes only; they are much too simplified to represent any real productive processes. Despite this simplification, the figure is useful for illustrating the connections between act structures and labor processes. As shown, labor processes encompass historical iterations of meta-acts. As such they encompass the impulses giving rise to productive acts as well as the consummatory values that can be realized within them. The important connection between a labor process and a productive act lies in how the social relations upon which a labor process is founded limit the impulses that can be satisfied in production by constraining the consummatory values it is possible to attain.

Appendix B: Notes on Data Collection

Data for this study were derived from three main sources: (1) on-site interviews and observations; (2) off-site interviews; and (3) self-administered questionnaires. The procedures by which the data were gathered are discussed below. Before discussing these procedures some background on the study's development is in order.

During the four-month period from June to September 1983, 33 manufacturing or engineering firms in southern California were requested to participate in a study of "the psychological effects of problem solving in work." While no more than five firms were being sought to participate in the study, more were contacted in anticipation of a high refusal rate. In each case the top plant manager (president, general manager, or plant supervisor) as listed in the local Chamber of Commerce directory was sent a letter describing the study and requesting an appointment to further discuss it. Follow-up phone calls found four firms out of business, 19 uninterested in participating, and 10 willing to hear more about the project in a personal interview. Of the latter, five eventually agreed to participate.

The study itself was not presented as one of the "psychosocial consequences of natural and alienated labor." Rather, relationships between work conditions, problem solving, self-esteem, and work stress (on which data were in fact collected) were emphasized as the primary interests of the study. Managers agreed to participate, or so it seemed, because of interests in the issue of work stress. Had this 'marketing' strategy not been used, it is unlikely that access to the capitalist workplace would have been obtained. It should be noted, however, that the data of interest to participating firms were collected as agreed and reported to them as agreed.

Of the five participating firms, four were manufacturing firms and the fifth as an engineering firm not directly engaged in manufacturing. Included were an aluminum casting machine manufacturer (approx. 130 employees); an aircraft battery manufacturer (approx. 145 employees); an aluminum sheet stock manufacturer (approx. 450 employees); an irrigation equipment manufacturer (approx. 650 employees); and an aerospace engineering firm (approx. 1100 employees). Once approval for the study was obtained, the chief personnel officer, or the equivalent, at each firm served as the primary liaison with the researcher. The identity of the researcher as a researcher was thus fully known to all participating firms and individuals.

Although the original plan was to conduct the study within a single firm, no single firm was willing to accept the time demands of the 100 on-site interviews felt necessary to obtain sufficient data for the qualitative phase of the study. So the study was spread out over five firms, each agreeing to 20 on-site interviews. This multi-site design facilitated access by greatly reducing the time demands placed on any single firm, and by offering managers what seemed to them an intriguing opportunity to see how their firms compared to others. All participating firms were offered anonymity in any published reports of the research, although only one insisted on this. All individuals were similarly guaranteed anonymity, both with regard to academic publications and to any reports of general findings reflected back to the firms themselves. To minimize potential suspicion regarding this 'management introduced' project, before field-work began attempts were made to contact and explain the project to union representatives at each of the three unionized firms in the study.

Once access was obtained, cooperation in data collection ranged from complete to grudging. In some cases, for example, initial restrictions on the length of interviews were relaxed, full access for observation was provided, employees selected for interviews were available as requested, and questionnaires and follow-up reminders were distributed according to specified procedures. However, where the project was perceived by the personnel manager to be of dubious value—a nuisance to be tolerated because the president or plant manager desired it—it was more difficult to arrange interviews with appropriate workers, observe closely, and make sure questionnaires were distributed properly. Such problems were virtually unavoidable in attempting to deal with five different firms, none having any significant commitment to the project. Nevertheless, useful data were collected at each firm as per initial requests to interview at least 20 employees on site and distribute 100-150 questionnaires. All the data were collected over a five-month period from September 1983 to January 1984.

With this as background, each phase of data collection can be described in more detail.

A total of 103 on-site interviews were conducted at the five firms. For purposes of obtaining an adequate sample of productive activities, employees in five principal job groups were interviewed: first-line supervisors (n = 16), maintenance mechanics (n = 13), engineers (n = 20), secretaries (n = 21), and production/assembly workers (n = 19). An additional 14 persons in various other occupations were also included in the sample: a custodian, a warehouseman, an accountant, two clerks, and nine computer programmers/program analysts. At each firm a request was made to interview four or five people in each principal job group, the only within-group selection criterion being tenure of employment (a distribution of 'new' and 'old' employees was sought). At two firms interviewees were 'selected' on a purely volunteer basis; that is, they selected themselves in response to a call for participants. At three firms interviewees were actively recruited by the personnel manager to constitute the sample as requested.

The on-site interviews consisted of a set of standard questions supplemented with probing questions as necessary. The standard questions included:

(1) What kinds of things do you do in your job?
(2) Can you see how your work contributes to a final product of some kind?
(3) Do you ever have to think about how someone is going to use or react to the results of your work?
(4) Of those things you do in your job, are there any you particularly dislike doing?—why?
(5) Of those things you do in your job, are there you particularly like doing—why?
(6) Do you ever have to solve problems in your work?—when?
(7) How much control do you feel you have in your work?
(8) If you think about the work you do, not your job as a whole, but just the work, would you say you enjoy it?—why?
(9) If you could start your work career over again and be assured of having job security and enough money to live comfortably no matter what you chose to do, what would you choose to do?
(10) How long have you worked for this company?
(11) How long have you been in your present job?
(12) How long have you been doing this kind of work?

Responses were recorded on an interview form during the interview. Average interview time was twenty minutes.

In only a few cases was it possible to conduct interviews at an individual's actual work site. Most were conducted at central locations within each plant (that is, people came to the researcher). Observation of work and work conditions, most important in the case of production workers, was thus undertaken apart from interviewing. Observation was not fully structured, but focused primarily on: (1) the overall production process at each plant; (2) the individual's location in the production process; (3) the actual operations performed by the individual; and (4) the degree of control the individual had over his or her work.

At the conclusion of the on-site interview people were asked to participate in a longer interview during off-work hours. This interview was portrayed as an attempt to go into more depth regarding job history and attitudes toward work. After a more thorough explanation of the project, approximately 75% of those asked agreed to an off-site interview. These were conducted at various locations, most often at people's homes. A total of 37 off-site interviews were conducted; interviewed were nine engineers, seven maintenance mechanics, nine secretaries, four production/assembly workers, six first-line supervisors, and one "computer program coordinator." These interviews were topically structured, focusing on: (1) job history; (2) worst jobs; (3) best jobs; (4) memorable innovations at work; (5) hobbies or crafts and their comparative relation to work; (6) depressing events at work; and (7) sources of special satisfaction in work. Interviews were taped and selectively transcribed later. Average interview time was one hour.

Surveys were carried out at each firm after all on-site and off-site interviews were completed. Sampling and distribution procedures varied somewhat from firm to firm. At the battery manufacturing plant all English-speaking employees (n = 130) received questionnaires. All employees at the casting machine manufacturing plant received questionnaires (n = 130). At firms with more than 150 employees, questionnaires were distributed by job group or department. At the aluminum sheet-casting plant questionnaires were distributed to 34 members of the maintenance department, 15 first-line supervisors, 11 secretaries and clerical workers, 20 machine operators, and 20 managerial personnel (n = 100). At the irrigation equipment manufacturing plant questionnaires were distributed to 18 first-line supervisors, 7 tool and die makers, 14 mold makers, 52 machine operators, 10 secretaries, 32 assemblers, 9 engineers, and 8 maintenance workers (n = 150). Only white-collar professional and technical workers and secretaries were available at the engineering firm. Here questionnaires were distributed to random samples of 50 professional-technical employees (including managers) and 50 secretaries. In most cases questionnaires were distributed by department supervisors or managers. In one case they were distributed directly by the personnel manager.

An attempt was made at each firm to inform prospective respondents as to the source and purpose of the survey prior to questionnaire distribution. Usually this was done by means of a memo from the personnel manager. All questionnaires were distributed in stamped, self-addressed envelopes ready for first-class mail return to the researcher. Within two weeks of initial distribution a follow-up reminder was sent (via company channels) to all those receiving questionnaires. The overall response rate was 43.6% (253/580); however, response rates ranged from 33% to 87% across firms.

The questionnaire contained items to measure the variables of interest discussed earlier. In most cases this involved creation of new scales for measuring such things as problem-solving and role-taking demands, means-ends comprehension, reification, etc. Pretesting with a 3% sample of working people similar to those at the firms studied revealed minor problems with early drafts of the questionnaire and led to appropriate modifications. Each of the scales used to measure key dependent and independent variables is described below.

Problem solving, role-taking, and means-ends comprehension were each measured using four-item scales, where each component item sought to tap a different aspect of these experiences. To measure problem-solving demands subjects were asked *how often* (never, once in a while, most of the time, or almost always) the following statements were true of their work:

(a) I can do my work and still keep my mind on other things
(b) I have to solve unusual problems in my work
(c) I have to deal with unexpected situations
(d) I have to figure out new ways to do things in my work.

Role-taking demands were measured in the same way using the following items:

(a) My work requires talking to others
(b) I have to think about how someone might use the results of my work
(c) I have to keep in mind how people are going to react to my work
(d) I can do my work and not think much about other people.

Means-ends comprehension was measured similarly using these items:

(a) I can see the direct results of my work
(b) I can see how my work contributes to the company as a whole
(c) I can see the relationship between what I do and a finished product
(d) I can tell when the results of my work are good or bad.

For each scale response categories were coded from 1 to 4 (i.e., never = 1, once in a while = 2, most of the time = 3, almost always = 4) and then scores on component items were summed, giving each scale a hypothetical range of 4 to 16. Cronbach's alpha, a coefficient of internal consistency, was calculated as a measure of reliability for each scale. For the problem-solving demand scale, the mean $(\overline{X})$ = 10.05, the standard deviation (sd) = 2.26, and Cronbach's alpha (a) = .41. For the role-taking demand scale, $\overline{X}$ = 11.99, sd = 2.44, and a = .58. For the means-ends comprehension scale, $\overline{X}$ = 12.77, sd = 2.55, and a = .77.

Two other independent work-experience variables potentially affecting opportunities for aesthetic experience—routinization and control—were measured similarly, with 4-item summated scales. The component items for the control scale were:

(a) I can talk to other people when I want to
(b) I can decide how best to do my work
(c) I can decide when to work fast and when to take it easy
(d) My boss keeps a close eye on me.

For this scale, $\overline{X}$ = 12.88, sd = 1.92, and a = .55. Routinization was measured with the following items:

(a) My work is the same from day to day
(b) I take on new tasks in my work
(c) I have to learn new skills on the job
(d) I have to follow standard rules and operating procedures in my work.

For this scale, $\overline{X}$ = 10.38, sd = 2.01, and a = .52.

The dependent variables of interest were measured using several different kinds of scales. The most simple was that used for measuring work enjoyment. For this people were asked to rate their work enjoyment on a 10-point scale between the extremes, "like actual work very little" and "like actual work very much." For this scale, $\overline{X}$ = 7.7 and sd = 1.95. On a single-item scale of this kind no reliability coefficient can be calculated from cross-sectional data.

Measuring a reified mode of consciousness was not as straightforward as measuring work enjoyment. For this purpose statements were devised to portray possible dimensions of a worldview through which collectively constructed social realities appear as things-in-themselves or sources of agency. People were asked to agree or disagree (on a four-point Likert-type scale) with these statements: (a) the economy in the U.S. operates pretty much independent of anyone's control; (b) it's possible for people to carry on their personal lives and be unaffected by the world around them; (c) technology will determine how we live in the future; and (d) people are largely helpless in the face of new social trends.

Agreement with these statements was taken to imply a view of constructed social realities ("the economy," "social trends," "technology") as forces operating independently of human agency, as entities with ontological status apart from human thought and action. Agreement with these statements was thus taken was evidence of a reified mode of consciousness. Response categories were coded from 1 to 4 strongly agree = 4, agree = 3, etc.) for each item; the item scores were then summed into a scale score. For this scale, $\overline{X}$ = 9.54, sd = 1.56, and a = .34.

Propensity to role-take was measured using a set of items adapted from Bernstein and Davis's Interpersonal Reactivity Index (Bernstein and Davis, 1982). This index was originally developed to measure distinct dimensions of empathy; specifically, perspective taking, tendency to fantasize, empathic concern, and personal distress (see also Davis, 1983). Here only those items pertaining to perspective taking were used. The five items included in the questionnaire were self-descriptive statements that respondents indicated described them "not very well," "somewhat," or "very well." Specifically:

(a) I sometimes find it hard to see things from the other guy's point of view (–)

(b) I try to look at everybody's side of an argument before I make up my mind (+)

(c) I try to understand my friends better by imagining how things look from where they stand (+)

(d) If I'm sure I'm right about something I don't waste much time listening to other people's arguments (–)

(e) Before criticizing someone I try to imagine how I would feel if I were in their place (+).

The plus or minus in parentheses indicate how the item was coded for propensity to role take if the respondent indicated the statement described him very well. The item responses were scored from 1 to 3, recoded unidirectionally, and summed into a single 'propensity-to-role-take' scale score. For this scale, $\overline{X}$ = 11.63, sd = 1.94, and a = .77.

Intellectual flexibility is a difficult trait to measure outside of a highly structured testing situation in which individuals must actually demonstrate the trait in some way. And in any attempt to measure intellectual flexibility there is the troublesome matter of just what to measure, *range* (the number of alternative perspectives an individual can adopt) or *depth* (the degree of familiarity an individual exhibits with regard to alternative perspectives). Such problems of measurement conceptualization are far from resolved among cognitive psychologists; as such, it was unrealistic to expect to resolve them here. Nevertheless, in keeping with the Meadian framework, a measure of intellectual flexibility was devised by using fifteen statements implying a predilection for adopting alternative perspectives. Subjects were asked to agree or disagree with these statements:

(a) I am usually one of the first people to try something new (+)

(b) There is a single right answer to almost every question (–)

(c) I am uncomfortable with people who have rigid opinions about social issues (+)

(d) the most enjoyable part of a conversation is finding out how other people think (+)

(e) children should not question their parents' values (–)

(f) I like to imagine different ways of doing things even if they seem impractical (+)

(g) the value of art lies in helping us see familiar things in new ways (+)

(h) There is usually one correct method for solving any particular problem (–)

(i) Rules are made for a reason and it is best not to question them (–)

(j) It's to be expected that people raised differently should have different values (+)

(k) When people disagree with one another there's not much point in further discussion (–)

(l) People should be willing to break away from tradition and try new ways of doing things (+)

(m) There is always a clear difference between right and wrong (–)

(n) The best way to solve a problem is to try looking at it from different points of view (+)

(o) Intuition is the best guide when it comes to deciding how to handle an unfamiliar situation (+)

The plus or minus in parentheses again indicates how an agree response was coded for intellectual flexibility. The scale score for intellectual flexibility was arrived at by counting the number of responses indicating a predilection to adopt alternative perspectives. The hypothetical range of this scale was thus 0 to 15, with $\overline{X}$ = 11.71 and sd = 1.95. For this scale the Kuder-Richardson reliability coefficient (KR20) was calculated to be .41. It should be acknowledged, finally, that this is not a true measure of ability to adopt multiple perspectives, but of a tendency or readiness to do so, which may reflect ability.

The survey questionnaire also contained standard items to determine social class position, occupation, number and type of off-work activities, age, sex, education, ethnicity, and income.

Appendix C: Analysis of Supplemental Data

The purpose of the survey phase of this project was to generate quantitative data documenting the psychological consequences of forms of productive activity. Using the procedures detailed in appendix B, a dataset containing 251 cases with measures of relevant work experience and psychological outcome variables was constructed. Cases in the dataset include 160 men (mean age = 46.3) and 90 women (mean age = 39.4). By occupational categorization it includes 36 engineers, 11 mechanics, 25 supervisors, 32 secretaries, 40 production workers, and 107 other in various other occupations. By social class categorization the dataset includes

18 managerial, 25 supervisory, 108 semi-autonomous professional/ technical, and 98 working-class subjects. Two basic connections are explored in analyzing these data: that between structural categorization (that is, class and occupation) and work experience, and that between work experience and psychological functioning.

The first connection is explored by analysis of variance, comparing mean scale scores on problem solving, role taking, means-ends comprehension, routinization, and control across class and occupational categories. In this context a brief reiteration of measurement conceptualization may be helpful. Problem solving and role taking were measured as *demands for* these cognitive activities in an individual's work; means-ends comprehension was measured as an individual's ability to see how various results followed from his work; routinization and control were measured as perceived work experiences. Based on previous theoretical arguments, these measures can be seen as roughly indexing an individual's opportunities for aesthetic experience in work. But since there is no direct measurement of aesthetic experience, I will refer to these scales as indicators of the dimensions of work experience noted above. The purpose of this initial analysis is, then, to explore variations in work experience across social class and occupational categories.

The second connection is explored in three steps. First, simple correlations between measures of problem solving, role taking, means-end comprehension, routinization, and control and psychological outcome variables are examined. This is to document relationships between work experiences and psychological effects in the most general way, placing no constraints on the data. The second step in exploring this connection involves using multiple regression to examine the relative effects of each work-experience variable on each psychological outcome variable. This is to document relationships between work experience and psychological functioning in a more qualified way, placing constraints on the data to determine which experiences are more consequential than others. The final step in this analysis uses the same statistical techniques to examine the possible effects of education, age, sex, tenure of employment, and off-work activities on each psychological outcome variable.

Table C.1 shows the mean problem solving (PROBSV), role taking (ROLETK) means-ends comprehension (MECOMP), routinzation (ROUTIN), and control (CONTRL) scale scores for each of the five job groups examined previously. It should be noted that the particular individuals making up each job group here were not all among those interviewed in the first phase of the study. In the first column of table C.1 we see supervisors, engineers, and mechanics scoring highest on the problem-solving demand scale; secretaries and production workers score lowest. With the exception of supervisors scoring slightly higher than engineers, these means fall out very consistently with the observations reported in chapter 4. The eta (.59) and F-value (18.53) calculated from this analysis of variance indicate a strong and significant (p < .01) association between occupation and problem-solving demands.

Table C.1   Relationship of Occupation to Opportunities for Aesthetic Experience

Job Group	N	PROBSV	ROLETK	MECOMP	ROUTIN	CONTRL
				Means		
Engineers	(36)	11.0	12.9	12.3	9.0	12.9
Mechanics	(11)	10.4	10.3	13.5	10.5	11.4
Supervisors	(25)	11.5	14.4	14.0	9.8	12.8
Secretaries	(32)	8.5	10.7	11.6	10.7	13.6
Production Workers	(40)	8.4	10.5	13.6	12.2	12.4
Eta =		.59	.58	.36	.57	.30
F =		18.53**	17.75**	5.08**	16.99**	3.68**

** = p < .01

PROBSV = problem solving; ROLETK = role taking; MECOMP = means-ends comprehension; ROUTIN = routinization; CONTRL = control

In the second column of this table we see supervisors scoring highest on role-taking demands, followed closely by engineers. Considering that this measure heavily weighted 'talking to others' and 'thinking about others', it is not surprising that first-line supervisors scored above engineers. Clustering close together farther down the scale are mechanics, production workers, and secretaries. These rankings are also quite consistent with the observations reported in chapter 4. And again, analysis of variance shows the association between occupation and role-taking demands to be strong (eta = .58) and significant (F = 17.75; p < .01).

The scale means displayed in the third column of table C.1 are somewhat less consistent with the observations reported in chapter 4. Although supervisors and mechanics score high on means-ends comprehension as expected, production workers unexpectedly score higher than engineers. In light of the qualitative analysis this can perhaps be explained with reference to the different meanings engineers and production workers attached to 'seeing the results of their work'. For engineers this usually meant seeing a contribution to a collective product often quite distant from their immediate efforts, and sometimes this was difficult. For production workers this usually meant seeing only the immediate results of their physical efforts, something they were nearly always able to do. Questionnaire items were apparently unable to tap this difference in experience and thus took only a surface reading of the phenomenon. There is also the possibility of some response bias among production workers, whose response rates were lowest. Those production workers who participated in the survey may have been more literate, aware, and motivated to seek means-ends comprehension than those who did not participate. Nonetheless, differences in means-ends comprehension across job groups are statistically significant (F = 5.08; p. ⟨ .01).

The fourth column of table C.1 is again quite consistent with previously reported observations. Engineers score lowest on routinization, followed closely by supervisors. Mechanics and secretaries score somewhat higher and in close proximity to each other. And, as expected, production workers score highest on routinization. The association between occupation and routinization is also shown to be strong (eta = .57) and significant (F = 16.99; p ⟨ .01).

The fifth column of table C.1 shows the mean scale scores for control. Like those for means-end comprehension, these scores are somewhat out of line with expectations. Here secretaries score highest on control, followed by engineers, supervisors, and then production workers. Surprisingly, mechanics score lowest. These scores seem to be more reflective of subjective perceptions influenced by social desirability factors than objective differences in actual control. As noted in the text, in on-site interviews people in all job groups tended initially to exaggerate the degree of control they had over their work. However, when pressed to be more specific, most promptly qualified their claims by saying, approximately, 'well, of course there are limits on what I can do, but within them my boss leaves me alone'. And here again there is the possibility of some response bias further contributing to the lack of expected variation. Those people who felt they had more control over their work may have been more likely to participate in the survey (again this would have the greatest distorting effect among those with the lowest response rates: production workers). The association between occupation and control is thus not especially strong, but statistically significant nonetheless (F = 3.68; p ⟨ .01).

In sum, the data presented in table C.1 generally corroborate observations presented in chapter 4. They also document the considerable differences in crucial work experiences arising across occupational categories. Thus if problem solving, role taking, means-ends comprehension, routinization, and control are necessarily linked to aesthetic experience, then it is further substantiated that opportunities for aesthetic experience vary within capitalist relations of production. Ultimately however, it is not the goal of this analysis to link occupation to aesthetic experience. The goal, rather, is to link work experiences to psychological outcomes. The prior link of key importance is between class and the work experiences associated with aesthetic experience. That link is explored below.

Table C.2 shows the mean problem-solving, role-taking, means-ends comprehension, routinization, and control scale scores for each of the four Marxist social classes represented in the survey sample (class categorization is based on the criteria used by Wright, et al., 1982). In the first column of table C.2 we see managers and supervisors scoring highest on problem-solving demands, followed closely by semi-autonomous professional/technical employees. Further down the scale, scoring lowest on problem-solving demands, are those in the working class. These results are in accord with theoretical expectations: those in the working class experience a significantly lower level of problem-solving demands in their work. Analysis of variance shows a strong (eta = .48) and significant (F = 24.82; p ⟨ .01) association between class and problem solving.

Table C.2   Relationship of Class to Opportunities for Aesthetic Experience

| | | Means | | | | |
Class	N	PROBSV	ROLETK	MECOMP	ROUTIN	CONTRL
Managerial	(18)	11.4	13.5	12.9	9.0	12.9
Supervisory	(25)	11.5	14.4	14.0	9.8	12.8
Semi-Autonomous	(108)	10.7	12.4	12.3	9.7	13.1
Working	(98)	8.8	10.7	12.9	11.4	12.6
Eta =		.48	.50	.22	.43	.12
F =		24.82**	26.84**	3.98*	18.59**	1.17

* = p ⟨ .05
** = p ⟨ .01

The second column of table C.2 is also consistent with theoretical expectations. Supervisors and managers experience the greatest role-taking demands in their work, followed then by semi-autonomous employees. Those in the working class experience the least role-taking demands. The association between class and role taking is also shown to be strong (eta = .50) and significant (F = 26.84; p < .01).

Theoretical expectations are not so well borne out by the mean scale scores in the third column of table C.2. With regard to means-ends comprehension, those in the working class score as high as managers. Indeed, there is very little difference between managers, semi-autonomous employees, and workers. Only those in the supervisory class stand out, scoring somewhat higher than the others. It seems likely that the same problems of measurement and response bias discussed in the previous section may be involved here. Based on the fieldwork conducted for this study it seems reasonable to suppose means-ends comprehension may be quite different for managers, supervisors, and semi-autonomous employees than it is for workers. The survey data, however, do not reflect these differences in experience, but rather the superficial similarities in reported subjective perceptions. Because the mean for supervisors stands out in this column, the analysis of variance yields a significant F-value (F = 3.98; p < .05)

The fourth column of table C.2 is again quite consistent with theoretical expectations. Those in the managerial class score lowest on routinization, followed closely by semi-autonomous employees and supervisors. Those in the working class score highest on routinization. The association between class and routinization is also shown to be strong (eta = .43) and significant (F = 18.59; p < .01).

The mean scale scores in the fifth column of table C.2 are not consistent with expectations. No significant differences in mean controls scores appear across classes. Clearly this does not reflect objective reality; the control scale is failing to discriminate between the real control of managers and the marginal autonomy of workers. And as discussed above, there may also be problems of social desirability and response bias that are especially pronounced with regard to this measure of control. Thus while these scores may accurately reflect subjective perceptions of control within class-based frames of reference, they do not accurately reflect control prerogatives as they actually vary across classes. Neither, therefore, is the relationship between class and controls shown to be significant.

Overall, the data in table C.2 support the propositions that class position is strongly and significantly related to demands for problem solving and role taking, and to work routinization. And while the results of field research showed important differences in means-ends comprehension and control experiences among people in different class positions, these differences did not appear in the survey data. Nonetheless, the survey data do show significant differences in opportunities for aesthetic experience across social classes, insofar as those opportunities arise out of problem solving, role taking, and variety in work. One important theoretical connection is thus established empirically: class is systematically associated with an individual's opportunities to engage in what have been argued to be psychologically consequential work experiences. The next link to be explored, then, is between these experiences and their proposed psychological effects.

The first *row* of table C.3 shows the Pearson product-moment correlation coefficients for the relationships between propensity to role-take and the work experience measures used above. As conceptualized here, propensity to role-take is the dependent psychological variable supposedly affected by the independent work experience variables. Looking across this row we see propensity to role-take is positively associated with role-taking demands (r = .14) and control (r = .12). Neither correlation is very strong, although the association between role-taking demands and role-taking propensity is statistically significant (p ⟨ .05). The positive relationship between role-taking propensity and role-taking demands in work is as theoretically expected. Expected relationships between problem solving, means-ends comprehension, and propensity to role-take do not appear, however.

Table C.3   Relationships Between Work Experiences and Cognitive and Affective Outcomes

| Conceptualized Outcome Variable | Pearson Product-Moment Correlation Coefficients | | | | |
	PROBSV	ROLETK	MECOMP	ROUTIN	CONTRL
Propensity to Role-Take	.08	.14*	.06	−.11	.12
Work Enjoyment	.19**	.23**	.30**	−.25**	.06
Reification	−.17*	−.20**	−.06	.16**	−.05
Intellectual Flexibility	.18*	.19**	−.02	−.22**	.05

* = p ⟨ .05
** = p ⟨ .01

The correlation coefficients in the second row of table C.3 consistently support theoretical expectations. Here work enjoyment is the outcome variable supposedly affected by work experiences. We see work enjoyment positively associated with problem-solving demands (r = .19; p ⟨ .01), role-taking demands (r = .23; p ⟨ .01), and means-ends comprehension (r = .30; p ⟨ .01). These experiences have all been argued to underlie aesthetic experience, which in turn was argued to produce a positive affective response to work. The correlations in this row are entirely consistent with this hypothesis. Further, we see routinization negatively correlated with work enjoyment ($r = -.25$; $p < .01$), as would be expected based on theoretical reasoning and previous research. Somewhat surprisingly, though, no relationship appears between control and work enjoyment.

In the third row of table C.3, reification or, as measured, 'tendency to hold a reified worldview', is considered the dependent variable. Again the relationships are as theoretically expected: problem-solving and role-taking demands are negatively correlated with reification ($r = -.17$; $p < .05$ and $r = -.20$; $p < .01$ respectively). In other words, as the Meadian theory predicts, problem-solving and role-taking experiences are associated with a decreasing tendency to hold a reified view of the world. It is also consistent that routinization is positively correlated ($r = .16$; $p < .01$) with reification; this is in one sense simply the obverse of the relationship between problem solving and reification. And here again control does not appear at all related to reification (no relationship was predicted); nor is means-ends comprehension related to reification. In the latter case an expected relationship does not appear.

In the fourth row of table C.3 intellectual flexibility is shown to be positively related to problem-solving demands ($r = .18$; $p < .01$) and role-taking demands ($r = .19$; $p < .01$), and negatively related to routinization ($r = -.22$; $p < .01$). These results are once again consistent with theoretical expectations. Specifically, it was predicted that greater role-taking demands would be associated with greater intellectual flexibility, as is the case. The negative relationship between routinization and intellectual flexibility may again by explainable as an inversion of the positive relationship between problem solving and intellectual flexibility. A predicted relationship between means-ends comprehension and the conceptualized dependent variable again fails to appear. No relationship appears between control and intellectual flexibility (none was predicted).

In sum, the survey data show significant relationships between measures of work experience and conceptualized psychological outcomes. Problem-solving demands in work were shown to be positively associated with work enjoyment and intellectual flexibility, and negatively associated with reification. Role-taking demands were shown to be positively associated with propensity to role-take, work enjoyment, and intellectual flexibility, and negatively associated with reification. Means-ends comprehension was shown to be positively associated with work enjoyment. All of these relationships were in the theoretically expected directions. However, several expected relationships failed to appear. Relationships between routinization and work enjoyment, reification, and intellectual flexibility were also consistent with theoretical expectations.

Although in this type of analysis one variable can be conceptualized as dependent, strictly speaking no causality is demonstrated. Nonetheless, the goal of this analysis was simply to explore relationships between work experiences and psychological functioning. The results were encouragingly supportive of the Meadian theory. Together with the analysis which demonstrated relationships between class and work experience, the relationships demonstrated here between work experience and psychological outcome variables logically imply the theorized connection between class and psychological functioning. Before distilling these findings for more pointed discussion, it will be useful to consider the relative contributions of each type of work experience to explaining the variation in each psychological outcome variable. And following that, to check for the possible effects of extra-theoretic variables on psychological functioning.

Each row in table C.4 represents the results of one regression equation. In the first row of table C.4 propensity to role-take is the dependent variable, the variation in which is being predicted by problem solving, role taking, means-ends comprehension, control, and routinization. Since we are dealing here with variables having no inherently meaningful scale, standardized regression coefficients (betas) are reported rather than the unstandardized coefficients. The betas in the first row of table C.4 show the relative contributions of each work-experience variable to predicting the variation in propensity to role-take. We see here that role-taking demands and control are of approximately equal importance in predicting increased role-taking propensity, and that routinization is of about the same level of importance in predicting decreased role-taking propensity. Problem-solving demands and means-ends comprehension have relatively little effects. The low overall R^2 (.03) and non-significant F-value (1.51) suggest that work experience may not be the most important factor affecting role-taking propensity. Attention is thus directed to extra-theoretic variables, which are examined below.

The second row of Table C.4 shows the betas for the equation predicting work enjoyment. Here we see that means-ends comprehension has the greatest effect on work enjoyment, nearly three times that of role-taking demands. Routinization is also shown to have a strong (negative) effect on work enjoyment, but overall its effect is less than that of means-ends comprehension. And here again problem solving fades in importance relative to role taking, means-ends comprehension, and

Table C.4   Regression Equations Predicting Psychological Outcomes From Work Experience

| Dependent Variable | Standardized Regression Coefficients | | | | | | |
	PROBSV	ROLTEK	MECOMP	ROUTIN	CONTRL	R^2	F
Propensity to Role-Take	−.01	.09	.03	−.07	.09	.03	1.51
Work Enjoyment	−.02	.11	.29**	−.21**	−.02	.16	9.16**
Reification	.00	−.15*	−.03	.11	−.01	.05	2.33*
Intellectual Flexibility	.02	.12	−.08	−.17*	.02	.07	3.46**

* = p ⟨ .05
** = p ⟨ .01

routinization. Nor is control of much relative importance in this equation. The R^2 (.16) and significant F-value (9.16; p ⟨ .01) suggest these work experiences are indeed important determinants of affective responses to work.

In the third row of table C.4 we see only role-taking demands and routinization accounting for much variation in reification when other work experiences are controlled. Indeed, problem solving, means-ends comprehension, and control contribute almost nothing to the equation relative to role taking (which has the greatest effect) and routinization. The R^2, though not substantively overwhelming, is nonetheless significant (p ⟨ .05). These results again suggest extra-theoretic variables merit some attention.

The betas in the fourth row of table C.4 show similar results to those above. Again role-taking demands and routinization have the greatest effects on the predicted variable, intellectual flexibility. In this equation, however, the overall negative effect of routinization is somewhat greater than the positive effect of role-taking demands. The relative contributions of problem solving, means-ends comprehension, and control are negligible. The R^2 (.07), although statistically significant (p ⟨ .05), once more suggests the need to examine other potential explanatory variables.

The results of this analysis suggest several things. First, that role taking and routinization may be the most important work experiences for predicting certain cognitive consequences, such as intellectual flexibility and a reified worldview. Second, that means-ends comprehension and routinization may be the most important work experiences for predicting affective responses to work (note that means-ends comprehension and routinization had significant independent effects on work enjoyment). And third, that more than work experiences must be considered in attempting to account for adult psychological functioning. In general this analysis supports theoretical expectations, but also indicates that further consideration of the relative importance of different work experiences for psychological functioning is in order.

It is largely an assumption in a study of this kind that the workplace is the most consequential context for shaping adult psychological functioning. Although this may seem a reasonable assumption on numerous grounds, it should properly be converted into an empirical question. While the present dataset is not adequate to answer such an ambitious question, it can be used to explore the possible effects of certain extra-theoretic control variables on the psychological outcomes of interest here. As discussed in the text, such things as education, off-work activities, tenure of employment, age, and sex might also affect psychological functioning. The assumption here is that experiences associated with each of these variables can be psychologically consequential, just as are experiences associated with class or occupation. The regression analysis presented in this section considers the independent effects of these control variables when work experiences are simultaneously taken into account. Table C.5 shows the results of this analysis when propensity to role-take is the dependent psychological variable.

Seven regression equations are presented in table C.5. It should be pointed out that this is not a 'stepwise' regression procedure. The purpose here is not to develop a model explaining the largest proportion of variation in role-taking propensity. The purpose, rather, is to assess the effects of extra-theoretic variables on psychological functioning, relative to the effects of work experience. This analysis may thus shed no light on the social-psychological dimensions of the Marxian/Meadian perspective, but it may tell something about its adequacy as a perspective on social structure and personality.

To return to table C.5: the first equation (EQI) is from table C.4; it predicts propensity to role-take from work experience alone. This is the baseline equation. Each subsequent equation introduces one of the five control variables. The last equation represents a 'full model' taking into account work experiences and all control variables. Much of table C.5 needs no discussion. Equations 2 through 5 show education (EDUC), the number of off-work activities (NUMACT), tenure of employment (TWORK), and age to have negligible effects on the outcome variable. In EQ6 we see sex having a significant effect on role-taking propensity, an

Table C.5 Regression Equations Predicting PROPENSITY TO ROLE-TAKE from Work Experience and Extra-Theoretic Control Variables

Standardized Regression Coefficients

| | Work Experience Variables | | | | | Control Variables | | | | | | |
	PROBSV	ROLETK	MECOMP	ROUTIN	CONTRL	EDUC	NUMACT	TWORK	AGE	SEX	R^2	F
EQ1	-.01	.09	.03	-.07	.09						.03	1.51
EQ2	-.03	.09	.04	-.06	.08	.04					.03	1.31
EQ3	-.02	.10	.03	-.08	.09		-.04				.03	1.31
EQ4	-.02	.09	.03	-.07	.09			.05			.03	1.34
EQ5	-.01	.09	.03	-.07	.09				.00		.03	1.25
EQ6	.04	.10	.03	-.06	.06					-.16*	.04	2.21
EQ7	.00	.11	.04	-.05	.05	.07	-.04	.09	.00	-.19**	.06	1.63

* = p < .05

** = p < .01

effect that holds up in the full model (EQ7). Since sex was included as a dummy variable coded 1 if male, 0 if female, the beta for sex tells us that being male has a significant negative effect on propensity to role-take, controlling for work experiences, age, education, and time working.

Table C.6 presents the same form of analysis looking at work enjoyment as the dependent variable. Equation 2 shows education having a small negative effect on work enjoyment, but not much altering the equation as a whole. Off-work activities (EQ3) have almost no effect, nor does sex (EQ6). As might be expected, however, age (EQ5) and time working (EQ4) both show significant positive effects on work enjoyment. Interpretation of this is straightforward: people are less likely to stay working at something they don't enjoy, thus time working and age (which are positively correlated) both show positive effects on work enjoyment. But these are not so much effects as artifacts. In the full model (EQ7) these effects are still present but non-significant. Means-end comprehension and routinization remain the best predictors of affective responses to work.

Table C.7 examines the effects of work experiences and control variables on reification. Not surprisingly, education (EQ2) has a negative effect on reification nearly as strong as that of role-taking demands. Taking education into account also diminishes the effect of routinization, which seems to partially mask the effect of education. In EQ5 and EQ6 we see age and 'being a male' also contribute modestly to reification. In the full model (EQ7), role-taking demands and education are shown to have the greatest effects on reification; the effect of routinization is here less than half what it is in the baseline model (EQ1).

Finally, table C.8 looks at intellectual flexibility as it is affected by work experience and control variables. Here EQ2 shows results similar to those in table C.7; education has a significant positive effect on intellectual flexibility; including it in the equation sharply diminishes the effect of routinization. Number of off-work activities (EQ3) shows a small positive effect on intellectual flexibility. Time working (EQ4) and age (EQ5) both show negative effects of approximately the same degree, but neither changes the effect of role taking or routinization. Sex (EQ6) appears to have little effect on intellectual flexibility. In the full model (EQ7), role-taking demands and education have the strongest effects; however, the effect of education is twice that of role-taking. In this equation the effect of routinization is again cut in half.

The interesting findings of the analysis can be summed up briefly. First, education has a strong and significant effect on intellectual flexibility independent of work experiences; in fact, its effect is twice as strong

Table C.6 Regression Equations Predicting WORK ENJOYMENT from Work Experience and Extra-Theoretic Control Variables

| | Work Experience Variables | | | | | Control Variables | | | | | | |
	PROBSV	ROLETK	MECOMP	ROUTIN	CONTRL	EDUC	NUMACT	TWORK	AGE	SEX	R^2	F
EQ1	-.02	.11	.29**	-.21**	-.02						.16	9.16**
EQ2	.00	.12	.27**	-.23**	-.02	-.06					.16	7.78**
EQ3	-.02	.11	.29**	-.20**	-.02		.01				.16	7.62**
EQ4	-.04	.12	.28**	-.23**	-.02			.12*			.18	8.48**
EQ5	-.05	.12	.29**	-.23**	-.03				.14*		.18	8.76**
EQ6	-.03	.11	.28**	-.21**	-.02					.02	.16	7.63**
EQ7	-.03	.12	.27**	-.24**	-.03	-.06	.02	.07	.10	.02	.19	5.40**

Standardized Regression Coefficients

* = p < .05
** = p < .01

Table C.7 Regression Equations Predicting REIFICATION from Work Experience and Extra-Theoretic Control Variables

Standardized Regression Coefficients

	Work Experience Variables					Control Variables						
	PROBSV	ROLETK	MECOMP	ROUTIN	CONTRL	EDUC	NUMACT	TWORK	AGE	SEX	R^2	F
EQ1	.00	-.15*	-.03	.11	-.01	-.12					.05	2.33*
EQ2	.04	-.14	-.06	.08	.00						.06	2.34*
EQ3	.00	-.15	-.03	.10	.00		-.06				.05	2.07
EQ4	.00	-.15	-.03	.11	-.01			.05			.05	2.03
EQ5	-.01	-.14	-.03	.10	-.02				.09		.06	2.33*
EQ6	-.02	-.15*	-.03	.11	.00					.08	.05	2.17*
EQ7	.00	-.14	-.06	.05	.00	-.11	-.05	.00	.08	.08	.07	1.77

* = p < .05
** = p < .01

Table C.8 Regression Equations Predicting INTELLECTUAL FLEXIBILITY from Work Experience and Extra-Theoretic Control Variables

Standardized Regression Coefficients

| | Work Experience Variables | | | | | Control Variables | | | | | | |
	PROBSV	ROLETK	MECOMP	ROUTIN	CONTRL	EDUC	NUMACT	TWORK	AGE	SEX	R^2	F
EQ1	.02	.12	-.08	-.17*	.02						.07	3.46**
EQ2	-.04	.11	-.03	-.11	.00	.21**					.10	4.36**
EQ3	.03	.11	-.08	-.14	.01		.09				.07	3.21**
EQ4	.04	.12	-.08	-.16*	.02			-.10			.08	3.34**
EQ5	.04	.12	-.09	-.16*	.02				-.08		.07	3.12**
EQ6	.02	.12	-.08	-.17*	.02					-.01	.07	2.88*
EQ7	.00	.10	-.03	-.08	.00	.20**	.07	-.09	-.02	.00	.11	3.00**

* = p < .05
** = p < .01

as any work experience variable. Second, education also has a modest (negative) effect on reification, although here role-taking demands have the greatest effect. Third, means-ends comprehension and routinization remain the best predictors of affective responses to work when all other variables are taken into account. And fourth, sex has the strongest effect on role-taking propensity of any work or non-work variable, although role-taking demands still have a positive independent effect. In general, what this analysis documents—quite consistently with earlier arguments—is that work experiences alone cannot account for all the variation in adult psychological functioning. Nevertheless, it also documents that even when other factors are considered, work experiences such as role taking, means-ends comprehension, and routinization still have significant effects on important dimensions of psychological functioning. Further, they remain the most important determinants of affective responses to work.

Notes

Notes to Chapter 1: Alienated Labor

1. Although it is not a matter that can be resolved by voting, a majority of accomplished Marxist scholars agree on the unity of Marx's philosophical thought from his early writings to his last (see Ollman, 1971; Meszaros, 1970; Plasek, 1974; Schaff, 1970; Avineri, 1968; Walton, et al., 1970). For a discussion of the young Marx versus old Marx debate, see Wartofsky (1982).
2. The change that is apparent in Marx's treatment of human labor is one of emphasis. In his early writings he was concerned with labor as a concrete human activity. In his later writings he was concerned with labor power as a commodity, especially as it fit into his economic analysis of capitalism (see Novack, 1970:64-70).
3. Marx alternately used the words *Entausserung* and *Entfremdung* to refer to the condition of alienation. The former, which translates as alienation, carries the connotation of failure. The latter denotes estrangement. For most purposes the two can be taken as synonymous; estrangement from species powers, for example, is a failure to realize them. This point is noted because of the tendency to interpret alienation strictly as separation, with little understanding of this as 'separation from a potentiality'.

4. Labor is what people do; labor power is the potential to do. That is to say, a capitalist who purchases one hour of labor power (the worker's time), buys only a potential—the worker may actually do a great deal or very little during that hour. It is thus up to the capitalist to try to 'get his money's worth' by getting the worker to do as much as possible during each unit of purchased time.

5. People can experience the cognitive and affective consequences of alienated labor and still, in general, be quite happy. One need only adapt psychologically to acting as the instrument of another's will, abdicate responsibility for one's actions, or accept the immutability of the world to alleviate much of the mental distress caused by alienated labor. Mainstream sociologists, misunderstanding the Marxist theory of alienation, falsely presume that if one is alienated one must feel bad, and conversely, if one doesn't feel bad, one cannot be alienated (cf. Heinz, 1981).

6. This is not to say Braverman does not use concrete examples. He does. The particulars he glosses are the day-to-day shopfloor struggles of workers resisting degradation, reconstructing the meaning of their work, and finding alternative forms of satisfaction within capitalist relations of production. To understand how people experience working for capitalism and how they are affected by it, requires a more in-depth social-psychological analysis than Braverman offers.

7. In a recent review of research on the working class in the U.S., William Form (1983) repeats a number of oft-heard criticisms of the Marxist view of alienation, based on the same old misunderstandings of the concept that have gripped American sociologists for decades. Form contends the Marxist theory of alienation is disproved, because research does not show U.S. workers to be experiencing "increasing alienation." The notion of alienation Form has in mind is that concocted by mainstream sociologists, not Marx.

8. Purely social-psychological interests in how work affects people are not without merit. It is worthwhile to know how all kinds of workplace experiences affect people. But if one's interest is in a coherent theoretical understanding of social structure and personality, one's social-psychological analysis should be linked theoretically to an explanation of the social structure in question. Since one goal of the present study is to formulate a Marxist theory of social structure and personality, only those variables that can be linked theoretically to Marx's structural analysis of capitalism are examined.

9. For a review of the numerous studies conducted in this tradition, see Seeman (1975).

10. Good examples of this can be found in Shepard (1977).

11. For a similar critique of subjective approaches to alienation, see Thibault (1981), who points up not only the theoretical and methodological shortcomings of these approaches, but also the fact that they have produced little knowledge of any value to workers.

Notes to Chapter 2: Natural Labor

1. Underlying Mead's formulation is an important issue of motivation. According to Mead organisms simply act to satisfy life-sustaining impulses. Some have argued that taking action as a given leaves Mead, like Dewey, with a 'problem of motivation'. But it is important to distinguish concerns with directional from non-directional motivation. Mead's theory is non-directional; he specifies only a general basis for action: to sustain life. A directional theory of motivation is concerned with specific patterns of action and the specific impulses they satisfy. The latter concern underlies contemporary sociologists' interests in predictive theories of motivation. Mead's general theory, however, is quite capable of subsuming a more specific, sociological theory of motivation (cf. Miyamoto, 1970).

2. There is evidence that higher apes, particularly chimps, are capable of self-awareness and self-reflective thought (see Meddin, 1979; Gallup, 1977). Unlike metaphysical views of human nature, Mead's naturalistic perspective is not in the least threatened by this fact. If chimps can use symbols in a rudimentary way, a modicum of self-awareness and primitive thinking should also be possible (see also Thompson and Church, 1981).

3. For more detailed discussions of role taking, see Coutu (1951) and Miller (1981).

4. For a more thorough treatment of the relationship between language and the self based on a Meadian perspective, see Schwalbe (1983).

5. See also Lewis's (1981) lucid and highly pertinent treatment of perception in the context of Mead's philosophy of the act.

6. Marx's lifelong collaborator Friedrich Engels also wrote about the importance of the hand and speech in human evolution. Given that Engels shared Marx's philosophical anthropology, this is not at all surprising. Once one recognizes the importance of coordinated action and complex transformations of nature to human development, as did Marx and Engels, it is only logical to explore the bases of these things. Numerous others have also recognized the importance of the hand, especially for tool use, in human evolution.

7. Mead himself did not write the introduction to *The Philosophy of the Act*, which was published seven years after his death. It was written principally by Charles W. Morris, a former student of Mead's, in collaboration with John M. Brewster, Albert M. Dunham, and David L. Miller. Morris also edited and wrote the introduction to Mead's better known *Mind, Self and Society*, which was also published posthumously by Mead's students.

8. In the Meadian view meaning consists in the response a gesture or object arouses in a hearer or observer. Thus any gesture or object that arouses a particular response or attitude in an individual can be called meaningful. An object or gesture that arouses no attitude, no response, no tendency to act on the part of an individual, can be called meaningless.

9. For parallel views on the importance of role taking for appreciating art objects, see Wartofsky (1975) and E. Fischer (1964).

10. Changing a flat tire on an automobile is an example of a mundane transformative act. In approaching a flat tire—acting on an impulse to fix it—one might imagine, as the object of consummation, an inflated tire. The inflated tire represents a transformed state, which various lines of action might produce. All that is necessary for aesthetic experience—given the other requisite conditions discussed in the text—is an understanding of the relationship between the imagined condition action is intended to produce (an inflated tire) and actions carried out to produce it. In principle it is just as possible to derive aesthetic experience from changing a tire as from composing a symphony.

11. Of course, all role taking in and at work does not occur via objects of production. A great deal must necessarily occur in face-to-face interaction. And this too would be expected to have consequences for psychological functioning. The argument here assumes this interpersonal role taking can be taken as a constant, at least theoretically. Ultimately, the question of which kind of role taking is more psychologically consequential is an empirical one.

12. Problem-solving abilities can be improved by learning general problem-solving strategies. But it seems that any particular kind of problem solving depends upon having both a strategy and much domain-specific knowledge (see Mayer, 1983, for a review). While contemporary theories of cognitive functioning in problem solving are much more elaborate than anything offered by Mead, in most cases they rely on many of the same basic assumptions set forth and philosophically defended by Mead. This is true of even the most sophisticated, currently popular information-processing models of problem solving.

13. There is hardly consensus on what constitutes intellectual flexibility, cognitive flexibility, ideational flexibility, or several similar concepts within cognitive psychology. In the work and personality area, Kohn and Schooler (1973, 1978, 1983) have used the term intellectual flexibility repeatedly without ever presenting a clear conceptualization of what it is. In their research it appears to constitute nothing more than whatever it is they allegedly measure with various indices of intellectual performance. No theoretical justification is offered for operationalizing intellectual flexibility in the manner they do. The theoretically-informed and philosophically-grounded Meadian interpretation of intellectual flexibility as the ability to adopt multiple perspectives, is thus as useful and defensible as any to be found in the mainstream of the social structure and personality literature today. See also Coser (1975) for parallel arguments.

14. In the Pragmatist tradition, and in that of the action psychologists such as Piaget, one learns about the world by attempting to manipulate it and observing the results. If one is not free to do both, then learning about one's

self and the world will be constrained. Alienated labor constrains this free-dom and so also constrains what individuals can learn about themselves and about the world. Natural labor, in contrast, involves this learning pro-cess operating at its highest level.

Notes to Chapter 3: Methodology

1. One need not adhere strictly to the labor theory of value to recognize that fundamental economic and social-psychological conflicts exist between workers and managers in a capitalist firm (see, e.g., Hill, 1981:16-44).

2. Social class is referred to in the Marxian sense of one's position in a system of production relative to the exploitation of labor. For attempts to opera-tionalize the Marxian concept of class suitably for analyzing the class struc-ture of the contemporary United States, see Wright, et al., (1982). A version of Wright's scheme adapted to the limitations of the present sample will be used here. Four class categories thus result: managerial, supervisory, semi-autonomous, and working.

3. By using seven supposed indicators of "intellectual performance in an inter-view situation," Kohn and Schooler contrive a measurement model of intel-lectual flexibility (1938:112). Principal component factor analysis of these various measures produced two dimensions, which Kohn and Schooler dis-tinguish as "ideational" and "perceptual." Following this statistical analysis, Kohn and Schooler thereafter refer to ideational flexibility as though its meaning had been clearly established. But in fact Kohn and Schooler have no theoretical understanding of ideational or intellectual flexibility, nor any theory-driven measures of these things. For them, ideational flexibility is no more than whatever they claim to be measuring with their atheoretical mea-surement model.

4. According to Kohn and Schooler (1982:1271), "the effects of job conditions on personality are readily interpretable as a learning-generalization process—learning from the job and generalizing the lessons to off-the-job realities." While it is undoubtedly true that work affects cognitive develop-ment to some extent via learning-generalization (see, e.g., Breer and Locke, 1965), this is hardly an adequate explanation of how work experiences af-fect people psychologically. It would be nice to know, for example, exactly what is learned on the job, how it is learned, and how this learning is trans-lated into various psychological consequences. Instead of answers to these questions Kohn and Schooler leave us with little more than a black box fes-tooned with all the most fashionable statistical wrappings.

5. Substantive complexity is related, however, to the *kinds* of problems people must solve in their work. And it is this, I believe, which is most important for cognitive development, not complexity per se. In all fairness, Kohn and

Schooler do recognize the importance of problem solving in assessing complexity (1983:325). But because they have no theory of psychological development or functioning they still get things backwards by focusing on complexity instead of problem solving.

6. These are not the only possible roles a field researcher might assume (see Schwartz and Jacobs, 1979:57). In the present study another alternative would have been to seek access by revealing my identity to an employer but not to employees. While this might have yielded valuable data, the moral cost of this approach would have exceeded available resources.

7. An analytic survey is a tool for exploring relationships among variables under non-experimental conditions (Rosenthal and Rosnow, 1984:55-56).

8. Theories are underdetermined by facts in that facts alone can never compel acceptance or rejection of a theory, since a theory can almost always be adjusted to fit the facts, or, as is more often the case in practice, discrepant facts can be ignored. On this matter see Kuhn (1970) and Feyerabend (1975, esp. ch.5).

Notes to Chapter 4: Exploration

1. While there was no evidence production workers perceived operational products resulting from their efforts, this is not proof they never perceived such products. It is possible that some did and simply never mentioned it. On the other hand, prior knowledge of their productive activities led me to believe that operational products were really not perceived by production workers as they were by secretaries or supervisors.

2. In other words, some production workers related their individual efforts to the collective product of their particular department, but did not relate their efforts to the firm's product. But again this is based on what production workers spontaneously reported about seeing how their work contributed to a final product of some kind. It is possible that, if pressed, production workers could have conceptualized relationships between their efforts and the firm's final product.

3. In some cases supervisors had extensive knowledge of a production process by virtue of special technical training or broad work experience. This was especially true of the foremen at the machine-building firm, all of whom were former machinists. In contrast, supervisors at the irrigation equipment firm were usually former assemblers who had been promoted off the line. These people had no prior technical training and as such had neither great range nor refinement of means-ends comprehension.

4. The machine operator's report of concern for the moral consequences of what he was producing was not specifically solicited. It was offered in response to the general question, "Do you ever have to think about how someone is going to use or react to the results of your work?"

5. People's thoughts on the moral implications of their weapons-building work had to be specifically solicited, carefully. This was an extremely sensitive issue at the aerospace firm. In fact, when a top manager learned (from his own secretary) that the matter had come up in some interviews, the survey phase of the study was temporarily held up until I explained why the matter was relevant to employee self-esteem.

6. People uniformly enjoyed seeing the consequences of their efforts, especially so when those consequences attested to their competence. Many of the things people cited as special sources of satisfaction and specially-liked aspects of work were occasions where they received objective feedback about their work performance.

7. Some views of schizophrenia see it as essentially an extreme form of alienation wherein the individual has lost all capacity to act back on the external world (Becker, 1965; Laing, 1965). It is perhaps through mundane self-objectification that most such 'acting back' on the external world occurs.

8. Like everyone else, mechanics also cited a host of disliked activities such as "having to do rush jobs," "having to fix up badly done work," and "dealing with two bosses at once" as problems. These were more often rhetorical than real problems.

9. From a Meadian perspective this would have to include the self as well. It's entirely possible that an individual might not respond to his own symbolic action (his thought) as anticipated. In Meadian terms this would amount to an inability to symbolically call forth an adaptive response in one's self, a situation that is not only conceivable but common.

10. Secretaries, however, did have white-collar status which allowed them to take a status-superior role when interacting with some blue-collar workers, particularly females. Further, secretaries were stratified among themselves, with executive secretaries at the top of the ladder, followed by administrative secretaries, secretaries, junior secretaries, and typists down the line. Thus some secretaries did have opportunities to engage in downward role taking in the workplace.

11. This is not to say there were no elements of domination in machine design. Domination could occur unconsciously as machines were designed with the operator's tolerances rather than preferences in mind. In other words, when design engineers took the role of the operator, it was not necessarily to imagine what the operator would prefer but what he would tolerate (by way of noise, hazards, effort required). Usually the operator's preferences were traded off against what was "profitably possible." In this way the design engineer contributed to the operator's continual subjugation to the preemptory demand for profit, both in building casting machines and in actually casting metal.

12. Some people described the need to separate different sets of motives for interacting with friends and family members in the workplace. One supervisor told of distancing himself from his son, who he once supervised,

because at work family relationships were irrelevant. A secretary faulted herself for being unable to do this. She would not make a good manager, she believed, because she couldn't separate her "personal feelings" from her "business feelings." These people were aware that from a managerial position too great a propensity to role-take could be a liability.

13. Role-taking accuracy has been the subject of some symbolic interactionist and other social-psychological research (e.g., Stryker, 1957; Thomas, et al., 1972; Davis, 1983). Typically this has been held to be the sum total of perspective-taking ability. Other dimensions of this ability (range and depth) have generally been ignored or not identified at all.

14. This situation was unusual in that the department this foreman supervised produced large discrete products: whole casting machines. Building a single machine was a project in itself, one that could take months to complete. Supervisors at the other manufacturing firms supervised more or less continuous processes or batch production operations.

15. One reason this was important for low-skill machine operators was that virtually anyone could be good at their type of work, and with very little training. In contrast, engineers and mechanics never cited such comparisons as sources of satisfaction or feelings of competence. Instead they emphasized their abilities to 'handle whatever was thrown at them'.

16. Some secretaries were salaried. But as discussed in the text, pay type did not appear to directly affect opportunities for aesthetic experience within job groups.

17. Autonomy, for example, was no less important to engineers than anyone else. If they cited it less often in on-site interviews than did production workers, it was because they took it for granted. Off-site interviews revealed a great deal about the importance of autonomy and control to everyone's satisfaction in work.

18. On an industry-wide level vertical integration has another meaning; it refers to a conglomerate's control of everything from parts supply to manufacturing to sales of a product within a particular industrial field. For example, all major auto manufacturers are vertically integrated in this sense.

19. In principle, the vertical integration concept could be applied to the aerospace firm, but in such a limited way as to make comparisons with the manufacturing firms cumbersome and largely useless. It should be understood, then, that the effects of vertical integration discussed in the text apply only to the four manufacturing firms.

20. Obviously, competence alone does not account for the distribution of resources in any capitalist enterprise. The point is simply that, *ceteris paribus*, competent individuals will tend to end up with more organizational resources at their disposal than incompetent ones. Of course this also presumes the competence at issue is relevant for profit making.

21. Most of those people who participated in sports activities, but had no other

hobbies or crafts, were production workers and secretaries. It was especially difficult for these people to compare sports to their work. Such comparisons would have required moving from a concrete to an abstract level, something these people seemed reluctant to do in the interview situation.

22. All of an individual's appreciative perspectives ultimately derive from others. In Meadian terms, these perspectives or attitudes are parts of the self that arise through interaction and are sustained and modified through interaction.

23. Those interviewed at each firm were included in the survey sample at each firm. Even so, the two samples were not identical because the latter included more persons than were interviewed. Furthermore, there is no way to be sure that all those who were interviewed returned questionnaires. For these reasons some real differences between the observation data and the survey findings are possible, though any such differences are likely to be small.

24. While this measure of means-ends comprehension may not reflect the subtle differences in the experience discussed in the text, it may still be useful as a measure of simple ability to see the results of one's work. It may well be that this is the most important level of means-ends comprehension for shaping affective responses to work. It may be more important, in other words, that an individual perceives *some* connection between his efforts and their consequences, than exactly how elaborately he understands it. Still, this would not change the fact that at a deeper level engineers experience means-ends comprehension differently than machine operators.

25. In on-site interviews many secretaries and production workers confused the marginal autonomy (freedom from direct supervision) they had in their jobs with control. The only real control most of them had was over their pace of work. But again this "control" was tenuous and narrowly circumscribed. Relatedly, see also Langer (1983) who argues there is a basic psychological need for people to maintain an "illusion of control" over their lives. This certainly seems to apply to the workplace.

26. Kohn and Schooler also find that, in cross-sectional data, education has a stronger effect on intellectual flexibility than work experience. Their longitudinal analyses, however, lead them to conclude that work experiences are ultimately more consequential (see Kohn and Schooler, 1983:154-189).

27. On this matter see Maccoby (1966), Maccoby and Jacklin (1974), Lever (1978), and Flavell (1968).

28. Just how consequential work actually is relative to other spheres of life is not simply a matter of speculation. Research undertaken from a variety of perspectives consistently shows occupational experience to more powerfully affect adult lives than experiences in other life spheres. Moreover, work has also been shown to be a powerful determinant of experiences in other adult life spheres (see Kohn and Schooler, 1983; Meissner, 1970; Champoux, 1978).

Notes to Chapter 5: Reassessment

1. Expected cross-class differences in mean scale scores for these outcome variables did in fact appear in the survey data. Analysis of variance showed these differences to be significant (p<.01) for intellectual flexibility and work enjoyment, and non-significant for reification and propensity to role-take. However, without representative class samples these results are not especially meaningful.

2. In off-site interviews people were asked about their most memorable innovations at work. Engineers and mechanics could almost always tell stories about their inventions or special problem-solving experiences. A few supervisors and secretaries could do the same. Those production workers interviewed off site could not tell of any such memorable experiences in their work.

3. From a structural perspective, under capitalism labor is always alienated in the form of value; that is, as long as surplus value is extracted from the working class, their labor is being 'alienated from them'. Here the primary concern has not been with alienation as expropriation of value, but with alienation as the denial of aesthetic experience. The latter, however, was argued to be predicated on the former.

4. The connection between the capitalist labor process and the role-set model is implicit in the roles and statuses themselves. But these are static connections that take for granted social relations of production without explaining how they arise from system imperatives. This is not to say, however, that models of role-set complexity could not be used within a Marxian framework; they could, if roles and statuses were accounted for theoretically and not simply assumed.

5. Perhaps among the very young or the mentally impaired one could find an absolute zero of role taking. But this would be of dubious value for making comparisons to normal adults. It is interesting to note, however, that young children who can use language (and thus must be able to role-take) can also be almost completely egocentric. Apparently there are different dimensions of role-taking ability involved in the "play" and "game" stages of early childhood development (see Mead, 1934:149-164; Denzin, 1972). For another relevant perspective on this matter, see Vygotsky (1962:9-24).

6. This issue might be resolved through experimental research. It would be possible to match individuals on role-taking ability and then manipulate aspects of an experimental situation to examine effects on role-taking propensity. One important situational variable would be the relative statuses of the subjects. Some experimental research examining perspective-taking ability has already been undertaken (e.g., Neale and Bazerman, 1983).

7. In the last major review of this literature Schweitzer (1981) calls for efforts toward formalizing alienation theory, supposedly so a program of cumulative research can begin. The goal, in this view, is theoretical consolidation

so a period of normal science, untroubled by epistemological disputes, can get underway. From a Marxist perspective, such consolidation for the purpose of 'carving out a niche in the discipline' would amount to bourgeoisification of the alienated labor concept.

8. Amazingly, some mainstream American sociologists (e.g., Form, 1983) still confuse occupation with class. Although the two are not unrelated, they are hardly the same; they can vary independently. For example, an individual might be an electrician by occupation. At the same time, he might be a small-scale capitalist if he employs others, petty-bourgeois if he works for himself by himself, semi-autonomous if he works as a salaried maintenance man, or working class if he works for wages for a capitalist employer. The basic premise here has been that it is class position rather than occupation that accounts for the most psychologically consequential work experiences people have.

9. For Piaget the stage of formal operations is the final stage of adult cognitive development. See Riegel (1973) for an attempt to begin with and go beyond Piaget's stages to the stage of dialectic operations.

10. The word "partially" is inserted to acknowledge whatever hereditary and non-experiential factors affecting cognitive development as might exist. However, even non-experiential factors, most notably nutrition, may be related to the political economy.

11. An early version of a political economy of cognitive development can be found in Georg Simmel's classic analyses of the individual/society relationship. Simmel's analyses run parallel in many ways to the Marxian/Meadian analysis developed here. Especially pertinent are his essays on the consequences for individuals of domination and subordination in economic and political life (see Simmel, 1950:181-303).

12. Research on political behavior shows that those in the working class are less likely to engage in political behavior on all levels of action (see Archibald, 1978:145-148, for a brief review).

13. Historically, the most skilled among the working class have been quickest to challenge management and, sometimes, capitalism itself (Mann, 1973; Thompson, 1963). These are the workers most likely to have engaged in natural labor within capitalist relations of production. From the natural labor perspective, their greater propensity to actively resist domination is not at all surprising.

Notes to Chapter 6: Praxis

1. To say that production under socialism would be free of domination is not to say it would be devoid of authority. The latter is necessary to ensure smooth operation of any large-scale productive enterprise, as Engels argued in his essay on authority ([1872], 1972:662-665). Under socialism, however,

authority would not be based on an employer's right to deprive an individual of his livelihood; rather, authority in production would presumably flow upward from workers and would be based on technical expertise or organizational skill.

2. The project of abolishing alienated labor is underway in some but not all socialist countries. In those state socialist countries where workers have no real control over production it cannot be said that alienated productive activity has been abolished. In the U.S., democratically operated cooperatives and collectives have had considerable success in abolishing alienated productive activity. However, the pressures of trying to survive in a capitalist economy have often limited the success of these alternative work organizations in transforming productive activities within them (see Rothschild-Whitt, 1976, 1979).

3. Employee stock ownership plans (ESOPs) are an example of worker ownership without any real worker control. These plans are typically schemes to make worker pension funds available as sources of investment capital, without giving workers any direct control over how these funds are used, let alone any direct control over production.

4. It is conceivable that some people might want to perform menial work if they desired no great responsibility for or participation in production decisions. If so, they should of course have the option of remaining marginal participants in the sphere of necessary production.

5. It was observed in this study that capitalist managers sometimes sought to induce aesthetic experience as a motivator. From the Marxian/Meadian view it seems this strategy may be a two-edged sword for the capitalist who tries to use it. While he may succeed in increasing work motivation, perhaps thereby increasing productivity, he may also be creating less controllable workers. From a capitalist perspective, aesthetic experience is thus best reserved for a select few who can be convinced it is a privilege generously granted them. To try to induce aesthetic experience to motivate the bulk of manual workers could, in the long run, prove disastrous for capitalist control of the labor process. As such, given the position taken here, advising capitalists to try motivating workers by encouraging problem solving, role taking, means-end comprehension, and self-objectification would seem to be the right thing to do.

6. These are the contextual variables previously identified as conducive to aesthetic experience. Given knowledge of the psychological advantages of organizing production in these ways, it seems a reasonable goal to try organizing a larger share of necessary production accordingly.

7. It should be emphasized that the reference here is to the necessity of autonomy and control in the sphere of freedom. Only given autonomy and control can individuals exercise true creativity and engage in marked self-objectification. By way of example it is useful to think of artistic production. Such production may be tied very closely to a particular commu-

nity context, but the work itself must be characterized by autonomy and control on the part of the artist. The possibility of this same degree of autonomy and control must be available to everyone in the sphere of freedom, otherwise the sphere of freedom is not that at all.

8. Attempts in socialist countries to abolish alienated labor and develop widespread socialist consciousness are indeed relevant as examples of how these projects might proceed. They are valuable sources of experience and knowledge about what to do and not do in order to make these projects successful. But in many cases these experiences are culture-specific and their lessons are not generalizeable to the contemporary U.S. Because of these complexities it is impossible to adequately make sense of other socialist projects in the limited context of this chapter.

9. The class consciousness that has arisen in many less-developed countries in the post-World War II period may be an exception to this trend. It seems many of the socialist movements in these countries have arisen from increased awareness of their exploitation by the U.S. in the international economy. But this is based on nationalist consciousness more so than on an internal class consciousness as predicted by Marx (cf. Sweezy, 1983).

10. Trends toward increased unionization among white-collar workers would seem to support the new working class thesis, as would the fact that skilled professional and technical workers have often been leaders in workers' control efforts in the U.S. and Europe.

11. These skilled workers had enormous confidence in their abilities to do just about anything that needed doing within the production process. Moreover, this sense of efficacy seemed to extend to most forms of technical problem solving. Although most of these workers respected the financial knowledge and organizational skill of top managers, they felt such people were largely superfluous to production. If any workers exhibited the potential to take over the reins of economic control, it was these.

12. A sense of efficacy or potential ability to achieve one's goals even in the face of resistance is often what the unskilled among the working class lack (cf. Gore and Rotter, 1963; Seeman, 1972; Della Fave, 1980). There are a number of ways such a sense of efficacy can be induced, one of the most powerful being demonstrating capacities for efficacious action to one's self via successes in attaining one's goals. This seems to apply on both an individual and a collective level (see Bandura, 1982; Archibald, 1978,140-144).

13/. If one believes, as a Marxist, in the inevitable collapse of capitalism and subsequent rise of socialism, there is nothing to do but sit back and wait for the revolution. To the extent such a belief keeps academic Marxists passive and unmotivated to engage in praxis, it preserves both their academic status, since their inaction threatens no one in the academy, and the status quo, since their inaction changes nothing in the outside world. Ironically, the Marxist belief in an inevitable socialist revolution can inadvertently become an ideological force serving capitalism.

14. Even hermits who choose to isolate themselves from the rest of humanity could not have become self-conscious and capable of living autonomously without socialization into some human community as children. They may thus reject community but could not even do so consciously without having been at one time part of a community. Feral children, those somehow surviving without being socialized into a human group, are only physiologically human. Without language they may at best have an inchoate awareness of self, but remain trapped in an unself-conscious animal world and thus cannot be said to live as autonomous humans.

Bibliography

Althusser, L.
    1969   *For Marx.*
        New York: Random House.

Anderson, C.H.
    1971   *Toward a New Sociology: A Critical View.*
        Homewood, IL: Dorsey.

Archibald, W.P.
    1976   "Using Marx's theory of alienation empirically." in R.F. Geyer and D. Schweitzer (eds.), *Theories of Alienation: Critical Perspectives in Philosophy and Social Science.* Leiden: Martinus Nijhoff.
    1978   *Social Psychology as Political Economy.*
        Toronto: McGraw-Hill.

Archibald, W.P., A. Owen, and J. Cartrell
    1981   "Propertylessness and alienation: reopening a 'shut' case." in R.F. Geyer and D. Schweitzer (eds.), *Alienation: Problems of Meaning, Theory and Method.* London: Routledge and Kegan Paul.

Avineri, S.
    1968   *Karl Marx: Social and Political Thought.*
        Cambridge: Cambridge University Press.

Balzer, R.
    1976   *Clockwork.*
        New York: Doubleday.

Bandura, A.
    1982   "Self-efficacy mechanisms in human agency." *American Psycholo-
           gist*, 37:122-147.
Basseches, M.
    1983   *Dialectical Thinking and Adult Development.*
           Norwood, NJ: Ablex.
Batiuk, M.E., and H.L. Sacks
    1981   "George Herbert Mead and Karl Marx: Exploring consciousness and
           community." *Symbolic Interaction,*4/2:207-224.
Baumann, B.
    1969   "George H. Mead and Luigi Pirandello: Some parallels between the
           theoretical and artistic presentation of the social role concept." in P.
           Berger (ed.), *Marxism and Sociology.* New York: Appleton.
Becker, E.
    1965   "Mills' social psychology and the great historical convergence on the
           problem of alienation." Pp. 108-133 in I.L. Horowitz (ed.), *The New
           Society.* New York: Oxford.
Berger, P., and T. Luckmann
    1967   *The Social Construction of Reality.*
           New York: Anchor.
Bernstein, B.
    1973   *Class, Codes, and Control, II: Applied Studies Toward a Sociology
           of Language.* London: Routledge and Kegan Paul.
Bernstein, W.M., and M.H. Davis
    1982   "Perspective-taking, self-consciousness, and accuracy in person per-
           ception." *Basic and Applied Social Psychology*, 3:1-19.
Blake, J.
    1976   "Self and society in Mead and Marx."
           Cornell Journal of Social Relations, 11:129-138.
Blau, J., and R.D. Alba
    1982   "Empowering nets of participation."
           Administrative Science Quarterly, 27:363-379.
Blauner, R.
    1964   *Alienation and Freedom.*
           Chicago: University of Chicago Press.
Blood, M.R., and C.L. Hulin
    1967   "Alienation, environmental characteristics and worker responses."
           Journal of Applied Psychology, 51:284-290.
Blumer, H.
    1969   *Symbolic Interactionism.*
           Englewood Cliffs, NJ: Prentice-Hall.
Bowles, S., and H. Gintis
    1976   *Schooling in Capitalist America.*
           New York: Basic.

Bramel, D., and R. Friend
  1981 "Hawthorne, the myth of the docile worker, and class bias in psychology." *American Psychologist,* 26: 867-878.
Braverman, H.
  1974 *Labor and Monopoly Capital: The Degradation of Work in the 20th Century.* New York: Monthly Review Press.
Breer, P.E., and E.A. Locke
  1965 *Task Experience as a Source of Attitudes.* Homewood, IL: Dorsey.
Burawoy, M.
  1979 *Manufacturing Consent.* Chicago: University of Chicago Press.
  1981 "Terrains of contest: Factory and state under capitalism and socialism." *Socialist Review,* 58: 83-124.
Champoux, J.E.
  1978 "Work, central life interests, and self-concept." *Pacific Sociological Review,* 21:209-220.
Coser, R.L.
  1975 "The complexity of roles as the seedbed of individual autonomy." Pp. 237-263 in L.A. Coser (ed.), *The Idea of Social Structure: Papers in Honor of Robert K. Merton.* New York: Harcourt Brace Jovanovich.
Coutu, W.
  1951 "Role-playing vs. role-taking: An appeal for clarification." *American Sociological Review,* 16:180-187.
Davis, M.H.
  1983 "Measuring individual differences in empathy." *Journal of Personality and Social Psychology,* 44:113-126.
Della Fave, L.R.
  1980 "The meek shall not inherit the earth: Self-evaluation and the legitimacy of stratification." *American Sociological Review,* 45:9 55-971.
Denzin, N.K.
  1972 "The genesis of self in early childhood." *The Sociological Quarterly,* 13:291-314.
Edwards, R.
  1979 *Contested Terrain.* New York: Basic.
Engels, F.
  1972 "On authority." in R.C. Tucker (ed.), *The Marx-Engels Reader.* New York: Norton.
Feuer, L.
  1963 "What is alienation: The career of a concept." in M. Stein and A. Vidich (eds.), *Sociology on Trial.* Englewood Cliffs, NJ: Prentice-Hall.
Feyerabend, P.
  1975 *Against Method.*

New York: Verso.

Fischer, C.S.
1976   "Alienation: Trying to bridge the chasm."
       British Journal of Sociology, 27:35-49.

Fischer, E.
1964   *The Necessity of Art.*
       Baltimore: Penguin.

Flavell, J.H.
1968   *The Development of Role Taking and Communication Skills in Chil-
       dren.* New York: Wiley.

Form, W.H.
1973   "Auto workers and their machines: A study of work, factory and job
       satisfaction in four countries." *Social Forces,* 52:1-15.
1983   "Sociological research and the American working class."
       The Sociological Quarterly, 24:163-184.

Fromm, E.
1955   *The Sane Society.*
       Greenwich, CN: Fawcett.

Gallup, G.G.
1977   "Self recognition in primates—a comparative approach to the bidi-
       rectional properties of consciousness." *American Psychologist,* 32:
       329-338.

Gans, H.
1962   *The Urban Villagers.*
       New York: The Free Press.

Gartman, D.
1978   "Marx and the labor process: An interpretation."
       Insurgent Sociologist, fall: 97-107.

Gecas, V., and M.L. Schwalbe
1983   "Beyond the looking-glass self: Social structure and efficacy-based
       self-esteem." *Social Psychology Quarterly,* 46:77-88.

Gerth, H.H., and C.W. Mills
1953   *Character and Social Structure.*
       New York: Harcourt, Brace and World.

Geyer, R.F., and D. Schweitzer (eds.)
1976   *Theories of Alienation: Critical Perspectives in Philosophy and So-
       cial Science.* Leiden: Martinus Nijhoff.
1981   *Alienation: Problems of Meaning, Theory and Method.*
       London: Routledge and Kegan Paul.

Goff, T.W.
1980   *Marx and Mead: Contributions to a Sociology of Knowledge.*
       London: Routledge and Kegan Paul.

Goldthorpe, J.H.
1966   "Attitudes and behavior of car assembly workers: A deviant case and
       a theoretical critique." *British Journal of Sociology,* 17:227-244.

Gore, P.M., and J.B. Rotter
    1963   "A personality correlate of social action."
           Journal of Personality, 31:58-64.
Gorz, A.
    1967   *Strategy for Labor.*
           Boston: Beacon Press.
    1976   *The Division of Labor* (ed.)
           Atlantic Highlands, NJ: Humanities Press.
    1980   *Farewell to the Working Class.*
           Boston: South End Press.
    1982   "Nine theses for a future left."
           Telos, 50(winter):91-90.
Hays, D.G.
    1976   "On 'alienation': An essay in the psycholinguistics of science." in R.F.
           Geyer and D. Schweitzer (eds.), *Theories of Alienation: Critical Per-
           spectives in Philosophy and Social Science.* Leiden: Martinus Nijhoff.
Heinz, W. R.
    1981   "Socialization and work: Notes on the normative acceptance of alien-
           ated work conditions." in R.F. Geyer and D. Schweitzer (eds.), *Alien-
           ation: Problems of Meaning, Theory and Method.* Leiden: Martinus
           Nijhoff.
Hill, S.
    1981   *Competition and Control at Work.*
           Cambridge: MIT.
House, J.S.
    1974   "Occupational stress and coronary heart disease: A review and theo-
           retical integration." *Journal of Health and Social Behavior,* 15:12-27.
    1981   "Social structure and personality."
           Pp. 525-561 in M. Rosenberg and R. Turner (eds.), *Social Psychol-
           ogy.* New York: Basic.
Hulin, C.L., and M.R. Blood
    1968   "Job enlargement, individual differences, and worker responses."
           Psychological Bulletin, 69:41-55.
Inkeles, A.
    1983   *Exploring Individual Modernity.*
           New York: Columbia University Press.
Inkeles, A., and D. Smith
    1974   *Becoming Modern: Individual Change in Six Developing Countries.*
           Cambridge: Harvard University Press.
Israel, J.
    1971   *Alienation from Marx to Modern Sociology: A Macro-Sociological
           Analysis.* Boston: Allyn and Bacon.
Janousek, J.
    1972   "On the Marxian concept of praxis." in J. Israel and H. Tajfel (eds.),
           The Context of Social Psychology: A Critical Assessment. London:

Academic Press.

Kagan, J.
   1972   "A conception of early adolescence." in J. Kagan and R.R. Coles
           (eds.), *Twelve to Sixteen: Early Adolescence*. New York: Norton.

Kanter, R.M.
   1977   *Men and Women of the Corporation*.
           New York: Basic.

Kohlberg, L., and C. Gilligan
   1972   "The adolescent as a philosopher: The discovery of self in a post-
           conventional world." in J. Kagan and R.R. Coles (eds.), *Twelve to
           Sixteen: Early Adolescence*. New York: Norton.

Kohn, M.L.
   1969   *Class and Conformity: A Study in Values*.
           Homewood, IL: Dorsey.

Kohn, M.L., and C. Schooler
   1973   "Occupational experience and psychological functioning: An assess-
           ment of reciprocal effects." *American Sociological Review*, 38:97-
           118.
   1978   "The reciprocal effects of the substantive complexity of work and in-
           tellectual flexibility: A longitudinal assessment." *American Journal of
           Sociology*, 84:24-52.
   1982   "Job conditions and personality: A longitudinal assessment of their
           reciprocal effects." *American Journal of Sociology*, 876:1257-1283.
   1983   *Work and Personality*.
           Norwood, NJ: Ablex.

Kuhn, T.
   1970   *The Structure of Scientific Revolutions*.
           Chicago: University of Chicago Press.

Laing, D.
   1965   *The Divided Self*.
           Baltimore: Penguin.

Langer, E.J.
   1983   *The Psychology of Control*.
           Beverly Hills, CA: Sage.

Lever, J.
   1978   "Sex differences in the complexity of children's play and games."
           American Sociological Review, 43:471-483.

Lewis, J.D.
   1981   "G.H. Mead's contact theory of reality: The manipulatory phase of
           the act in the constitution of mundane, scientific, aesthetic, and eval-
           uative objects." *Symbolic Interaction*, 4:129-141.

Lichtman, R.
   1970   "Symbolic interactionism and social reality: Some Marxist queries."
           Berkeley Journal of Sociology, 15:75-94.

Lindenfeld, F., and J. Rothschild-Whitt (eds.)
    1982   *Workplace Democracy and Social Change.*
          Boston: Porter Sargent.
Littler, C.R., and G. Salaman
    1982   "Bravermania and beyond: Recent theories of the labor process." *Sociology*, 16:251-269.
Ludz, P.C.
    1976   "Alienation as a concept in the social sciences." in R.F. Geyer and D. Schweitzer (eds.), *Theories of Alienation: Problems of Meaning, Theory and Method.* Leiden: Martinus Nijhoff.
Maccoby, E.
    1966   *The Development of Sex Differences.*
          Stanford: Stanford University Press.
Maccoby, E., and C.N. Jacklin
    1974   *The Psychology of Sex Differences.*
          Stanford: Stanford University Press.
Mackinney, A.C., P.F. Wernimont, and W.O. Galitz
    1962   "Has specialization reduced job satisfaction?" *Personnel*, 39:8-17.
Mallet, S.
    1963   *The New Working Class.*
          New York: Spokesman Books.
Mann, M.
    1973   *Consciousness and Action in the Western Working Class.* London: Macmillan.
Marcuse, H.
    1955   *Eros and Civilization.*
          Boston: Beacon.
Marglin, S.A.
    1974   "What do bosses do? The origins and functions of hierarchy in capitalist production." *Review of Radical Political Economics*, 6:60-112.
Markovic, M.
    1981   "Alienated labor and self-determination." in R.F. Geyer and D. Schweitzer (eds.), *Alienation: Problems of Meaning, Theory and Method.* London: Routledge and Kegan Paul.
Marx, K.
    1959   *Marx and Engels; Basic Writings on Politics and Philosophy.*
          L.S. Feuer (ed.), Garden City, NY: Anchor.
    1963   *Karl Marx: Early Writings.*
          T.B. Bottomore (ed. and trans.), London: C.A. Watts.
    1971   *The Grundrisse.*
          D. Mclellan (ed. and trans.), New York: Harper and Row.
    1972   *The Marx-Engels Reader.*
          R.C. Tucker (ed.), New York: Norton.
Mayer, R.E.

1983　*Thinking, Problem Solving, Cognition.*
New York: W.H. Freeman.

Mead, G.H.
1932　*The Philosophy of the Present.*
A.E. Murphy (ed.), Chicago: University of Chicago Press.
1934　*Mind, Self and Society.*
C.W. Morris (ed.), Chicago: University of Chicago Press.
1938　*The Philosophy of the Act.*
C.W. Morris (ed.), Chicago: University of Chicago Press.
1982　*The Individual and the Social Self;* Unpublished Work of George Herbert Mead. D.L. Miller (ed.), Chicago: University of Chicago Press.

Meddin, J.
1979　"Chimpanzees, symbols, and the reflective self." *Social Psychology Quarterly,* 42:99-109.

Meissner, M.
1970　"The long arm of the job: Social participation and the constraints of industrial work." *Industrial Relations,* 10:239-260.

Meltzer, B.N., J.W. Petras, and L.T. Reynolds
1975　*Symbolic Interactionism; Genesis, Varieties and Criticism.*
London: Routledge and Kegan Paul.

Meszaros, I.
1970　*Marx's Theory of Alienation.*
New York: Harper and Row.

Miller, D.L.
1973　*George Herbert Mead; Self, Language, and the World.*
Chicago: University of Chicago Press.
1981　"The Meaning of Role-Taking." *Symbolic Interaction,* 4:167-175.

Miller, G.A.
1967　"Professionals in bureaucracy: Alienation among industrial scientists and engineers." *American Sociological Review,* 32:755-768.

Mills, C.W.
1956　*White Collar.*
New York: Oxford University Press.

Miyamoto, S.F.
1970　"Self, motivation, and symbolic interactionist theory." in T. Shibutani (ed.), *Human Nature and Collective Behavior,* Englewood Cliffs, NJ: Prentice Hall.

Moore, T.S.
1985　"The class patterning of work orientation." *The Social Science Journal,* 22:61-76.

Neale, M.A., and M.H. Bazerman
1983　"The role of perspective-taking ability in negotiating under different forms of arbitration." *Industrial and Labor Relations Review,* 36:378-388.

Noble, D.
    1979   "Social choice in machine design: The case of automatically-
           controlled machine tools." Pp. 18-50 in A. Zimbalist (ed.), *Case
           Studies on the Labor Process*. New York: Monthly Review Press.
Novack, G.
    1970   *The Marxist Theory of Alienation.*
           New York: Pathfinder.
Ollman, B.
    1971   *Alienation: Marx's Conception of Man in Capitalist Society.* Cam-
           bridge: Cambridge University Press.
Olsen, M.E.
    1968   "Perceived legitimacy of social protest actions." *Social Problems,*
           15:297-309.
Pfeffer, R.
    1979   *Working for Capitalism.*
           New York: Columbia University Press.
Plasek, W.
    1974   "Marxist and American sociological conceptions of alienation." *So-
           cial Problems,* 21:316-328.
Popper, K.
    1950   *The Open Society and Its Enemies.*
           Princeton, NJ: Princeton University Press.
Riegel, K.
    1973   "Dialectic operations: The final period of cognitive development."
           Human Development, 16:346-370.
    1979   *Foundations of a Dialectical Psychology.*
           New York: Academic press.
Ropers, R.
    1973   "Mead, Marx, and social psychology." *Catalyst,* 7(winter):42-61.
Rosenberg, M.
    1979   *Conceiving the Self.*
           New York: Basic Books.
Rosenthal, R., and R.L. Rosnow
    1984   *Essentials of Behavioral Research.*
           New York: McGraw-Hill.
Rothschild-Whitt, J.
    1976   "Problems of democracy."
           Working Papers for a New Society, 4(fall):41-45.
    1979   "The collectivist organization: An alternative to rational-
           bureaucratic models." *American Sociological Review,* 44:509-527.
Roy, D.
    1959   "Banana time: Job satisfaction and informal interaction." *Human Or-
           ganization,* 18:158-164.
Russell, R.

1982   "The rewards of participation in the worker-owned firm." Pp. 109-124 in F. Lindenfeld and J. Rothschild-Whitt (eds.), *Workplace Democracy and Social Change,* Boston: Porter Sargent.

Schacht, R.

1970   *Alienation.*
        Garden City, NY: Doubleday.

Schaff, A.

1970   *Marxism and the Human Individual.*
        New York: McGraw-Hill.

Schlesinger, M.B., and P.B. Bart

1982   "Collective work and self-identity: Working in a feminist illegal abortion collective." Pp. 139-153 in F. Lindenfeld and J. Rothschild-Whitt (eds.), *Workplace Democracy and Social Change.* Boston: Porter Sargent.

Schwalbe, M.L.

1983   "Language and the self: An expanded view from a symbolic interactionist perspective." *Symbolic Interaction,* 6:291-306.

Schwartz, H. and J. Jacobs

1979   *Qualitative Sociology: A Method to the Madness.* New York: The Free Press.

Schweitzer, D.

1981   "Alienation theory and research: Trends, issues and priorities." *International Social Science Journal,* 33:523-556.

Seashore, S.E., and T.D. Taber

1975   "Job satisfaction indicators and their correlates."
        American Behavioral Scientist, 18:333-368.

Seeman, M.

1959   "On the meaning of alienation."
        American Sociological Review, 26:753-758.

1972   "Alienation and knowledge seeking: A note on attitude and action."
        Social Problems, 20:3-17.

1975   "Alienation studies."
        Annual Review of Sociology, 1:91-123.

Sève, L.

1978   *Man in Marxist Theory.*
        J. McGreal (trans.), New Jersey: Humanities Press.

Shepard, J.M.

1977   "Technology, alienation, and job satisfaction."
        Annual Review of Sociology, 3:1-21.

Sheppard, H.L., and N.Q. Herrick

1972   *Where Have All the Robots Gone? Worker Dissatisfaction in the 70s.*
        New York: Free Press of Glencoe.

Sieber, S.D.

1973   "The integration of fieldwork and survey methods."
        American Journal of Sociology, 78:1335-1359.

1974   "Toward a theory of role accumulation."
        American Sociological Review, 39:567-578.
Simmel, G.
    1950   *The Sociology of Georg Simmel.* K.H. Wolff (trans., ed.). New York:
            The Free Press.
Staples, C.L., M.L. Schwalbe, and V. Gecas
    1984   "Social class, occupational conditions, and efficacy-based self-
            esteem." *Sociological Perspectives,* 27:85-109.
Stone, G.P., and H.A. Farberman
    1981   *Social Psychology Through Symbolic Interaction* (second edition).
            New York: John Wiley and Sons.
Stone, K.
    1974   "The origins of job structures in the steel industry."
            Review of Radical Political Economics, 6:1113-173.
Straus, M.A.
    1968   "Communication, creativity, and problem-solving ability of middle-
            and working-class families in three societies." *American Journal of
            Sociology,* 73:17-430.
Stryker, S.
    1957   "Role-taking accuracy and adjustment."
            Sociometry, 20:286-296.
Susman, G.I.
    1972   "Process design, automation, and worker alienation." *Industrial Re-
            lations,* 11:34-45.
Swanson, G.
    1974   "Family structure and the reflective intelligence of children." *So-
            ciometry,* 37:459-490.
Sweezy, P.M.
    1983   "Marxism and revolution 100 years after Marx." *Monthly Review,*
            34(March): 1-11.
Szymanski, T.
    1977   "The practice of Marxist social science." *Insurgent Sociologist,* 7:53-
            59.
Terkel, S.
    1972   *Working.*
            New York: Avon.
Thibault, A.
    1981   "Studying alienation without alienating people: A challenge for soci-
            ology." Pp. 275-283 in R.F. Geyer and D. Schweitzer (eds.), *Aliena-
            tion: Problems of Meaning, Theory and Method.* London: Routledge
            and Kegan Paul.
Thomas, D., D. Franks, and J. Calonico
    1972   "Role-taking and power in social psychology." *American Sociological
            Review,* 37:605-614.
Thompson, E.P.

1963 *The Making of the English Working Class.*
London: Gollancz.

Thompson, C.R., and R.N. Church
1981 "Explanations of the language of a chimpanzee."
Science, (Jan.):86-88.

Thompson, P.
1983 *The Nature of Work.*
London: Macmillan.

Twining, J.E.
1980 "Alienation as a social process."
The Sociological Quarterly, 21(summer): 417-428.

Vanek, J. (ed.)
1975 *Self-Management: The Economic Liberation of Man.*
Baltimore: Penguin.

Vygotsky, L.S.
1962 *Thought and Language.*
New York: MIT Press and John Wiley and Sons.

Walton, P., A. Gamble, and J. Coulter
1970 "Image of man in Marx."
Social Theory and Practice, 1:69-84.

Wartofsky, M.W.
1975 "Art as humanizing praxis."
Praxis, 1:56-65.

1982 "Marx among the philosophers."
in B. Ollman and E. Vernoff (eds.), *The Left Academy.* New York:
McGraw-Hill.

Wells, M.
1981 "Alienation, work structure, and the quality of life: Can cooperatives
make a difference?" *Social Problems,* 28:548-562.

Welsh, J.F.
1983 "The structure of self in dramaturgical society: The mutable self and
role-distance as forms of self-estrangement." *Transforming Sociology
Series,* Livermore, CO: Red Feather Institute.

Wright, E.O.
1983 "Capitalism's futures."
Socialist Review, 68:77-126.

Wright, E.O., C. Costello, D. Hachen, and J. Sprague
1982 "The American class structure."
American Sociological Review, 47:709-726.

Wrigley, J.
1982 "The division between mental and manual labor: Artisan education
in science in nineteenth-century Britain." *American Journal of Sociology* (supplement: Marxist Inquiries): S31-S51.

Zeller, R.A., and E.G. Carmines
    1980 *Measurement in the Social Sciences.*
          London: Cambridge University Press.
Zimbalist, A. (ed.)
    1979 *Case Studies on the Labor Process.*
          New York: Monthly Review Press.
Zipp, J.F., P. Luebke, and R. Landerman
    1984 "The social bases of support for workplace democracy."
          Sociological Perspectives, 27:395-425.
Zwerdling, D.
    1980 *Workplace Democracy.*
          New York: Harper Colophon.

Index

Act, Mead's philosophy of, 3, 34-36
Acts, types of, 36
Aesthetic experience: and ability to adopt multiple perspectives, 115; in capitalist labor process, 98-104, 126-127; contextual variables affecting, 108-113; and control over work, 110-111; denial of, 3, 46; moral dimensions of, 40-41; and motivation for self-objectification, 114; and motivation to understand productive activity, 113; nature of, 39-41; outside workplace, 116-120; personality variables affecting, 113-116; and plant size, 110; and problem solving, 51; and production for exchange, 51; and product standardization, 111-112; and projects, 101-102, 110-111; researchable questions regarding, 69-70; and role taking, 50; as source of motivation, 103-104, 212n; and specially-liked activities, 105; and task competence, 114; and vertical integration, 108-110; and work satisfaction, 107-108
Alba, R.D., 160

Alienated labor: abolition of, 159-162, 212n; act structures in, 173-176; adjustment to, 202n; affective consequences of, 14-16; cognitive consequences of, 12-14; concept, criticisms of, 21-25, scientific utility of, 22; in Marxist thought, 1-2, 10-12; Meadian analysis of, 48; nature of, 16
Alienation and Freedom (Blauner), 20
Alienation: as denial of aesthetic experience, 44-48; concept of in mainstream sociology, 1, 15, 18,26-27, 141-142, 202n; and schizophrenia, 207n;
Althusser, L., 7
Anderson, C.H., 44
Archibald, W.P., 18, 26, 141, 211n, 213n
Artisan production, 10, 40, 49-50, 212n; impulses underlying, 175
Avineri, S., 7, 18, 201n

Balzer, R., 63
Bandura, A., 213n
Bart, P.B., 160
Batiuk, M.E., 44
Basseches, M., 149

229